D0098771

Building Better Boards

David A. Nadler, Beverly A. Behan,

Mark B. Nadler, Editors

Foreword by Jay W. Lorsch

—ᴡᴡ— Building Better Boards

A Blueprint for Effective Governance

JOSSEY-BASS
A Wiley Imprint
www.josseybass.com

Copyright © 2006 by Mercer Delta Consulting LLC.

Published by Jossey-Bass
A Wiley Imprint
989 Market Street, San Francisco, CA 94103-1741   www.josseybass.com

No part of this publication may be reproduced, stored in a retrieval system, or transmitted in
any form or by any means, electronic, mechanical, photocopying, recording, scanning, or otherwise, except as permitted under Section 107 or 108 of the 1976 United States Copyright Act,
without either the prior written permission of the publisher, or authorization through payment
of the appropriate per-copy fee to the Copyright Clearance Center, Inc., 222 Rosewood Drive,
Danvers, MA 01923, 978-750-8400, fax 978-646-8600, or on the Web at www.copyright.com.
Requests to the publisher for permission should be addressed to the Permissions Department,
John Wiley & Sons, Inc., 111 River Street, Hoboken, NJ 07030, 201-748-6011, fax 201-748-6008,
or online at http://www.wiley.com/go/permissions.

Limit of Liability/Disclaimer of Warranty: While the publisher and author have used their best
efforts in preparing this book, they make no representations or warranties with respect to the
accuracy or completeness of the contents of this book and specifically disclaim any implied
warranties of merchantability or fitness for a particular purpose. No warranty may be created
or extended by sales representatives or written sales materials. The advice and strategies contained herein may not be suitable for your situation. You should consult with a professional
where appropriate. Neither the publisher nor author shall be liable for any loss of profit or
any other commercial damages, including but not limited to special, incidental, consequential,
or other damages.

Readers should be aware that Internet Web sites offered as citations and/or sources for further
information may have changed or disappeared between the time this was written and when
it is read.

Jossey-Bass books and products are available through most bookstores. To contact Jossey-Bass
directly call our Customer Care Department within the U.S. at 800-956-7739, outside the U.S.
at 317-572-3986, or fax 317-572-4002.

Jossey-Bass also publishes its books in a variety of electronic formats. Some content that
appears in print may not be available in electronic books.

Library of Congress Cataloging-in-Publication Data

    Building better boards : a blueprint for effective governance / David A. Nadler,
Beverly A. Behan, Mark B. Nadler, editors ; foreword by Jay W. Lorsch.
         p. cm.
    Includes bibliographical references and index.
    ISBN-13 978-07879-8180-8 (alk. paper)
    ISBN-10 0-7879-8180-X (alk. paper)
    1. Boards of directors. 2. Corporate governance. 3. Boards of directors—Canada.
  4. Corporate governance—Canada. 5. Boards of directors—Great Britain. 6. Corporate
  governance—Great Britain. I. Nadler, David. II. Behan, Beverly. III. Nadler, Mark B.
  HD2745.B85 2006
  658.4'22—dc22   2005028782

Printed in the United States of America
FIRST EDITION
HB Printing   10 9 8 7 6 5 4 3 2

—⁓— Contents

—⌇— Foreword

I am pleased to write this foreword to *Building Better Boards* for two reasons. First, I have long had a high regard for David Nadler and his colleagues at Mercer Delta Consulting. I first encountered David in 1972 at Harvard Business School, where he was a first-year student enrolled in my course on human behavior in organizations. I soon realized that David had unusual insight and a special skill for understanding how groups of people function. With a great deal more education and experience, he has become one of the world's foremost experts on top management teams and groups.

David also practices what he preaches. He has built a first-rate and highly collaborative consulting firm, and he and his colleagues understand top management teams very well. Now, in this book, they are applying that understanding to an even higher-level group: boards of directors.

This is the second reason I am pleased to be writing this introduction. Boards of directors are critically important institutions to the success of business firms, and in fact, to the global economy. If boards fail, companies fail. We have seen this simple but important truth play out time and again in the United States over the past several years, and there is similar evidence in the United Kingdom and other advanced economies of Europe. Some of these failures are the products of accounting misconduct and fraud, such as Ahold and Parmalat in Europe and Enron, Tyco, and WorldCom in the United States. But there are other, less dramatic examples of the connection between board failures and company failures. The performance shortfalls, management succession problems, and strategic missteps at companies like Hewlett-Packard, Merck, and Morgan Stanley are clear recent indicators that when companies have problems, they can be traced back to dysfunction in the boardroom.

Most proposed solutions to fix such boardroom failings have been in the form of new laws (Sarbanes-Oxley in the United States), new guidelines (the Higgs Review in the United Kingdom), or new regulations (U.S. listing requirements at NYSE and Nasdaq). Although new requirements help pressure boards to be more effective, they only take us so far. The real action is around the board table and among the groups of people we call boards of directors. That is what this book is about—how to improve the actual functioning of boards. Like my own recent book *Back to the Drawing Board: Designing Corporate Boards for a Complex World* (with Colin Carter), David and his colleagues put the focus on where the real action is—in the boardrooms of the world's companies.

This book presents sound and practical advice about how to build effective boards. It is thorough in that it examines who should be on the board and how to judge the performance of these individuals, the leadership of the board, and the critical activities that boards should perform. In my judgment, the advice is sound. Although each board must adapt these ideas to its own circumstances, I have no doubt that doing so will lead to boards that are truly effective in governing their companies.

JAY W. LORSCH, *Louis E. Kirstein Professor of Human Relations at Harvard Business School*

—ᨓ— Preface

It says something fairly significant about the evolution of corporate governance that throughout the first fifteen years of my career as a consultant to CEOs, I hardly paid any attention to boards. They just didn't matter.

For twenty-five years now, my colleagues and I have worked with CEOs on issues of organization, leadership, and change. This is close-in, sometimes intense work on issues at the top of the CEO's agenda: the design of the organization, change management, leadership development, culture transformation, and strategy. But for our first fifteen years as a firm, through the mid-1990s, our work never directly involved the board of directors. Sometimes we'd help our clients prepare for board presentations on matters such as management succession or changes in the organization or the strategy. But we never engaged directly with the board; in fact, we rarely spent much time talking about the board with our clients. The board, as such, wasn't an important element of governance; it was just another meeting, a passive audience for presentations.

Things began to change in the 1990s. Like everyone else, we watched with considerable interest the dramatic and unprecedented boardroom upheavals of 1992–93, when directors suddenly shook off their lethargy and unceremoniously removed the CEOs of some of the leading U.S. companies. In addition, we had the good fortune to encounter some forward-thinking CEOs who wanted to engage their boards in new and different ways. They asked us to help them figure out how to involve their boards constructively in critical issues such as strategy and CEO succession. As we began to work with these CEOs and their boards, we started to form some new insights into the board's historical problems and potential value.

We realized that boards were, at their essence, groups or teams of people trying to get work done, albeit in a very unique context and set of circumstances. We realized also that we had something to contribute, because we brought expertise in leadership and team effectiveness based on our years of consulting to executive teams in organizations.

Although we knew a lot about the dynamics of teams and behavior at the top of major corporations, we concluded we needed to learn more about boards. We put together a study group in our firm, led by our colleague Chuck Raben. We used a variety of means to explore the phenomenon of boards and corporate governance, including asking my "old" professor, Jay Lorsch, of Harvard Business School, to help us learn about the specific dynamics of boards. Finally, in the year 2000, as our company (Delta Consulting Group) was acquired by Mercer and we changed our name to Mercer Delta Consulting, we decided to officially launch a practice in corporate governance and board effectiveness. We added new talent with deep expertise, most notably David Nygren, a renowned expert on governance and adviser to numerous corporate and nonprofit boards, and Beverly Behan, a lawyer with extensive board-level experience.

Little did we know in the summer of 2000 how prescient our moves would turn out to be. This was before Enron, Anderson, and World-Com imploded. No one had yet heard of Sarbanes-Oxley or the New York Stock Exchange listing requirements. It was a different world, but one that was soon to change.

So we began to work with boards, both as direct clients and through our CEO relationships. In the beginning, in the wake of the corporate scandals and the avalanche of new laws and listing requirements, most boards were narrowly fixated on the issue of compliance. But as time went on, and it became obvious that minimal compliance was only remotely associated with improved governance, many boards began thinking about how to make a meaningful contribution to improving their companies' leadership and performance.

As our work expanded and our insights deepened, we followed our long-standing tradition of publishing what we were learning in a variety of venues. At a certain point, we concluded that we had something of value to offer to a larger audience—hence, this book.

Building Better Boards draws heavily from three sources of information. First and foremost, it builds on the work that we have done at Mercer Delta over the past decade with more than fifty corporate boards in the United States, Canada, and Western Europe. This opportunity to observe, advise, and interact with boards has provided us with a front-row seat on the inner workings of corporate governance, grounding our insights in real experience.

Second, this book draws on a broad and rigorously structured stream of research that has expanded our understanding beyond our firsthand experiences. In collaboration with Ed Lawler and the Center for Effective Organizations at the University of Southern California's Marshall School of Business, we conducted annual surveys of directors in 2003 and 2004. These surveys provided us with important insights into the changing practices at more than two hundred U.S. corporate boards. Throughout this book, we'll frequently refer to data derived from these USC/Mercer surveys.

Third, in 2004 we were active participants in the National Association of Corporate Directors (NACD) Blue Ribbon Commission on Board Leadership. Jay Lorsch and I cochaired this commission, and we were aided by our colleagues from Harvard Business School and Mercer Delta Consulting. The NACD has conducted many Blue Ribbon Commissions over the years, and they have made outstanding contributions to our knowledge of corporate governance. For this commission, we decided to take a different approach, however. We formed a broad-based commission composed of about fifty directors, CEOs, chairmen, academics, and corporate governance experts (see the appendix for a list of commissioners). In advance of our commission meeting, our staff conducted in-depth, one-on-one interviews of at least an hour with each of the commissioners. We used direct transcripts to do a computer-aided content analysis of the interviews as input to our commission meeting and the final report. The interviews provided us with a rich database of more than two thousand discrete comments (usually a paragraph in length), and we have used this database (with the kind permission of the NACD) as a basis for important parts of this book. (These comments will be referred to as the NACD or Blue Ribbon Commission interviews.)

Our goal was to bring together our experience, the USC/Mercer quantitative data, and the NACD interview qualitative data into a meaningful set of insights. Our hope is that these insights, and the perspectives offered through this book, will be of use to all those engaged in the critically important work of building better boards.

October 2005　　　　　　　　　　　　　　　　DAVID A. NADLER
New York City

PART ONE

Board Leadership and Dynamics

CHAPTER ONE

A Blueprint for Building Better Boards

David A. Nadler
Mark B. Nadler

T here's a story once told by Felix Rohatyn, the renowned investment banker who served on literally dozens of corporate boards during his illustrious career. In the 1960s, he joined his first board, at the Avis car rental company, and was welcomed by the CEO with this piece of wisdom: "A really good board is one that only reduces the efficiency of the company by 20 percent."[1]

That pretty well sums up the low esteem in which boards have been held over the years. It certainly captures the disdain harbored by many CEOs who viewed their boards as inconsequential at best, and at worst, as meddlesome obstacles to the efficient exercise of executive power. The possibility that boards might actually contribute some element of value just didn't factor into the equation.

It's time for some new math.

Today, boards have reached a historic fork in the road. In the wake of an unprecedented series of corporate scandals in both the United States and Western Europe, maintaining the status quo simply isn't an option. We've known for years that traditional boards were generally passive, compliant, and unproductive assemblages of individuals who would gather periodically to rubber-stamp the CEO's edicts. It turns out that was the best scenario. The corporate scandals of recent years aimed the spotlight on one board after another where the pervasive cronyism, cowardice, and collusion produced a toxic combination of sloth and sleaze. Those revelations, and the public demand for corporate reform, are forcing boards to look in the mirror and ask themselves profound questions about what role they should play in governing their organizations and how to constructively manage the shifting balance of power between the board and the CEO.

Every board faces a choice. On one hand, they can take the path of least resistance—minimal compliance with the new technical requirements imposed by legislators and stock exchanges. To be sure, compliance is important, but in our view it represents nothing more than the lowest common denominator of sound governance, a corporate version of the Hippocratic oath: "Above all, do no harm."

Our firm belief—and the premise of this book—is that directors and CEOs should choose the more difficult but ultimately more rewarding path of building better boards that actually contribute substantial value to the organizations they serve and the shareholders they represent.

It's easy to understand the overwhelmingly legalistic thrust of the so-called reforms enacted in recent years. Yet, although they might provide comfort to those whose main concern is ensuring that boards do no harm, they do little to help boards create value. Transparency in financial reporting, appropriate expertise on the board audit committee, and an explicit code of ethics represent little more than the "table stakes" of adequate governance; they're aimed at forcing boards to meet the basic legal requirements they should have been living up to all along. There's no added value in any of that.

Now, as CEOs experience a diminution of their "imperial" powers and boards contemplate the best way to fill the leadership vacuum, there's a unique opportunity for directors to commit themselves to a higher standard of performance. We are absolutely convinced that active and appropriately engaged boards, drawing on their members' collective experience, insights, and intellect, can partner with senior management in an environment of constructive contention to produce better decisions than management would have made on its own.

Here's the rub: boards can do that only if they learn to operate as high-performance teams, a role that represents a fundamental, even radical, departure from their deeply entrenched customs and practices. As we'll explain throughout this book, building a better board is a transformational exercise, one specifically designed to overcome the inherent and powerful obstacles to the board's capacity to function well as a team. Our goal here is to provide a blueprint for doing just that: for creating boards composed of the right people using the right processes to do the right work in an environment shaped by the right culture.

Here's an example of what we mean by boards adding value.

Henry Schacht, the retired chairman and CEO of Lucent Technologies, recalls that when Lucent was spun off by AT&T in 1995, the new company set up shop in the Bell Labs headquarters, a serviceable but somewhat outdated building that had seen better days. Schacht, something of an architecture buff, asked world-renowned architect Kevin Roche to begin working on plans for a brand-new headquarters building. After months of planning, Schacht proudly took his proposal to the Lucent board, which essentially asked him if he was out of his mind in light of all the other issues Lucent was dealing with at the time. "You know what? They were right," Schacht told us later. "We had a tough discussion, and we ended up making a different decision than I would have made on my own, and that's a good thing. That's an operational definition of value-added."

It's more than an academic question to ask how much value Enron's board would have contributed if it had questioned the bewildering off-the-books partnerships management was creating, or if WorldCom's board had halted top management's questionable accounting practices or loans to themselves, or if Disney's board had exercised some control over Michael Eisner's hiring and firing of top executives, or if Time-Warner's board had stood up to Gerald Levin and blocked the merger with AOL, a move that ultimately erased more than $200 billion in shareholder value.

In each of those cases, the board not only failed to add value, it even failed to preserve value. The good news is that in recent years we've seen more and more opportunities where boards have been adding value—at TRW, for instance, where the board stepped in and held the company together following the new CEO's sudden departure to Honeywell; at Lucent, where the board prevented Schacht's successor from making a series of potentially disastrous acquisitions; at Best Western International, where a badly fragmented board came together to block the CEO's proposed spin-off of the company's non-U.S. operations and then took an active role in working with management to rethink the strategy, design robust new performance metrics, and reshape the corporate culture.

THE DUELING PHILOSOPHIES OF GOVERNANCE

Just to be clear: the idea that boards can be a source of value isn't new. There's long been a school of thought that the board—or more specifically, its individual members—might constitute a *resource*. Through their personal networks, directors could help the company establish contact with new customers or partners, tap into new sources of capital, or gain a foothold in new markets or technologies. Ideally, some directors might actually provide the CEO with sound advice and wise counsel from time to time.

But the resource perspective has traditionally taken a distant backseat to the prevailing view that the board's central purpose is *control*—to act as a watchdog to make sure that the shareholders aren't robbed blind by "the agency," the hired managers who run the company. The control perspective has provided the philosophical underpinnings for the governance reform movement in the United States. That movement surfaced quietly in the late 1980s, then took on new urgency with the boardroom revolts of the early 1990s, which saw the ouster of CEOs at iconic U.S. institutions such as General Motors, American Express, and Kodak. Shareholder activism gained momentum throughout the 1990s, fueled by the manic merger and acquisition activity that resulted in so many ill-considered, poorly executed deals that erased billions of dollars of shareholder wealth.

And then came the opening years of the new century. The tech bubble burst, the post–9/11 economy went into a tailspin, and the unraveling of artificially inflated corporate results revealed an alarming pattern of questionable business schemes, fraudulent accounting practices, and appalling management excesses. At first, the unprecedented scandals seemed to be a U.S. phenomenon, involving a now-familiar list of corporate culprits—Enron, Tyco, WorldCom, Adelphia, Rite-Aid, HealthSouth, and Hollinger, to name a few. But Europe saw its own share of scandals at leading companies such as ABB, Skandia, Ahold, and Parmalat, while Canada added Nortel to the list.

Society's ire was targeted both at the CEOs who had abused their positions, either for financial gain or personal aggrandizement, and at the boards that had failed to stop them from running amok. It seemed that one board after another had either been bedazzled by a larger-than-life CEO, befuddled by business schemes they barely understood, or simply were asleep at the switch.

The response was swift and harsh, and it clearly reflected the control theory advocated for years by self-described governance watchdogs. The Sarbanes-Oxley legislation and the new listing requirements adopted by the New York Stock Exchange and Nasdaq had one clear purpose: to impose new structures and formal procedures that would minimize opportunities for financial mismanagement and conflicts of interest. Nearly all the reforms were about maintaining tighter control through tougher oversight.

At one level, it's hard to argue that reforms weren't needed. No one disputes that the governance process was badly broken at some companies. Yet so much of the public discourse and institutional response to the governance crisis has been shaped by the control theory and fixated on legal compliance as the source of good governance. For us, that creates some real concerns.

First, we reject the underlying notion that you can legislate board effectiveness. You can't mandate independent judgment, intellectual curiosity, constructive dissent, broad participation, or any of the other hallmarks of truly great boards. To quote Bill George, the highly respected retired CEO/chairman of Medtronic, Inc., "A lot of people who have not served on the inside think the reforms can be imposed from the outside. These are necessary, but not sufficient conditions for good governance."[2]

Second, the governance reform dogma rests on some shaky articles of faith; for example, the conventional wisdom is that boards dominated by a majority of independent directors are superior to those that aren't. In fact, a widely cited meta-analysis of fifty-four different studies "showed no statistical relationship" between board independence and company performance.[3] The same holds true of splitting the chairman and CEO roles, an arrangement that prevails in the United Kingdom and Canada but is still resisted by more than 70 percent of U.S. boards. There are good arguments for both models, but no clear evidence that bifurcating the roles results in better performance. In fact, a recent study by Booz Allen Hamilton found that companies in both North America and Europe in which the roles were split actually averaged lower returns for investors.[4]

Third, the obsession among some governance watchdogs and journalists with the technical aspects of corporate reform perpetuates a "governance by the numbers" mind-set that directs attention away from the most meaningful elements of sound governance. Take *Business*

Week's annual ranking of the "Best and Worst Boards," which is partly based on a point system that rewards compliance with various good governance criteria. Using those standards, both Sunbeam (1997) and Lucent (2000) made the list of best boards just as their CEOs were driving them to the brink of disaster. Yet Apple Computer was named one of the worst boards in 2002 because CEO Steven Jobs flunked *Business Week*'s requirement for purchasing his own company's stock—although Jobs somehow went on to mastermind one of the most stunning turnarounds in recent corporate history.

Perhaps the most extreme example of governance by the numbers is the continuing campaign to have Warren Buffet, perhaps America's most astute investor, removed from the Coca-Cola board's audit committee. The argument goes that Buffet, the chairman of Berkshire Hathaway, can't properly represent Coke's shareholders because two of Berkshire's units have purchased $185 million in Coke products. The implication that Buffet is somehow a management stooge who can't look out for the shareholders' best interests ignores the fact that Buffet's company is itself Coke's biggest shareholder (owning stock valued at more than $8 billion) or that Buffet personally played a key role in the board's ouster of CEO Douglas Ivester. The campaign defies logic and common sense, but it illustrates the dangers of the watchdog mind-set at its most rigid and unreasonable.

Our fourth concern is that the new regulations may be forcing boards to spend disproportionate time on activities that aren't likely to create value. Our own research, for example, found that more than 40 percent of directors feel they're now spending more time on compliance and less time on corporate strategy.[5] We're also finding the Sarbanes-Oxley reporting requirements shower directors with more financial data than they can possibly put to good use, exacerbating the growing concern that directors are choking on meaningless data but starved for useful information.[6]

Our final concern is that a narrow focus on compliance can actually prove dangerous if it creates a false sense of security. There's a risk that far too many companies will spend way too much time and money convincing themselves and their shareholders that they have created good governance when, in point of fact, they've done little to reduce the risk of meltdowns or improve their leadership and governance. It's all too easy to have good governance on paper and bad governance in practice; let's not forget that the Enron and HealthSouth boards were widely hailed as models of quality and independence.

It would be a wasted opportunity of historic proportions if all the attention now being focused on boards resulted in nothing more than a few technical fixes and a thicket of audit reports. We should demand more than that, searching for ways to build better boards that add real value to the organizations they serve.

THE BOARD AS A HIGH-PERFORMANCE TEAM

As we mentioned earlier, there has always been a school of thought that individual directors could act as resources, providing value on an ad hoc basis. What's new is the idea that the board, effectively constituted as a high-performance team, can provide ongoing collective value that's far greater than the sum of its individual parts. It's based on the belief that a board's collective experience, skills, and insights, when properly engaged, can enable management to make better decisions and run the company more effectively than it would have if left to its own devices. We've been suggesting that idea since the mid-1990s, and it's been gratifying to see others espouse the same notion over the years.[7, 8]

But it's easier said than done. As we'll discuss more fully in later chapters, the board operates under unique circumstances that inhibit its ability to function like other teams. It has unique legal requirements, meets infrequently and for only short periods of time, consists of a group of powerful people who are accustomed to leading their own teams, and involves fluid roles and ambiguous power relationships—for example, when the same person is both CEO and chairman, the person who leads the board as chairman simultaneously reports to the board as CEO.

So it's not enough to say the board should function as a team. The real question—and the question we hope to answer in this book—is this: Exactly how does a board go about transforming itself from a ritualistic appendage to a real team? Not only that, but in today's perilous corporate environment, how does it strike the proper balance between a do-nothing rubber stamp and an out-of-control lynch mob ready to assume management's rightful duties or prematurely toss the CEO overboard at the first sign of trouble? More specifically, a value-adding board has to address these three challenges:

• How do you create a board that is truly effective—one that not only meets its minimum legal obligations but also becomes a source of added value to its company?

- How do you design the work of the board so that it achieves an appropriate level of engagement without overstepping its proper role, which is to ensure that the company is managed effectively rather than to manage the company?
- How do you build an effective relationship between the board and the CEO, one that empowers the board without hampering the CEO's ability to lead?

Our research and experience indicate that a few boards have already figured out the answers, but not many. Most boards have a general sense that something's not working, but no clear idea of where they want to be, or how to get there. We hope that's what this book will provide: a blueprint for building better boards.

THE BLUEPRINT: BUILDING BETTER BOARDS

Every board is unique; each faces a particular set of challenges, and there's no quick fix that will solve every problem for every board. Nevertheless, based on our work over the years with more than fifty boards in the United States, Canada, and Western Europe, we have developed a board-building framework that suggests both a conceptual framework and some specific processes that apply in a multitude of situations. In this section, we'll describe the framework and explain how the remainder of the book is organized to provide a deep look at each step (see Figure 1.1).

Initial Steps: Taking Stock and Setting Direction

Later in this chapter, we'll dive into the first two steps in the process. The first step is what we refer to as *taking stock*. This is essentially a diagnostic phase, the necessary precursor to all the work that follows. The goal here is twofold: to identify the precise problems that are preventing the board from being as effective as it should, and then, even more importantly, to use a carefully facilitated process to build consensus about what the problems are and a board commitment to doing something about them. To be effective, board-building can't be forced; if the majority of directors don't think the work is important and worth the time and effort, the process will collapse in the starting block.

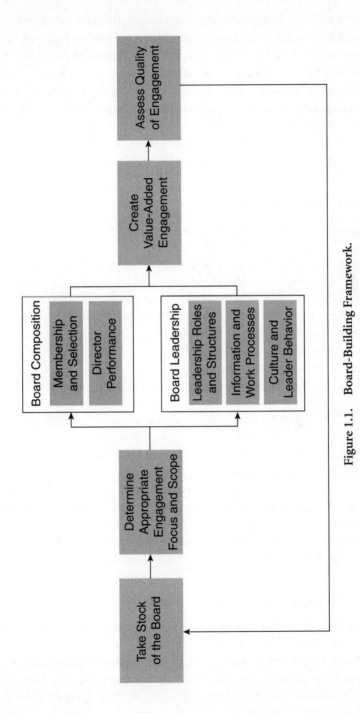

Figure 1.1. Board-Building Framework.

In the second step, the discussion turns into real work when the board and management survey the entire landscape of governance responsibilities and reach agreement on which work is primarily the board's, which is primarily management's, and which should be shared. This step is absolutely critical to shaping the board as a team. The outcome provides both a road map for moving forward with real work—and an appropriate level of engagement—and the foundation for the final step in the process, which is to assess the board's effectiveness and to evaluate how closely its activity matches its aspirations.

Board Composition

Fundamental to the success of any team is having the right people around the table, and the board is no exception. As we'll discuss in Chapter Two, recruitment of new board members is one of the areas where the shift in power from the CEO to the board has been most dramatic. It's crucial for board leaders to create explicit profiles that will guide their recruitment and enable them to use each appointment to help shape a board that has the collective experience, skills, and personal attributes to do real work collaboratively and effectively. That will require robust recruitment strategies that search beyond the personal networks of the CEO and the board—the "usual suspects"—to find qualified candidates.

Selection is only the first step in making sure the board has the right people. In Chapter Three, we'll explore the aspect of composition that boards have been much more reluctant to address: the performance of individual directors. As directors often tell us, it's generally easier for most boards to remove an underperforming CEO than an underperforming director. In both the United States and the United Kingdom only about a quarter of all boards have established rigorous processes for regularly evaluating each director's performance and using the feedback to either improve performance or initiate removal. We'll describe some effective tools we've developed with boards to do just that.

Board Leadership

The next set of chapters focuses specifically on the role of board leaders in building high-performance teams.

Chapter Four sets the scene by exploring the emerging leadership roles and structures of boards. In the United States, the CEO's control over the board was unchallenged and absolute at most companies until very recently. In the wake of the corporate scandals, and the structural changes that followed, CEOs no longer control the powerful compensation, nominating, and audit committees. Independent directors are filling a variety of leadership roles, as lead directors, presiding directors, and nonexecutive chairmen. Boards are required to meet periodically in executive session without the CEO present. We're now in a period of experimentation, and each board has to decide what division of responsibilities works best for it.

In Chapter Five, we take a close look at what leaders can do to improve the quality and productivity of their ongoing work processes. Specifically, we'll explore ways in which leaders can improve the absolutely essential flow of information to the board, how they can shape agendas to make the best possible use of the board's limited opportunity for working together face-to-face, and how they can maximize the value of the independent directors' executive sessions, perhaps the single most valuable change to come out of the recent governance reforms.

The first five chapters deal with how to get the right people doing the right work, using the right processes. Any board—or any team for that matter—can get those first three approximately right, but without the right culture, which is the topic of Chapter Six, the other three won't matter. This is perhaps the biggest challenge for board leaders: to reshape a deeply entrenched, traditional culture of passivity, deference to management, and excessive formality into a culture that encourages independence, constructive dissent, broad participation, unfettered openness, and spirited inquiry. The burden falls squarely on the shoulder of board leaders; no one else can change the culture or keep it from either slipping back to the old ways or hurtling out of control into dysfunctional acrimony.

Value-Added Engagement

If the board has successfully mastered the requirements up to this point, then ideally the outcome will be engagement that adds value to the organization. Beyond the area of audit and financial reporting, which has been the primary focus of the recent governance reforms, we think there are four critical areas where the board is uniquely positioned to add significant value to the overall quality of an organization's governance.

- *Corporate strategy* (Chapter Seven): Many directors believe that the development and oversight of corporate strategy is one of the board's most critical functions (the other being hiring and firing of CEOs), but it's also an area where they believe they've been least effective. A high-performing board, through its collective experience, expertise, and rigorous questioning, can add immense value to management's thinking. Ineffective boards either rubber-stamp management's plans or get too involved in the details. We will describe a process that, based on our experience, allows for appropriate engagement and added value.

• *CEO performance evaluation* (Chapter Eight): Traditionally, the board mainly relied on lagging indicators of financial performance to determine the CEO's compensation. But an effective evaluation process should do much more. Although it should recognize the importance of the financials, it should also evaluate the CEO's leadership based on outcomes that are directly within his or her control, and use the evaluation process to shape organizational goals for the coming year.

• *Executive succession* (Chapter Nine): Increasingly, boards are demanding an active role in deciding who will be the next CEO. It's not sufficient for the CEO to come up with a single candidate and ask the board to ratify that choice. Boards need to get involved early to ensure identification of a range of candidates who will be evaluated, provided with opportunities to broaden their skills and experience, and exposed to the board in various settings. Boards are also realizing that their role doesn't end when the new CEO is selected; they have a unique responsibility to help the new chief executive get off to a good start.

• *Risk assessment and crisis management* (Chapter Ten): The board is uniquely positioned not only to oversee a rigorous process for assessing risk and planning for crises but also to take center stage when the CEO is the focal point of a crisis, a situation that's not uncommon these days. The board can also contribute substantial value by insisting on a thorough analysis of the underlying institutional problems that might have led to the crisis in the fist place.

Assessment of Engagement

The final step in the board-building process is for the board to regularly assess the quality of its engagement (Chapter Eleven). Annual assessment was among the new requirements imposed on U.S. boards in 2002. But it's a stark example of the difference between minimum compliance and a robust process. A board can easily fulfill the NYSE listing requirements by checking off the boxes on a pro forma report cobbled together by some other company's lawyers, verifying whether it is in compliance with all the other technical requirements. But that won't tell you a thing about whether the board is doing the right work and doing it well. As we suggested earlier, the assessment should flow from the board's decisions about what work it thinks is important and how deeply it should be engaged, and measure the gaps between its intentions and accomplishments.

Board Issues in Canada and the United Kingdom

Corporate governance has developed in different ways in the United States, Canada, and the United Kingdom. Each country has its own set of laws, listing regulations, and governance guidelines reflecting its history, traditions, and culture. Overall, we're struck more by the similarities than the differences (the differing attitudes toward splitting the CEO and chairman roles notwithstanding). Based on our work with boards in all three countries, we are convinced that the framework and underlying concepts of the board-building framework apply in all three. However, acknowledging the heavy emphasis on the United States throughout much of this book, the final chapters focus on current governance issues of particular significance in Canada (Chapter Twelve) and the United Kingdom (Chapter Thirteen).

BOARD-BUILDING: TAKING STOCK

With that framework in mind, let's begin the board-building process with the first step: taking stock of the board.

The process of board-building rarely starts with a blank page (although there is the special case of a new company or spin-off that is creating a brand-new board). Each board enters the process at a different place, based on its own history, assumptions, culture, composition, and leadership. The first step is to understand the feelings, perceptions, and evaluations of both directors and senior managers about how the board operates today. More often than not, the challenge is how to take an existing board and reshape it into a productive team. Without some initial diagnostic work, it's practically impossible to know where to start.

For example, in recent years we worked with a number of Fortune 100 companies, in vastly different industries, where the initial diagnosis in each case pointed unequivocally to composition as the board's biggest problem. In one case, the problem was behavior; certain board members were so disruptive, disloyal, and dysfunctional that the board couldn't get any work done or be confident that any of its deliberations would remain private. In others, the boards just didn't have enough directors who knew enough about the company and its industry to make any worthwhile contribution. In those situations, it was pointless to work on any other changes until there'd been a major change in the cast of characters.

Yet we've also been brought into situations where the board's makeup was just fine; the members just weren't spending their time on the right work, or if they were, they didn't know how to move the ball forward. Those situations suggested a course of action unrelated to composition.

To be effective this initial phase requires a more open-ended diagnostic process than what you'd normally find in a formal assessment. Asking people to check off boxes on a structured survey won't get the job done. This requires in-depth, confidential interviews with everyone involved.

Gathering the information is only the first step. The real goal is to use the feedback as the basis for discussions that will create consensus about the board's challenges and generate collective energy to do something about them. There has to be general agreement that the pursuit of greater effectiveness is a sufficiently worthwhile goal to merit the time and effort the work is likely to take. Every board is squeezed for time; a rigorous and often-uncomfortable process of self-examination and change isn't likely to win much time on the agenda unless the board first decides that this work really is a priority.

(This is one of those situations—and, just to give fair warning, there will be a few others sprinkled through this book—where it makes sense to enlist the help of outsiders. There are a number of ways to find out how directors and executives are feeling about the board, but confidential interviews with impartial outsiders who have experience in gathering, analyzing, and constructively presenting the feedback often work best.)

THE KEY ISSUE: APPROPRIATE ENGAGEMENT

The new relationship between boards and management is what most often triggers a board's reexamination of its work. The rules of the game have changed, and the key players in corporate governance are trying to figure out how to play their new positions.

In general terms, there's widespread confusion about what work is properly the board's, what work should be management's, and what work ought to be shared. More specifically, our work with one board after another has started with the CEO or chairman telling us something like this: "I have some directors who are very traditional, very passive, and they just sit and wait for the CEO to tell them what to do. And I have others who think their job is to manage the company, and they want to run the place. We can't get anything done."

From every corner, boards are told the answer is simple: they need to overcome their traditional passivity, and become active and empowered. In a perfect world, the board would:

- Bring deep wisdom and broad perspective to the table, providing the CEO with useful advice and acting as a sounding board and source of support.
- Help influence critical outside constituencies.
- Create a solid front to the outside world during crises.
- Assist in effectively managing succession.
- By doing all of the above, safeguard shareholder interests.

But it's not that simple; activism and empowerment can be double-edged swords. Taken to extremes, they can lead to:

- Meddling and micromanagement that distract executives, consume inordinate chunks of their time, and interfere with the orderly operation of the company
- Power struggles at the top of the company
- Damage to the CEO's credibility outside the company
- Inappropriate limits on the CEO's compensation
- Interference with orderly executive succession
- Hasty dismissal of the CEO as an expedient solution to more complex problems

Our point is that it's not enough simply to decide that a board should be active, independent, and empowered. The real question is what does engagement look like for a particular board in a given situation, and what are the options? One way to engage directors in a preliminary discussion is to have them describe their own view of where their board sits on the continuum, ranging from the least to the most engaged boards. Broadly speaking, there are five general archetypes of boards (see Figure 1.2):

- *Passive:* The traditional model. The board's activity and participation are limited, and at the CEO's discretion. The board has limited accountability, and its main job is ratifying management decisions.

Figure 1.2.   Degree of Board Engagement.

- *Certifying:* Places a heavy emphasis on the importance of outside directors, and certifies to shareholders that the business is being managed properly and that the CEO is doing what the board requires. Directors stay informed, oversee an orderly succession process, and are willing to change management if necessary. They are credible to shareholders.

- *Engaged:* Partners with the CEO, providing insight, advice, and support on key decisions and implementation. This kind of board recognizes its ultimate responsibility for overseeing CEO and company performance; meetings typically involve substantive discussion of key issues and decisions. Board members need some level of industry and financial expertise to provide value. They actively work at defining their roles and required behavior, as well as the boundaries of CEO/board responsibility.

- *Intervening:* Most common mode during crises. The board holds frequent and intense meetings, and becomes deeply involved in key decisions.

- *Operating:* The deepest level of ongoing involvement. The board makes key decisions, and management implements them. This model is frequently found in the early stages of start-ups, when top executives often bring some special expertise but lack broad management experience, which the board helps to provide.

Of course, these archetypes are just that—examples of each type of engagement in its purest form. In the real world, boards slide back and forth across the scale, exhibiting different degrees of engagement with regard to different issues. A passive or certifying board, for instance, can suddenly find itself facing a crisis in which it has to act as an intervening board to remove the CEO, and it may then play the role of operating board until a new CEO is in place.

The purpose of the engagement archetypes isn't to squeeze a particular board into a particular box. Rather, the framework provides a useful starting point for a discussion within the board as it begins to grapple with questions such as, "Where are we on this scale?" and "Where and how can we best add value?" Ideally, that discussion leads to the next step in the board-building process: moving beyond generalities and specifically identifying exactly what work the board should be doing, and with what intensity and engagement.

MAPPING THE BOARD'S FOCUS AND ENGAGEMENT

The initial stage of the process is fairly straightforward. It involves creating a framework that lists all of the areas in which the board, at some time or another, might possibly be involved, and then asking each director to rate each area on the degree to which the board is actually involved, and the level at which he or she thinks the board *should* be involved (see Exhibit 1.1).

The trick here is to think in specific terms that go beyond the fairly general legal obligations of the board. These include approving major corporate actions such as making acquisitions; providing counsel to senior management; hiring, firing, setting compensation, and evaluating the performance of the CEO; ensuring effective audit procedures; and monitoring the company's investments for legal compliance.[9] The new requirements call on boards to spell out those duties in written charters, and at the end of each year, to go down the checklist and affirm, "Yes, we did that." But that's a recipe for compliance, not necessarily for good governance.

It's much more useful for boards to translate those legal mandates into specific areas of work, which might be grouped this way:

- Strategy, including strategic direction, plans, and implementation
- Strategic transactions, such as major investments, mergers, acquisitions, and spin-offs
- Operations, including research and development, manufacturing, marketing and sales, and information technology
- Human resources and organization, involving issues such as leadership development, executive compensation, human capital, organizational structure, and corporate culture
- Financial management, including financial strategy, capital structure, liquidity management, dividend policy, and financial reporting
- Risk management, including enterprise risk management, ethical performance and compliance, and audit
- External relations, which might involve the positioning and integrity of the brand, shareholder relations, legal and regulatory affairs, and relations with other major constituencies such as customers, communities, regulators, and government officials
- CEO effectiveness, including critical responsibilities such as performance appraisal, compensation, and succession

Exhibit 1.1. Areas of Potential Board Engagement.

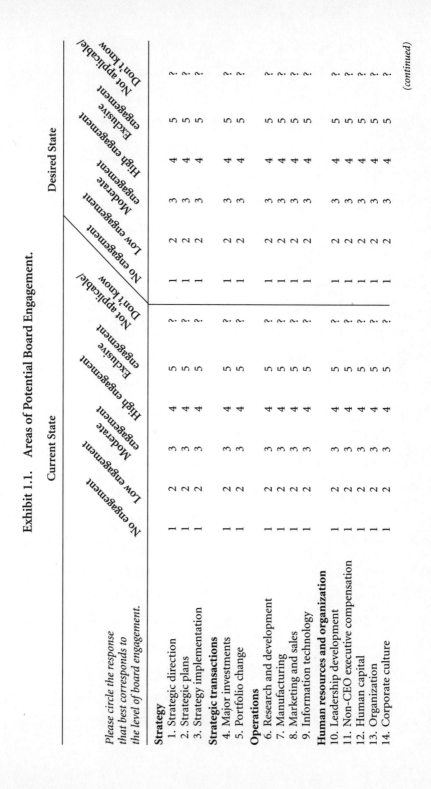

Please circle the response that best corresponds to the level of board engagement.	Current State						Desired State					
	No engagement	Low engagement	Moderate engagement	High engagement	Exclusive engagement	Not applicable/Don't know	No engagement	Low engagement	Moderate engagement	High engagement	Exclusive engagement	Not applicable/Don't know
Strategy												
1. Strategic direction	1	2	3	4	5	?	1	2	3	4	5	?
2. Strategic plans	1	2	3	4	5	?	1	2	3	4	5	?
3. Strategy implementation	1	2	3	4	5	?	1	2	3	4	5	?
Strategic transactions												
4. Major investments	1	2	3	4	5	?	1	2	3	4	5	?
5. Portfolio change	1	2	3	4	5	?	1	2	3	4	5	?
Operations												
6. Research and development	1	2	3	4	5	?	1	2	3	4	5	?
7. Manufacturing	1	2	3	4	5	?	1	2	3	4	5	?
8. Marketing and sales	1	2	3	4	5	?	1	2	3	4	5	?
9. Information technology	1	2	3	4	5	?	1	2	3	4	5	?
Human resources and organization												
10. Leadership development	1	2	3	4	5	?	1	2	3	4	5	?
11. Non-CEO executive compensation	1	2	3	4	5	?	1	2	3	4	5	?
12. Human capital	1	2	3	4	5	?	1	2	3	4	5	?
13. Organization	1	2	3	4	5	?	1	2	3	4	5	?
14. Corporate culture	1	2	3	4	5	?	1	2	3	4	5	?

(continued)

Exhibit 1.1. continued

	Current State						Desired State					
Please circle the response that best corresponds to the level of board engagement.	No engagement	Low engagement	Moderate engagement	High engagement	Exclusive engagement	Not applicable/ Don't know	No engagement	Low engagement	Moderate engagement	High engagement	Exclusive engagement	Not applicable/ Don't know
Financial management												
15. Financial strategy	1	2	3	4	5	?	1	2	3	4	5	?
16. Capital structure	1	2	3	4	5	?	1	2	3	4	5	?
17. Liquidity management	1	2	3	4	5	?	1	2	3	4	5	?
18. Dividend policy	1	2	3	4	5	?	1	2	3	4	5	?
19. Financial reporting	1	2	3	4	5	?	1	2	3	4	5	?
Risk management												
20. Enterprise risk management	1	2	3	4	5	?	1	2	3	4	5	?
21. Ethical performance and compliance	1	2	3	4	5	?	1	2	3	4	5	?
22. Audit	1	2	3	4	5	?	1	2	3	4	5	?
External relations												
23. Brand positioning, integrity	1	2	3	4	5	?	1	2	3	4	5	?
24. Shareholder relations	1	2	3	4	5	?	1	2	3	4	5	?
25. Legal and regulatory	1	2	3	4	5	?	1	2	3	4	5	?
26. Other constituencies	1	2	3	4	5	?	1	2	3	4	5	?

CEO effectiveness

	1	2	3	4	5	?		1	2	3	4	5	?
27. CEO performance appraisal	1	2	3	4	5	?		1	2	3	4	5	?
28. CEO compensation	1	2	3	4	5	?		1	2	3	4	5	?
29. CEO succession	1	2	3	4	5	?		1	2	3	4	5	?

Corporate governance

	1	2	3	4	5	?		1	2	3	4	5	?
30. Board effectiveness	1	2	3	4	5	?		1	2	3	4	5	?
31. Director selection	1	2	3	4	5	?		1	2	3	4	5	?
32. Director assessment	1	2	3	4	5	?		1	2	3	4	5	?

Other (please specify)

	1	2	3	4	5	?		1	2	3	4	5	?
33. _____	1	2	3	4	5	?		1	2	3	4	5	?
34. _____	1	2	3	4	5	?		1	2	3	4	5	?

• Corporate governance, which covers activities relating to the board's own leadership, performance, and composition

For each specific area of responsibility in each general group, directors rate the board's actual and optimal level of engagement on a sliding scale that describes the relative intensity of engagement by the board and senior management, respectively, ranging from no engagement to exclusive engagement. At one end of the scale are activities that are the primary responsibility of management and in which the board has no involvement; at the other end are areas that fall exclusively within the purview of the board, which merely keeps management informed of its decisions. Boards that have had the greatest success with this form of assessment have asked senior managers to fill out the same rating form.

For example, using a similar approach, the board of a Fortune 500 company where the CEO's predecessor had recently been ousted developed the following comparison (see Figure 1.3) of its current and desired levels of engagement. Interestingly, there was only one area—operations—in which the board did not seek significantly more engagement than it already had, a view that mirrors a concern common among many boards that feel too bogged down in operational details. In contrast, the board expressed a clear desire for much more active engagement in such critical areas as CEO effectiveness, corporate governance, strategy, strategic transactions, and risk management.

This information can be used in several important ways. The first is a gap analysis reflecting whether directors feel the board is appropriately involved in the right work. Reconciling the "shoulds" and "actuals" is an essential step in matching the board's real work with its general view of its role. The second gap analysis illustrates how directors' views differ from those of managers regarding the board's appropriate role, an issue that's often lurking in the background but that no one feels comfortable in raising. It's worth noting that the data sometimes provide some pleasant surprises; at one large media company, directors were surprised to find that in some areas management rated the board's involvement more highly than the board had rated itself.

SUMMARY

Looking back at the first two steps of the process we've just described, and thinking ahead to the steps that follow, we'd like to highlight two themes that will recur throughout our discussion.

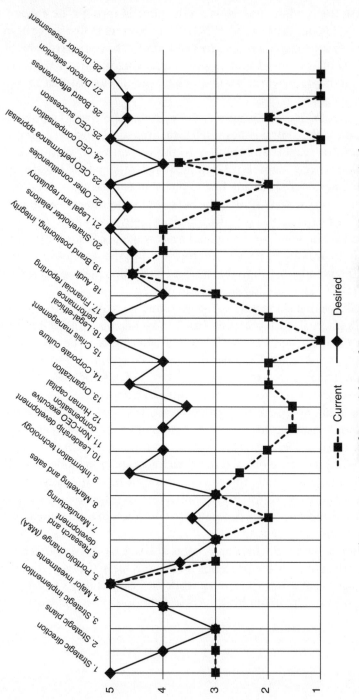

Figure 1.3.   Areas of Potential Board Engagement: Current Versus Desired.

First, the fundamental issue on the table is appropriate engagement. So far, our discussion has been fairly abstract in that we've been talking about engagement in terms of defining the respective responsibilities of the board and senior management. But as we work through the framework, it will quickly become evident that there's nothing abstract about it.

In Chapter Two, for example, as we discuss the board's composition, one of the central issues will be what role the board, its committees, and its leaders should play in the recruitment, vetting, and selection of new members. Until fairly recently, most CEOs in the United States were basically free to pick and choose whomever they wanted to fill the seats around the table, and appointments were routinely used to pack the board with management allies and a couple of celebrities who might or might not have any qualifications for the job. Clearly, boards are quickly assuming much of the responsibility for selecting members. But that leaves open the important question of what role, if any, the CEO should still play.

We'll see that same question played out as we move through the board's internal work processes (such as agenda planning and information management) to specific content areas such as development of corporate strategy, CEO performance evaluation, and succession planning. In each case, the work has to begin with some shared vision of the respective roles of the board and management.

The second theme is that process really is important; sometimes, it's what is most important. It's not enough to say that the goal is a board that is active, engaged, and functioning as a high-performance team. The processes employed by board leaders have to model the culture they hope to create. You can't mandate a culture of engagement. You can't have two or three senior directors go off on their own and set the ground rules for broad participation. You can't order members to think and act independently.

In short, the culture the board wants to create has to be reflected by, and consistent with, the processes it uses to achieve that goal. Board-building is about more than what work the board chooses to do; just as importantly, it's about how the board chooses to do that work.

CHAPTER TWO

Board Composition

Beverly A. Behan

Until quite recently, designing a board's composition was a lot like decorating a Christmas tree: the CEO would pick out a nice selection of glittering ornaments, then top off the tree with a flashy star.

That may be an exaggeration—but not by much. For decades, the appointment of outside board members was an informal, even incestuous process. CEOs took the lead, frequently nominating their personal friends and professional acquaintances. A "balanced" board included one or two CEOs and a sprinkling of bankers, lawyers, academics, community leaders, and retired politicians. There was no shortage of candidates; the job was easy, the pay and the perks were good, the prestige was always welcomed, and performance just wasn't an issue—the job was yours as long as you wanted it.

Times have changed. Perhaps what has changed most of all is how actively the board is now engaged in a realm that was almost entirely dominated by the CEO until just a few short years ago. As we'll see in this chapter and the next, the board has significant opportunities—some still unfulfilled—to shape the board's composition in ways that can enhance its ability to work as a high-performance team.

Today, the independent directors, not the CEO, control the nominating process. Seven out of ten directors in the 2004 USC/Mercer Delta Corporate Board Survey said that their board's nominating/governance committee had the most influence in selecting nominees, whereas only 14 percent said the CEO still reigned over the process. The traditional "butcher, baker, candlestick-maker" approach to populating the boardroom is giving way to a more disciplined and systematic process. Many boards are striving to align the skills and experience of directors with the challenges of their particular company and industry, and trying hard to recruit people with personal qualities that will foster constructive working relationships in the boardroom. And as we'll see in Chapter Three, some boards are finally stepping up to the thorny issue of director performance and dealing with members who fail to carry their own weight.

At the same time, the recruitment process is becoming more complicated, and more difficult, for everyone involved. Just when boards need them most, highly qualified, independent directors are getting harder to find. The imbalance between supply and demand started in 2002, when boards were first required to ensure that a majority of their members were outside directors who met tougher new definitions of independence. As a result, boards had to start searching for nominees beyond the list of "usual suspects," people with business connections with the company and its CEO.

But just as boards began searching for new blood, the pool of obvious candidates was shrinking. The same corporate scandals that led to more exacting requirements for board membership also raised grave concerns among potential directors about whether they really wanted to assume the new rigors and risks associated with the job. A quarter of the directors in the 2004 USC/Mercer Delta Corporate Board Survey said they were more hesitant than before about serving on boards, and that survey was conducted before the precedent-setting cases in which Enron and WorldCom directors were forced to make personal restitution for their boards' negligence.

Add to that the increasing scarcity of CEOs who are willing or able to sit on boards. Traditionally, sitting and retired CEOs have made up the biggest source of directors—around 45 percent, by some estimates. But according to the directors we surveyed, half of their boards— nearly double the percentage just three years earlier—had imposed limits on how many outside boards their CEOs could belong to. In some cases, the limits are superfluous; more and more CEOs are deciding they have their hands full just doing their day job. Either by choice or by policy, CEOs are becoming a scarce commodity as outside directors. Spencer Stuart, the executive search firm, found in its 2004 annual board survey that the average number of outside directorships held by CEOs was only 0.9, the first time it had ever dropped below 1 and a great decrease from an average of 1.6 in 1999.[1]

Matthew Barrett, chairman of the British bank Barclays PLC, is a case in point. He told an interviewer that he had abandoned his practice of routinely sitting on one or two outside boards, no longer belonged to any, and had rejected about ten approaches in the previous year. "I will go through a degree of risk analysis that I wouldn't have gone through in the past," he explained.[2]

As we said, it's a challenging situation, but boards that are serious about meeting their new responsibilities have no choice but to rise to the challenge. The board's composition—the individual skills and collective capabilities it brings to the table—constitutes a cornerstone of the board-building process, and lies at the heart of any board's ability to perform its duties effectively.

In this chapter, we'll discuss the issues that have the strongest impact on board composition:

- Alignment of board composition with the work to be done and the working dynamic the board wants to create and maintain
- Practical issues in designing a director nominating process
- Due diligence that savvy candidates pursue before accepting a board invitation
- Integration of new directors onto the board

ALIGNING COMPOSITION WITH ENGAGEMENT

The key to effective board composition is ensuring that the people gathered around the board table can leverage their experience to contribute in meaningful ways, to understand the issues, ask the right questions, demand the right information, and make the best possible decisions. Many of the recent attempts to strengthen boards have focused on the control function, the board's responsibility to closely monitor management's performance. But a well-constituted board can go further and add value by providing a source of counsel, questions, and expertise as the company pursues its strategic objectives. That requires a much more disciplined approach to board composition than most boards have taken in the past.

Board Competencies: Three Key Elements

There are three important elements to consider when it comes to making sure that you have the right people in your boardroom (see Figure 2.1):

SKILLS AND EXPERIENCE. Develop a profile of the skills and experience that should be present around the table in order for the board to thoroughly understand the company and make substantive contributions to the quality of its management and strategic direction. Many boards have used a board skills inventory to identify the gap between the current board's collective portfolio of skills and the ideal portfolio the board ought to have.

INDIVIDUAL ATTRIBUTES. Define the individual attributes that you want all board members to demonstrate—independence, business credibility, confidence, courage to raise challenging issues, ability to manage one's ego, for example.

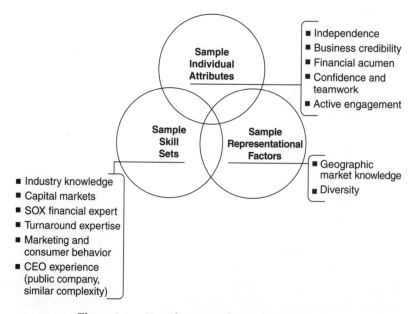

Figure 2.1.   Key Elements of Board Competency.

REPRESENTATIONAL FACTORS. Address representational factors—demographic and geographic diversity, for example—that are important in terms of board composition.

All three elements are critical to optimizing the board's composition. A director who has impeccable professional credentials but lacks the personal attributes to work comfortably within the board culture you're trying to create will be marginally effective at best and dysfunctional or disruptive at worst. Similarly, achieving demographic or geographic diversity at the expense of critical skills or experience is risky. The fact is, some trade-offs are inevitable, but unless you've developed an explicit board composition profile, it's hard to know precisely what they are or how to weigh them.

Board Skills Inventory

The first step is for the nominating/governance committee and the CEO to agree on which skills are the most crucial given the company's strategic direction and issues. The key question: What kinds of experience and backgrounds will enable a board to ask the right questions and engage in informed discussions as it tackles the strategic issues the company is likely to face over the next few years?

For example, if mergers and acquisitions are a strategic priority, board members experienced in planning, reviewing, and implementing M&As would clearly raise the level of board discussion and decision making on these matters. Moreover, directors with experience in the arenas that the company is confronting typically provide the most value for the CEO and senior management, who can benefit tremendously from these directors' experience. Most CEOs will tell you they get the greatest value from directors who have already "walked through the fire" on issues the CEO is confronting for the first time.

Deep understanding of the company's core technologies is another valuable asset directors can bring to the table. Several years ago, our colleagues worked with a major communication services company where board meetings were generally unproductive. Managers would march in, deliver fully scripted, highly technical presentations that left the board befuddled, then go back to work. The board finally added two new members with outstanding high-tech credentials; from that moment on, board meetings were never the same. The first managers who had to sweat their way through intensive questioning from the new directors went back to their colleagues and announced that the "cakewalk" was over.

No single director is expected to bring all of these skills and experiences into the boardroom. Rather, the goal of the nominating/governance committee is to ensure that the board overall has every one of them. When determining which skills are most important, keep in mind three considerations:

- First, avoid a cookie-cutter approach and resist the temptation to simply adopt another board's profile. There is real value in tailoring the list of skills to your own company's particular needs; moreover, the actual exercise of thinking this through creates healthy dialogue and focuses much needed attention on the importance of board composition.

- Second, consider whether any of the skills on your list should be "purchased" rather than incorporated into the fabric of the board. For example, every board has to wrestle with legal issues from time to time, but that doesn't necessarily mean you should have a corporate lawyer on the board when you can easily retain legal counsel when you need it.

- Finally, create an ideal board profile without regard to your current board composition. Some boards fall into the trap of simply listing the backgrounds of their existing directors and calling that their skills inventory. This defeats the purpose of the exercise. Instead, start with a blank sheet; if you were putting together a board from scratch, what combination of skills would you seek in light of the issues you're likely to confront over the next two to five years?

Once you've developed this list, the next step is to match the skills your board needs with those it already has, and then to recruit directors to fill the gaps.

Examples of Board Skills Inventories

Table 2.1 provides a sample board skills inventory prepared by the nominating/governance committee of a fast-growing NYSE-listed defense company. Table 2.2 shows an inventory prepared by the nominating/governance committee of a community bank that had recently

Table 2.1.   Defense Corporation Board Skills Inventory.

Competency	Board Members Who Possess This Competency
U.S. defense experience, government or industry	Briggs Cooper Jones King
CEO or other senior executive, public company	Rutherford King
International business or government experience	Briggs Cooper
Engineering-technical expertise, practical or academic	Jones
Financial or accounting experience, professional	Briggs Martin Newman
Operational management experience, large-scale implementation of strategy, M&A, and major cost controls	Jones King Newman Rutherford
Financial management or portfolio investment experience	Lawrence Newman

Table 2.2.   Community Bank Board Skills Inventory.

Competency	Board Members Who Possess This Competency
Experience-knowledge of financial services industry	Morris Sloane White
Public company CEO experience, preferably active public company CEOs	Kates
Financial or accounting experience, professional	White
Capital markets experience-knowledge	Morris Sloane
Mergers and acquisitions experience, large-scale implementation of M&A or review of M&A deals	Kates Madden
Knowledge or expertise in retailing	Franklin
Active or newly retired CEOs of companies with similar complexity to the bank, public or private	Carter Franklin Yarborough
Knowledge of peer financial services sectors, such as insurance	Madden
Knowledge of towns and municipalities, a significant client base for the bank	Sloane Yarborough

completed its IPO on the Nasdaq. These examples, although quite different, illustrate how two boards defined their optimal board skills profiles to reflect their respective businesses and corporate strategies.

PRACTICAL ISSUES IN THE DIRECTOR NOMINATION PROCESS

As we noted early in this chapter, good directors are becoming harder to find. That simple fact has significant implications for boards when it comes to how and where they look for qualified candidates.

In our 2004 directors survey, 37 percent agreed that it's getting more difficult to find qualified directors. Tom Neff of Spencer Stuart said in 2003 that his firm was engaged in 50 percent more director searches than the previous year, and he attributed the "supply crunch" to the new rules requiring a majority of independent directors and banning nonindependent directors from the audit and compensation committees.[3] And although the number of vacancies is rising, the number of acceptances is plunging. Neff's colleague Dennis C. Carey told the *New York Times,* "Five years ago, four candidates might have turned down each job; today, it may be ten."[4]

No doubt this is due at least in part to a growing concern about potential legal and financial liability, and the possibility of a reputation being destroyed. It also reflects the tremendous amount of time now required for board business. Directors who responded to the 2004 USC/Mercer Delta survey indicated that they sat only on two boards on average, and spent 188 hours a year on board matters (including preparation time, travel time, attendance at board and committee meetings) for each board on which they served. Nearly two-thirds said they were spending more time on board work in 2004 than they had in 2003.

There's also the fact that the traditional pool of directors is shrinking. As already noted, CEOs have been cutting back on their outside board memberships since 2000, and many don't serve on any outside boards at all. The same trend is evident among directors in general; those we surveyed in 2004 belonged to an average of only 2.5 boards. Although the boards represented in our survey are more willing to limit their CEO's outside directorships than their own, the trend is clear: the number of respondents who said their boards have membership limits rose to 37 percent in 2004 from only 3 percent in 2001.

One implication of this shrinking pool of candidates is obvious: boards have to expand the pool by thinking more creatively about who should be included in it. Retired CEOs are becoming more attractive; at the same time, boards that typically favored seasoned CEOs should take a close look at relatively new CEOs, who are often much more interested in sitting "on the other side of the board table" in part for their own professional development.

In addition, boards may want to consider qualified candidates a level or two below the CEO. Many boards, like that of Target Corporation, find they can discover outstanding people at those levels who have relevant operating experience, are younger, and are more diverse. Indeed, the imperative to cast a wider net—which 54 percent of our survey respondents said their boards have done—is gradually weakening the traditional reliance on the "old boys network" of potential candidates. Although the overall percentage of women on boards of the largest publicly traded U.S. companies has gradually increased over the years (from 12 percent in 1999 to 16 percent in 2004), 24 percent of the new independent directors appointed in 2004 were women, the largest single-year increase ever recorded for the S&P 500.[5]

Search Firms Versus Board Network

"In the past," recalled one member of the NACD Blue Ribbon Commission on Board Leadership, "when CEOs did all the board recruiting, there was a temptation for them to say, 'Here's my frat brother. He'll be good on my board.' What we can't have happen now is for the new board members to just be the frat brothers of the people on the nominating/governance committee. That's not really much better." In other words, simply shifting the responsibility for director recruitment from the CEO to a committee of independent directors doesn't guarantee a better process.

That raises the issue of search firms, and members of the Blue Ribbon Commission offered decidedly mixed views on whether it's preferable to rely on the board's personal network or to retain outside help.

Some felt strongly that a director network yielded superior talent. "The best directors are recruited through other directors," said one commission member. "I don't worry about cronyism because candidates need to be approved by all the board members, so people are careful with their recommendations." Others pointed out that board members can best sense whether a particular candidate will be a good fit with their board's culture. Moreover, when a board member recommends a director candidate who is ultimately endorsed, the nominator tends to have a vested interest in that individual's success and often takes on a mentoring role.

Others, however, strongly advocated using headhunters to go beyond the board's own network of contacts. A commission member said, "I know that many good people have been found through board networks, but I think it's a mistake to just continue to limit yourself to the people around the table for recruitment. It's a very small pool and can provide a very insular perspective and many interlocks."

As a practical matter, many boards end up using both sources. One commission member whose board does just that, explained, "It can be useful to use search firms to surface candidates beyond our immediate network. But it's also a good idea to use your own board and say to them, 'Can you recommend people who bring this skill set that we're looking for who you feel would be effectively engaged?'"

Role of the CEO

Now that nominating/governance committees have taken the lead in director recruitment, many boards are struggling to define the appropriate role for the CEO in the process. As a first step, the CEO should be engaged with the board in defining and mapping board competencies and setting priorities for each search; for example, if the CEO feels strongly that she needs someone on the board with more industry experience and the nominating/governance committee was planning to focus on financial expertise, that's a serious issue that should be addressed before recruitment begins rather than midway through the process.

The CEO, like any other board member, should also have the opportunity to recommend candidates. As one commissioner noted, "The chairman/CEO shouldn't lead the recruitment effort but . . . he or she should be able to raise potential candidates just like everyone else on the board, and that candidate should be put in the hopper with other candidates."

The CEO should also have the opportunity to interview every serious candidate, though it's hardly necessary to mandate that as part of the process. The fact is, it's almost impossible to imagine any candidate accepting a board position without first meeting the CEO.

Finally, when it comes time to recommend candidates, the nominating/governance committee has the ultimate responsibility, but the CEO's point of view should certainly be considered. It's rarely helpful to nominate a director who has an acrimonious relationship with the CEO. Some commissioners went so far as to suggest that the CEO should be given a veto over board candidates. "It's a check-and-balance thing," said one commissioner, "but I think it creates a lot of dysfunction right from the start when the CEO and a new board member really don't like each other. I'd tend to give the CEO a veto to avoid that."

Interviewing Director Candidates

Historically, the board recruitment process was perfunctory at best. It generally involved one or two conversations, after which the CEO would extend an offer and provide the date of the next board meeting.

Those days are gone. Today, few nominating/governance committee chairs would dream of recommending a candidate before that person had been interviewed by the CEO and several members of the board. The challenge, however, is to design a process that allows the nominating/governance committee and the CEO to make a deliberate assessment without making the candidate feel that she's jumping through an endless series of hoops. That's especially important when qualified directors are in such high demand.

In practice, once a candidate has been interviewed—particularly a high-profile one—nominating/governance committees are often hesitant to reject that candidate because of the potential embarrassment to everyone involved. But short-term embarrassment is clearly preferable to long-term dysfunction, and that's what's really at stake in these situations.

Despite growing attention to director performance (see Chapter Three), the typical board is still more likely to fire the CEO than to oust one of its own members. As one commissioner noted, "When you are recruiting people onto your board, they are going to be with you for a very long time. It's amazing how little you really know about these people when you're making that sort of decision. You meet and you're both in sales mode and being very charming to each other. There's a real element of luck involved many times, because you often don't really get to know a person until they come onto your board, and then it's too late if there's a problem."

Unfortunately, the typical candidate interview doesn't offer any magic solution. It generally takes place over lunch or dinner, begins with an exchange of pleasantries about families, hobbies, and shared acquaintances, and sometimes ends there as well. Members of the Blue

Ribbon Commission suggested some interview questions that are likely to give a decent indication of a candidate's suitability without being overly intrusive:

"In recruiting directors, I always ask, 'Why would you consider being on this board?' What I don't want to hear is, 'It would be a great honor' or 'I like the other board members.' What I want to hear the person say is that they understand the challenges facing the company, they spell out some of those challenges, and then they tell me how they think their background and experience could be beneficial to the board of a company facing those challenges."

"Ethics is one of the key things we are looking for in recruiting directors. The question we always ask in interviews is: 'Give me an example of where you have had to make a tough ethical decision.' We have rejected a board candidate based on how they answered that question because it's so important to us."

Other questions that can yield helpful insights include these:

- What would you describe as your best board experience either on a public company or not-for-profit organization, and why? Conversely, what was your worst experience?

- What are the two or three key attributes that make someone a really good director? Why are those qualities important?

- What do you hope to get out of your experience serving as a director on our board? When you are considering a board invitation, what are the most important factors? Why would you decide to join one board over another? When you look at our board, what do you find most appealing about the opportunity? What are you most concerned about?

Personal interviews are also the best way to gauge how well a candidate matches the personal attributes you're looking for in a board member. Although skills, experience, and representational factors can usually be gleaned from the candidate's biographical information, only interviews and references can help you assess a candidate's "fit" on this personal dimension. Thus you may want to focus your conversation to try to get some insights on the personal attributes you're looking for, particularly those that may be unique to your board or corporate culture.

As one commissioner told us, "Our company has a core value of giving back to society. We've always made significant charitable contributions and taken great pride in what we do in this area. When we're talking to prospective board members, we try to ascertain whether this person embraces that value or not. Because, frankly, a Scrooge McDuck type wouldn't be a very good fit on our board." Another board chairman we worked with recently told us, "This is a down-to-earth midwestern company with a down-to-earth midwestern board. There's no room here for arrogance or pretension, so that's what we're screening for when we talk to people that we're considering as potential directors."

Director References

Reference checks on director candidates, which have increased in recent years, can be challenging. As one commissioner stated, "There's a lot more due diligence that goes into checking out a potential board member now. I would add that potential board members are doing the very same thing. We do background checks to make sure that there are no arrests, SEC violations, etc. That didn't used to go on as rigorously as it's going on now. We also look into whether there are any conflicts of interest or foreseeable conflicts."

The discovery of a conflict, arrest, or SEC violation makes the choice pretty clear. What's harder to find is genuinely helpful feedback about a candidate's character and suitability for board service. Many boards now require one or two references from the CEO or directors who serve on a board with the candidate, and they try to identify people in their own networks who can provide firsthand references.

Legal concerns involving privacy rights have made reference checks more problematic than ever, and the same holds true for director searches. One commission member noted, "There is often reluctance to speak candidly over the phone about a candidate. You often find out too late that this guy can't keep a confidence, or that he talks too much or has a self-interested agenda that you didn't anticipate. Reference checking should be done in person, and not by the headhunter. When you do it face-to-face, you usually get the real 'goods' because there are no memos or potential litigation."

DUE DILIGENCE BY CANDIDATES

It's not just boards that are getting more rigorous about searches. Considering all the risks involved, potential directors are increasingly gun-shy about which boards they're willing to join, and they are doing much more due diligence before accepting an invitation. Whether you're a director anticipating questions from a candidate or you're a candidate pursuing your own due diligence, it's important to understand the issues that weigh heavily in the decision about whether or not to join a particular board.

Public Information

The most basic research starts with a corporate profile to get a snapshot of the company—its recent performance and an overview of some key corporate issues—supplemented by the latest annual report and recent financial statements. Many director candidates track down or ask for recent industry analysts' reports about the company and news reports or media articles on the company over the last twelve to eighteen months. They generally go to company Web sites looking for director and management biographies as well as committee charters and corporate governance guidelines. Frequently, nominating/governance committees have anticipated this need and prepared a package of such information that can be sent to candidates.

A company's latest proxy circular is usually the most important document for a prospective director to review. It not only contains biographical data on fellow directors but also indicates how long each director has served on the board. A potential director will want to know if there has been turnover on the board or if she is the first new recruit in many years. Most prospective directors also review the level of stockholdings of the other directors, disclosure of related party transactions, and the level of CEO compensation in light of corporate performance.

Board Information

Many candidates ask to see the agendas and reading packages for the last two board meetings. That material provides an immediate picture of the issues the board is working on and enables the prospective director to make some judgments about the quality of board information. Two packages provide a pattern; if both are poor, it's a problem, not an anomaly.

Many candidates also request the results of the most recent annual board assessment. A seasoned director can discern whether it was a superficial exercise or a meaningful process that effectively raised and addressed important issues. A board assessment that suggests there are no issues is actually a red flag, signaling either a poorly designed assessment process or a board that's not really interested in improving.

Finally, many prospective directors will ask to see a company's score from a governance rating service such as Institutional Shareholder Services (ISS) or Governance Metrics International (GMI). These ratings should be taken with a grain of salt. Most are based on structural best practices that an outside "rater" can glean from proxy or other public information, but they omit crucial elements that can significantly affect how a board functions; for example, board processes are considered at a superficial level, and board dynamics aren't factored in at all. Consequently, a low score should raise concerns, but a high score is no guarantee of excellence.

Boards should also provide candidates with information on two other important issues: director compensation, and the directors' and officers' liability insurance program. Although the annual proxy circular provides some details, it seems appropriate to let a prospective director know right away what he can expect to be paid and what expectations there may be (formal or informal) about maintaining a certain level of company stockholdings while serving on the board. Moreover, in today's litigious environment, D&O insurance is increasingly important to prospective directors. It's a good idea to have the company's risk manager walk each candidate through the D&O policy and its limitations.

Interviews

For most directors, the single most important factor in the decision to join a board is their assessment of the CEO. Is this CEO someone they can respect and support? Do they share the same values? Does the CEO's assessment of her company and board sound reasonable and candid?

When the director recruit meets the CEO, the conversation typically focuses on the CEO's vision for the company—key strategic objectives and challenges. During this discussion, the candidate will be gauging the CEO's leadership style and his own level of comfort with that style. He may ask the CEO directly how the board adds value for her, where the board has been most helpful and most frustrating in the past, and how the board could be better. The CEO's answers to these questions provide excellent insight into the relationship between the CEO and the board, and in particular how the CEO views contributions from board members.

In conversations with the chair of the nominating/governance committee, lead director, and other board members, the candidate will again be gauging the working relationship between the board and management, though this time it will be done through the board's lens. Most will ask current directors for their assessment of management's effectiveness. Answers yield insight as to whether there is a constructive relationship between the board and management, whether there is disharmony, or (worse yet) whether board members appear spellbound by management and unlikely to voice dissenting views.

Although boards and top executives are often tempted to "sell" a prospective director in these conversations by pitching an overwhelmingly positive story, that strategy frequently backfires. Candidates aren't dumb; they understand a company's reluctance to spill secrets to an outsider. But a stream of endless happy talk leads to three possible conclusions, none of them good: the board is either uninformed, seriously dishonest, or in collective denial.

One former CEO told us why he turned down an invitation to join the board of one of the best-known U.S. companies: "I've been a CEO long enough to know that no company is perfect, and every company can do better, and this company's problems were a matter of public record. But nobody I talked to would acknowledge anything had to be fixed. I had no interest in joining a board where everyone would just wink and nod and pretend that everything's fine."

It can also be helpful for the candidate to talk with the last director to join the board, especially if this individual has served on the board for at least six months. It's useful to find out what the new director has most enjoyed about the board and what she has been disappointed or surprised by. It also provides a good opportunity for the recruit to ask candid questions about director orientation.

INTEGRATION OF NEW DIRECTORS

In past years a typical response from new directors when asked about their board orientation was: "They gave me a big binder."

Now, however, the fundamental shift from the ornamental to the working board requires a more thoughtful and thorough integration for new board members. And it needs to be done more quickly. An accelerated learning curve can give board members the knowledge and comfort level they need to quickly start contributing to board discussions and deliberations. As one of the commissioners noted, "When we recruit directors, we give them a full-day orientation session and then tell them, 'We expect you to contribute from Day One. We don't want you to hang back to make a contribution until you get to know the business. We recruited you for your experience and your knowledge and you know enough now to start to make a contribution—so don't hang back.'"

One-on-One Meetings

Far more comprehensive orientation sessions are becoming the norm at progressive boards. Although binders may still be one component of the orientation process, most incoming directors are now being offered opportunities, either before or shortly after their first board meeting, to talk privately with the CEO and other senior executives about the company, its industry, and its key issues. These sessions not only facilitate director learning but also help build rapport between the new directors and members of the executive team.

One senior executive of an NYSE-listed utility told us, "It used to be that you'd come into the boardroom and just see a new face. Now, every member of our executive team spends an hour with each new director one-on-one. So when you see them for the first time at a board meeting, you have a sense of who they are and they also know us a little bit, which makes it easier. I also take comfort in the fact that they have at least some understanding about what we're going to be discussing; they're not hitting this stuff cold. And the new people seem to engage more readily once they've been through this type of orientation."

Some companies also offer new board members a similar opportunity to sit down one-on-one with the chairs of each of the board committees and to attend the meetings of all committees. That gives them valuable exposure, and the opportunity to decide which committee they'd like to serve on.

Role of Board Leadership

Members of the NACD Blue Ribbon Commission emphasized the role of board leadership—the lead director or chair of the nominating or governance committee—in the integration of new board members. "Once you go out and recruit some good new people onto your board, don't abandon them," one commissioner said. "By this I mean that the lead director needs to spend some time with the new people and help them understand things about the history of the company and how the board works—not just one meeting, but checking in regularly. That really helps the new person get comfortable and gets him or her integrated more readily into the board."

One of the commissioners who had particularly extensive experience recruiting new board members noted, "In cases where new people come onto the board who have never served on a board before, the chair of the nominating or governance committee can do a great deal to get the newbie comfortable. One thing I used to do was to sit down with the new director and talk about matters to be discussed at the next meeting so that the new director got more background and understanding. Then, it's a good idea to strategize for a question that the new director can ask at the meeting that relates to his or her particular area of expertise. That's a good way to draw the person in, and it gets him or her more comfortable because they've then participated in the boardroom."

Site Visits

Company site visits are also being added to director orientation programs at many companies. New board members are invited to visit some of the larger company facilities to give them a greater hands-on feeling for the business at the outset. If a company's business is integrally linked to relationships with a small number of key customers or suppliers, new directors are sometimes given an opportunity to spend time with one of them.

Orientation site visits come with a warning, however. They can be problematic unless directors are given some "rules of the road" before visiting. There is almost nothing worse from a CEO's perspective than getting a call from a plant manager at the end of a director site visit and hearing, "Your new board member agreed with me that I should have been given the expansion money that you took out of my budget last year!" This is a sure way for a CEO and a new director to get off on the wrong foot, and the faux pas is almost always unconscious on the part of the board member.

Directors—whether new to the board or long-serving—need to be cognizant of the impact of any commitments or statements they might make to company personnel or customers during site visits, particularly about matters that are properly within the purview of management. If and when that happens (as it frequently does), the director should indicate that he will raise the issue with the CEO who can respond as appropriate, and then follow through and do so. Although directors should be given as much freedom as possible in their discussions with site personnel, establishing a few ground rules at the outset can avoid potential problems and enable the directors to feel more comfortable in handling questions during their visits.

SUMMARY

The new regulations and guidelines—prompted by the high-profile corporate scandals of recent years—that have had an impact on so many areas of corporate governance have also changed board recruitment practices. Finding new directors, a process that only a few years ago lay firmly in the CEO's grasp, has shifted to the nominating/governance committee, which now bears responsibility for board composition. At the same time that this shift has occurred, the scandals and new regulations have had another significant impact on the recruitment process: highly qualified directors are more difficult to find.

However, because board composition is one of the most important factors in a board's overall effectiveness, it's worth the effort to get the right mix of directors sitting around your board table. Without the appropriate individual skills and collective capacity, no board, even one with the best of intentions, can successfully develop into a high-performing team. An understanding of four crucial issues—alignment of board composition with corporate strategy, practical issues in designing a nominating process, due diligence by director candidates, and integration of new members—can help boards rise to the challenge.

CHAPTER THREE

Director Performance

Beverly A. Behan

T he lead director of a major financial services company was about to do the unthinkable: he was going to ask a member of his board to resign.

For the past three years, the director—a high-profile CEO of a large manufacturing firm—habitually arrived unprepared for board meetings, then sat and read documents from his own company's business as board discussions swirled around him. A few directors had gently admonished him—"Hey, Phil, you're in the wrong meeting, buddy!"— but to no avail. He also made himself unavailable between meetings. When the CEO called for his advice, he would be told by the director's assistant, "I'm sorry, but this is not a good time for him."

In short, his behavior was unacceptable. So why was it allowed to persist for three years? At a time when midlevel managers face extensive annual reviews and incessant pressure to perform or pack up, why don't companies pay closer attention to performance at the very top?

The answer, quite simply, is that the reluctance of boards to face up to their members' poor performance remains one of the most resilient artifacts of the old boardroom culture. Resistance to change runs high; various studies show that in both the United States and the United Kingdom only about one-fourth of all public boards have instituted some form of systematic peer review for directors. It's easy to understand why. When you think about the professional and social status of most directors, the idea of sitting one of them down and telling him he's doing a crummy job is almost too painful and embarrassing to contemplate. And yet, it's impossible to imagine how any board can hope to function as a high-performance team without finding some way to demand high performance from its members.

As it turned out, the lead director we just described was actually saved from the awkward conversation by a new process some boards are adopting: peer review of individual directors. In this case, the board had supplemented its annual assessment with a process allowing members to give each other feedback on their performance. The peer review was designed for professional development, not for renomination decisions, but it turned out to be enough. The disengaged director knew he'd been coasting; faced with candid feedback from his peers, he admitted to himself that he either had to get serious about the board or get off. Given the demands of leading his own company, he resigned.

Peer review is just one of the tools boards are considering as they tentatively come to grips with the impact of individual performance on the board's overall effectiveness. In this chapter, we'll discuss a variety of issues relating to individual director performance:

- Director roles and expectations
- Types of problem directors
- Director performance issues
- Tools for evaluating individual directors

This is an area where most boards still have a lot of work to do. From the standpoint of board-building, selecting the right people to fill vacancies represents only half of the composition equation. The other half is to find ways to enforce the same standards of behavior and performance on directors once they're on the board.

DIRECTOR ROLES AND EXPECTATIONS

Most definitions of director roles, which are typically crafted by lawyers, use terms such as *stewardship* and *fiduciary duties*. These descriptions are valid, and actually look quite elegant on a Web site. But they miss the mark in two ways.

First, it is the board members themselves who should be taking the lead in defining their roles and discussing what should be expected of them. The board's involvement in the process builds a level of commitment that simply can't be achieved by borrowing a job description developed for other boards and then circulating it for cursory review and approval. Second, the real ways in which directors can add value to the board can easily become shrouded in relatively meaningless legalese.

This means having a conversation about expectations of directors that goes beyond the legally mandated duties of "loyalty" to the interests of the corporation and its shareholders and "care" in making deliberate and informed decisions. That kind of conversation, involving concrete examples of ways a board could make significant contributions, goes much further than any neatly packaged guidelines toward generating real understanding of the directors' roles and expectations.

Watchdogs and Sounding Boards

Directors play two distinct roles. The first is as watchdog, aggressively questioning, challenging, and monitoring management. Top-notch watchdog directors have an instinctive feel for just the right question that will get to the heart of a matter. The most effective watchdogs know how to make their points in a way that's constructive, not combative. They appreciate the difference between oversight and management, and they focus their concerns on substantive issues rather than wallowing in minutiae.

Directors also play a second and much different role as sounding board for the CEO and senior management on critical ideas and strategies. Drawing on their personal knowledge and experience, they provide management with advice and differing perspectives. Excellent sounding-board directors foster a constructive working relationship with management, generally characterized by their ability to offer honest feedback and contrary views tactfully, without making the CEO feel defensive.

Most directors are naturally inclined toward one role or the other. Those with financial or legal backgrounds often feel most comfortable as watchdogs; former or active CEOs of other companies typically feel at ease in the sounding-board role. The best directors actually play both roles well, switching effortlessly between the two during a single meeting. But those are the exceptions. So it's essential for boards to recognize that both roles are important, and then to ensure that the board's membership provides some degree of balance between the two.

Defining Director Expectations

The board of a company that had recently spun off one of its largest business units took an important step in preparing for its first off-site following the spin. Prior to the meeting, all directors and the members of management who regularly worked with the board were interviewed and asked these questions:

- What does the board expect of management? What can and should management be able to expect of the board? What do directors expect of each other?

- How would you characterize the climate or culture you'd like the board to develop as we become a new company? How might this compare or contrast with our board culture prior to the spin? What are the implications in terms of what will be required of individual directors?

- Describe the working relationship that should exist between the board and management. What are the strengths of the current relationship? What concerns, if any, do you have about it? Are there any challenges or impediments that you think might get in the way of creating the type of working relationship that you'd like to see?

A set of proposed expectations was distilled from the feedback (see Exhibit 3.1) and then discussed by the board and senior management for more than an hour at the off-site. As a result, the directors were able to clarify their expectations and develop a common view of the implications for their own performance.

A similar exercise was undertaken by the board of a midcap company that had recently completed its IPO. The chairman synthesized the feedback from the interviews and created a five-point list of what he expected from directors (see Exhibit 3.2). The items were discussed at length in the first board meeting after the IPO. Although the first three points on the list generated minimal debate, the fourth and fifth came as genuine surprises to some of the directors and yielded some important discussions and clarifications.

Exhibit 3.1.   Board and Management Expectations.

Management expectations of the board
- Investment of necessary time, energy, and effort to understand the business and prepare for meetings.
- Open, honest, and constructive feedback. Board members should be respectful in expressing their views, but please say what's on your mind and say it in the boardroom.
- Active engagement and participation in board discussions.
- Timely and sound decision making. Once a decision is reached, support management.
- No micromanaging.

Board expectations of management
- Honesty, integrity, and the highest ethical standards.
- No surprises—keep the board informed of significant issues. Be honest if there's a problem.
- Come to the board with a point of view, but provide a balanced perspective. What are the pros and cons of other alternatives? What are the risks and implications of the proposed course of action?
- Run the company's business effectively and execute on the strategy.

Desired climate-culture of the board
- The board should be open, inclusive, candid, respectful, and friendly.
- Board members should challenge management and each other, and be willing to ask the dumb question and express the contrary viewpoint.
- Guard against polarization among directors, which could potentially occur on two fronts: geographic divisions and the long-serving director group versus the newer director group.

Working relationship between the board and management
- It should engender mutual respect.
- The openness, good communication, and transparency that have characterized the relationship so far should continue.
- Professional and friendly but not too cozy.
- A practice should be established in terms of board members contacting members of management below the CEO level outside of board meetings, and vice versa.

Exhibit 3.2.   Five Things the Chairman Expects from the Board.

1. *Effective engagement:* The board should be thoughtful, comfortable with debate, honest with their views, prepared to give constructive feedback, and able to make decisions.
2. *Equal participation:* All members of the board should express their views in board discussions and decision making.
3. *Mutual respect:* Board members should demonstrate respect for one another, and mutual respect should exist between the board and management.
4. *No surprises:* Any significant concerns should be vetted with the chairman offline so that they can be effectively addressed either before or during the board meeting. Governance by ambush is not OK.
5. *External relations:* Board members are expected to play an active role in community relations and business development for the company.

In these examples, significant events—an IPO and a spin-off—provided the impetus for bringing the board together to redefine the expectations for directors' performance. Other triggering events—the appointment of a new CEO or nonexecutive chairman, for instance—present good opportunities for revisiting the topic. Absent such events, boards should consider building a component on director expectations into the annual board assessment process as a means of getting this important issue onto the table.

TYPES OF PROBLEM DIRECTORS

So far, we've focused on setting standards for director performance. Needless to say, some directors fall far short of those standards. They miss the mark in a variety of ways, and their impact on the board's overall effectiveness can range from relatively benign to downright toxic. In this section we'll describe some of the most common problem directors, explore some of the reasons for how they develop, and discuss their impact on overall board effectiveness.

The CEO Wannabe

This director would rather be running the company than serving on its board. In some cases, the CEO wannabe is a director who was frustrated in past attempts to become a CEO and sees this as his opportunity to prove himself to the dimwits who failed to recognize his talent. In others, it is a former CEO who's restless in retirement and simply can't "kick the habit." Either way, the problem usually manifests itself in two ways:

- *Constantly second-guessing the CEO.* As one member of the NACD Blue Ribbon Commission on Board Leadership said: "This is the kind of person who says things like, 'Well, I'm not the CEO, but here's where the company really needs to go.'"
- *Chronic micromanaging.* As described by one CEO, "You know, there's always one director who insists on a detailed explanation of the variance on line 37 of the Philadelphia plant's monthly operations report."

Most boards are guilty of micromanaging from time to time. However, when one director constantly wastes the board's limited time with endless excursions into minutiae, the damage can be significant. The board's allocation of time is a zero-sum game; time spent on the trivial is no longer available for the vital.

Somewhat more insidious is the CEO wannabe with a personal agenda, someone who is either making a play for the CEO's job or would just like to be viewed as someone who could do a better job of running the company than the CEO. At the very least, the CEO becomes defensive; in extreme cases, the entire board becomes polarized and politicized. These situations almost inevitably arise when the CEO's performance is an issue, and that's not necessarily a bad thing. But when the CEO is doing fine, or there's a new CEO who is still trying to establish leadership, the CEO wannabe can be particularly destructive.

There's also a major problem when a wannabe assumes the chair of the compensation committee and takes the lead in assessing the CEO's performance and recommending her compensation. At that point, an annual process that should be constructive (see Chapter Eight) can easily become bitterly contentious, poisoning the relationship between the CEO and the board.

The Pit Bull

This is the overly aggressive and combative director. His questions of management and fellow directors always sound accusatory rather than inquisitive. In more extreme cases, the pit bull director becomes verbally abusive in the boardroom. Pit bulls generate unnecessary tension in board discussions and are prone to bully both management and their fellow directors. We sometimes see inexperienced and insecure directors who are merely trying to establish their credibility exhibit this behavior; of much greater concern are those who demonstrate over time that this is their normal operating style.

Pit bulls can have an enormously corrosive impact on a board's culture. They inhibit open discussion and put nearly everyone around them on the defensive. Although some CEOs can manage a pit bull, other senior executives lack the standing to do that, so they go to great lengths to avoid all contact. The result is anything but an open and constructive board-management relationship.

Extended and highly aggressive pit bull behavior in a boardroom is so disruptive that it can seldom be ignored. As one Blue Ribbon commissioner noted, "When you have a director who is counterproductive, asking questions in an aggressive and antagonistic way, creating problems, and micromanaging, you have to do something about that."

An even more extreme situation arises when directors resort to pit bull behavior because of emotional instability. When things don't go their way—or sometimes, for no discernible reason at all—they throw tantrums, shout, curse, pound their fist on the table, and storm out of a meeting. Their behavior in the room would be bad enough, but frequently it doesn't stop there. In some cases their mere presence, even when they're on relatively good behavior, makes it impossible for the board to conduct serious work because there's always the chance that they will freely discuss the most confidential matters the minute they leave the meeting.

The problem becomes most serious when the pit bull, through the force of his strong personality, secures the position of lead director or nonexecutive chairman. At that point, it's not at all clear who should, or even can, engage that person in the kind of frank conversation that's required to address this behavior.

The "Superdirector"

On some boards, there is one particular "superdirector" whose experience and credentials are so far superior to everyone else's that she assumes inordinate influence over the entire group. To paraphrase the ubiquitous ads of the now-defunct brokerage house E. F. Hutton, when a superdirector talks, everybody listens. Every time an important issue comes before the board, the other directors look first to see how the superdirector is voting.

In extreme cases, having a superdirector is almost like having a one-person board, because the other directors become hesitant to challenge her views. Although the individual's credentials might be outstanding, the group dynamic is dysfunctional, with minimal engagement and limited effectiveness.

Most often, the real problem is rooted in the board's composition. The solution is to recruit enough directors with strong credentials to create more balance. A more dangerous situation arises when the superdirector wields his influence to create an "opposing camp" at odds with the CEO. Those situations often lead to a showdown resulting in the departure of one—and sometimes both.

The Management Lapdog

This is the director who rarely challenges management and tries to downplay or deflect issues that might create problems for the CEO.

As one commissioner commented, "The least effective directors are those that always let management off the hook. They let them postpone and take the easier route."

Management lapdogs have little credibility with their peers—and even less respect. (In fact, in the course of our interviews with the members of a Fortune 500 board, one director derisively described another director, a former senior government official, as a "sycophantic lapdog.") They become marginalized, and their opinions are dismissed out of hand. It's not just that they're perceived as management's mouthpieces; in the most extreme cases, they really are unwilling or unable to think critically and act independently.

Not surprisingly, some CEOs wish they had a board full of management lapdogs. They should be careful what they wish for, however, because CEOs who mistakenly look to lapdogs as bellwethers of board sentiment risk some major miscalculations; for example, the other directors aren't likely to discuss their concerns about the CEO's performance with the management lapdog. Even if the lapdog realizes there is an issue, he typically downplays it when discussing it with the CEO. Consequently, a CEO who assumes he's closely monitoring the pulse of the board by routinely checking in with the lapdog can easily find himself blindsided.

Several years ago, a CEO who was going through a particularly rough period assured us, "I'm not concerned about my board. I know they're with me." It turned out that on the very day he was expressing his confidence to us, a group of his directors had convened a clandestine meeting to talk about ousting him—and would have, if their chosen successor hadn't turned down the job.

Despite his obvious willingness to do so, the management lapdog is actually incapable of "carrying the water" for the CEO on tough issues because he lacks credibility with the rest of the board. Appointing a management lapdog as chairman of the compensation committee, for example, virtually assures that all compensation decisions will be rehashed by the full board.

Nearly every board has at least one director who falls into this category, and the problem rarely rises to the level of a serious performance issue. It usually falls to the individual to recognize that he is regarded in this way by the other directors and that his credibility would be enhanced by taking a more balanced perspective.

The real problem arises when the lapdog mentality pervades the entire board. As we've seen all too often in recent years, deferential boards can fail to recognize warning signs or act decisively to stave off corporate failures. One Blue Ribbon commissioner provided this anecdote: "I was once invited onto the board of a company that was in a tailspin. I left the board after a year because the other directors just ignored what was going on and talked about how well the company had done in the past. Everybody was proud of the company, and they were in complete denial about the problems. Rather than try to understand or address the issues we were facing, they just took management's side on everything and said things like, 'Those regulators are a bunch of communists.' Even as the problems were growing, they kept telling management, 'Don't worry about it. You're doing fine.' "

The "Checked-Out" Director

Anyone who has spent time with boards has seen this type. He arrives at meetings late (or sometimes not at all), he hasn't read the pre-meeting package, he sits silently or occasionally lobs in a completely off-the-wall question or comment. These days, he whiles away his time reading e-mail, tapping out messages on his BlackBerry, or even taking calls in the back of the room on his cell phone. One checked-out director we observed would routinely keep busy doing crossword puzzles. Another—a lawyer who was named to countless boards because of his personal connections to important politicians—was renowned for dozing during meetings, and sometimes had to be awakened by his colleagues when his snoring became too distracting.

By and large, checked-out directors have little direct impact on their board's effectiveness, apart from the fact that they're filling a chair that could be used by someone who actually contributes to the board's work. Many boards still prefer to find a way to work around these noncontributors. As one commissioner described it, "Most boards have an attitude that if the underperforming director is not causing any real harm, it's better to leave that person in place until they retire."

Nevertheless, we're seeing signs that more progressive boards are facing up to this age-old problem. A former board chairman who served on the commission noted, "A board is not a club. Everyone's there for a purpose, and when there are twelve directors and one's not shouldering his load, it creates disharmony amongst the other eleven." Another chairman was even more adamant: "How can you go to your management team and tell them that you are an organization committed to performance of the highest standards and then, when they walk into the boardroom to make a presentation, they see people there who are half-asleep and practically drooling on the board table? You have to address performance issues within your board or you lose credibility with your executive team."

The Overwhelmed Director

Some directors are just lost in the boardroom; they're in so far over their heads that they can hardly see the bottom of the board table. During substantive discussions of the company's finances or business strategy, they become paralyzed. You can quickly pick them out by the "deer in the headlights" expression on their faces.

Sometimes these are the marquee directors who have been invited to join the board to add a little luster; they have a recognizable name but lack the requisite business acumen to effectively participate in board discussions. Other times they are family members without a strong business background who have not been effectively integrated onto the board of a family-controlled company. (Chapter Twelve discusses the importance of a thoughtful orientation process for such companies.) And even today, there are directors who were asked to join the board by the CEO in years past when friendship, rather than business experience, was a strong determining factor in extending board invitations.

Regardless of how this situation develops, it is ultimately unfulfilling on both sides. Overwhelmed directors are typically uncomfortable in board meetings and sense that they are not respected by the others. They often say little—even when they have something worthwhile to contribute—for fear of being off the mark. In other cases, they say too much when striving to make a worthwhile point and demonstrate their value. Sadly, an overwhelmed director's "off-the-wall" statements are often met with considerable eye-rolling and frustration, which only exacerbates the problem.

DIRECTOR PERFORMANCE ISSUES

Unless they are particularly acute, director performance issues have long been ignored. More and more chairmen, CEOs, and lead directors, however, are stepping up to this awkward but critical issue.

Retirement Ages and Term Limits

One commissioner noted: "The issue of individual director performance often goes unaddressed or is addressed only through a retirement age, which is the primary means I have seen used to get rid of underperforming directors. Now, if you have a younger board member that's not doing a good job, then obviously the retirement age isn't the answer." Indeed, board retirement ages have been implemented at 75 percent of U.S. companies; another 18 percent have adopted term limits.

The difficulty with these practices is that the sword cuts both ways: both ineffective and highly effective directors are forced off the board on reaching the same age. One board we worked with lost its best and most seasoned director at the time of a significant international acquisition simply because he turned seventy. The chairman/CEO asked him to stay on, to which the director replied, "I appreciate that. But this is the way things work in the boardroom. Don't try to change the rules just for me."

One commissioner expressed dismay about the prevalence of retirement ages and term limits as the means of dealing with director performance: "While I believe there is value in getting new blood onto a board and rotating off those who may have served too long, I've never been a fan of term limits or retirement ages. They are used instead of evaluating director performance."

Apart from retirement ages and term limits, there's another practice boards use to remove directors under difficult circumstances without it becoming "personal." A number of boards have followed Target's lead and adopted this rule: if an outside director's full-time job changes for any reason other than promotion or retirement, that person is automatically required to submit a resignation from the board. This is particularly useful for companies that recruit second- or third-level executives with great CEO potential who, for whatever reason, don't live up to expectations.

Handling Director Performance Problems

A willingness to address director performance problems is a hallmark of effective board leadership. It is often easier for a board leader, rather than the CEO, to deal with these problems. One commissioner advised, "If there is a performance issue with a director, the CEO should stay out of it. Let the lead director or nonexecutive chairman deal with it. It's too awkward for the CEO to do it even if he has the combined title of chairman/CEO, because the board is the CEO's boss." Another noted, "A good lead director can add a lot of value by delivering tough messages to the board or to individual directors; for example, if you have a director who's micromanaging, that's an awkward situation for a CEO to address. A lead director can be very helpful in dealing with this."

If a performance problem is recognized, the following advice from one of the commissioners is useful: "You should consider the impact of the performance problem and put it in context. First, how long does this person have to the normal retirement age? If it's only one year and if the performance problem isn't really dragging down the rest of the board, you might just want to let them serve it out."

The director who takes the lead on formally addressing performance issues should sit down with the problem director and discuss the situation honestly but diplomatically. Several useful examples were provided by members of the Blue Ribbon Commission. One chairman noted, "If there is an issue with director performance, I usually raise it in my annual one-on-one meeting with him or her. I'll say, 'Here are some observations on my part: Sometimes when you ask questions, the tone seems a bit accusatory rather than simply a question being asked for information. Do you agree with this observation, or am I off the mark?'" Another suggested, "It is up to the leader of the board to sit down with a director who isn't contributing very much and say, 'Listen, we need your help more than you've been giving it.' Give the person a year after that to see if they perform better. If they don't, then I think you can come back and say, 'We need your board seat for someone who can contribute more.'"

There seems to be general agreement that once a performance issue has been brought to a director's attention, fairness dictates that he should be given an opportunity to remedy the situation. However, if the problem persists or simply can't be resolved, then the board leader must manage the process so that the director can depart with dignity.

Again, some of the insights of the Blue Ribbon commissioners are instructive. "The key is to give the person a graceful way out so that you don't burn bridges or create a rift within the board," said one. "You need to address performance issues with board members, but you have to do it in a way that allows the individual to address the situation on their own terms," suggested another. "If you are trying to create a culture of openness and mutual respect on the board, you undermine that if someone is publicly drummed off the board. If the board is too openly critical of its members, this can quickly inhibit openness in board discussions."

The Demise of the Director Emeritus?

In the 1990s, shareholder activists took aim at director retirement programs. In response, director pensions were significantly curtailed. Spencer Stuart found nearly 80 percent of the one hundred companies surveyed for its 1995 board index had director pensions; by 2000, fewer than 10 percent of the S&P 500 had them.[1] The director emeritus—a role sometimes created for a retiring director who continues to draw some sort of compensation or benefits—consequently fell from grace.

However, there's some evidence that the director emeritus role might be making a comeback. John R. Engen reported in *Corporate Board Member* magazine in 2005 that the Corporate Library's review of two thousand U.S. proxies found 107 board members with titles of director emeritus or honorary director in the year 2004 compared with only 60 in 2003.[2]

It's probably no coincidence that the revival of this role comes at a time when boards are acting more aggressively to address their members' performance issues. For one thing, it provides a "graceful way out" for directors leaving the board for performance issues. It can also be useful in situations where board membership must be adjusted in order to meet the new requirements for board independence (as at Krispy Kreme) or to keep the board from ballooning to an unmanageable size following a merger (as at Independence Community Bank).

INDIVIDUAL DIRECTOR EVALUATIONS

Individual director assessments are widely recognized as a corporate governance best practice. Although not found among the new stock exchange rules of the NYSE or the Nasdaq, the British Combined Code, Canadian TSX Corporate Governance Guidelines, and other guidelines applicable to public companies outside of the United States often include them. In the United States, the practice of evaluating the performance of individual directors was recommended by the Conference Board's 2003 Commission on Public Trust and Private Enterprise.[3]

And yet, it's not at all clear that this "best practice" is practiced well. Only 43 percent of the respondents to the 2004 USC/Mercer Delta survey whose boards used individual director evaluations found them to be effective or very effective. The remainder of this chapter explores approaches that maximize the effectiveness of these evaluations as performance management tools in the boardroom.

Self-Assessments Versus Director Peer Reviews

Self-assessments typically ask directors to evaluate themselves against a list of performance criteria. If the board has developed expectations for directors, as outlined earlier in the chapter, the criteria used in the self-assessment should reflect these expectations. Exhibit 3.3 illustrates a director self-assessment created for the same board used as an example in Exhibit 3.2.

Individual director self-assessments—where directors rate themselves, but not each other, against a list of criteria—are largely used as a consciousness-raising exercise and can be particularly helpful for new boards. They help reinforce director expectations at a time when directors may not have worked together long enough to be comfortable assessing one another's performance. Other boards use self-assessments as a relatively nonthreatening first step down the path of more rigorous performance assessment.

One strategy that's not particularly helpful, in our experience, is to have directors fill out their self-assessments and then hand them in to the nominating/governance committee. It's not unheard of for directors with performance problems to give themselves outlandishly positive ratings. This leaves the chair of the nominating/governance committee in a quandary. Should the chair advise the director that his self-assessment is inconsistent with the board's perception of him? And what evidence does the chair have, other than her own observations, to back that up? Should confidential, informal hallway observations be the basis for such a conversation? Or will this simply create a political maelstrom? Not surprisingly, most chairs simply avoid the issue, allowing the director to keep stumbling along in a satisfied state of self-delusion.

Under even the best of circumstances, self-assessments lose their luster and value after one or two rounds. As one director described it, "This sort of thing is fine in the beginning to get everyone thinking about their own performance as a director. But after you do it once, I'm not sure there's much value in repeating the exercise. Knowing what the other people at the board table think about you as a director is where you can actually learn something."

Exhibit 3.3. Director Self-Assessment.

The purpose of this component of the survey is to enable you to reflect on your own performance as a director. Please read each statement carefully and circle the number that best describes your opinion.

To what extent . . .	To a very small extent	To a small extent	To some extent	To a great extent	To a very great extent	Not applicable/ Don't know
1. . . . do I diligently prepare for board meetings?	1	2	3	4	5	?
2. . . . do I engage effectively in board discussions and deliberations?	1	2	3	4	5	?
3. . . . do I ask constructive and thought-provoking questions?	1	2	3	4	5	?
4. . . . am I frank and honest in expressing my views?	1	2	3	4	5	?
5. . . . am I willing to listen to other points of view?	1	2	3	4	5	?
6. . . . do I exercise sound judgment in decision making?	1	2	3	4	5	?
7. . . . am I responsive to the need for timely decision making (as opposed to putting things off)?	1	2	3	4	5	?
8. . . . do I understand and respect the line between governance and management?	1	2	3	4	5	?
9. . . . am I available to management or other board members when required?	1	2	3	4	5	?
10. . . . do I support management in implementing corporate strategy-direction?	1	2	3	4	5	?
11. . . . have I established a constructive working relationship with my fellow directors?	1	2	3	4	5	?
12. . . . have I established a constructive working relationship with senior management?	1	2	3	4	5	?
13. . . . do I vet any significant concerns with the chairman/CEO off-line so that they can be addressed either before or after the meeting?	1	2	3	4	5	?
14. . . . do I play an active role in community relations for the company?	1	2	3	4	5	?
15. . . . do I play an active role in business development for the company?	1	2	3	4	5	?

Comments (optional):

In a director peer-review process, board members provide structured feedback on each of their fellow directors. Because this switches the focus from the group to the individual, it naturally involves a greater degree of personal anxiety than a board assessment. Boards must grapple with these questions: Will the peer review be used solely for professional development, in which case only the individual director will see her feedback? Or will a summary of the feedback be reviewed by the nominating/governance committee as a form of due diligence as it decides whether to renominate incumbent directors?

Either design can work well. In fact, using peer review exclusively for professional development offers some distinct advantages. First, the process engenders less anxiety. Second, because boards are usually made up of accomplished and well-respected business leaders, most directors take the feedback from their peers quite seriously. As such, they can choose to respond to negative feedback either through improved performance or resignation—as in the anecdote at the start of this chapter—even when it was provided for their eyes only.

The key to a successful director peer review is to make the process constructive. For example, one board member we interviewed as part of a peer review was seething over the boardroom behavior of three fellow directors and welcomed a forum to give them a piece of his mind. Once he had finished letting off some steam, however, we began asking him more probing questions; his initial comment, "These guys are self-important jerks," was followed up with questions such as, "Give me an example of what they've done that struck you as inappropriate, and tell me how it had an impact on the board as a whole." In every case, there was a rich kernel of advice underlying the emotional outbursts. Because the feedback focused on constructive suggestions instead of personality issues, it was well received and actually taken to heart.

Director Peer-Review Methodologies

Feedback is typically collected for an individual director peer review either through a survey or an interview format. Because individual director peer reviews are particularly sensitive, it can be helpful to have a third party collect, tabulate, analyze, and provide feedback. The interview format enables the interviewer to probe and ensures that the feedback is constructive. When a survey is used, it's often necessary to edit comments that are overly personal and without value.

SURVEY METHODOLOGY. With a survey, board members rate each of their peers on a number of key indices of director effectiveness using a numeric rating scale. Figure 3.1 depicts a sample feedback report from a survey-based director peer review.

There are two downsides to a survey: First, the underlying reasons for the scores may not be apparent, leaving the recipient to wonder why he was rated highly by his peers on a certain element and lower on another. Most surveys provide for write-in comments, but therein lies the second downside. If the comments are merely personal and not at all constructive, they have limited use and the potential to foster ill will, if they are shared.

On the upside, director peer surveys can be quite comprehensive. They also generate quantitative feedback that lends itself to year-over-

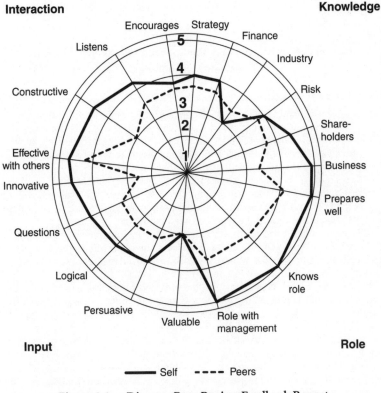

Figure 3.1. Director Peer-Review Feedback Report:
Survey Methodology.

year comparisons as a means of tracking individual progress. A survey can be even more effective when used in conjunction with in-depth interviews.

INTERVIEW METHODOLOGY. Using the interview methodology, board members are asked to provide comments on their fellow directors' strengths and weaknesses. This can involve either highly structured interview questions or a more open-ended format, such as asking where each individual is particularly strong, where she has made a significant contribution to the board in the past year, and where she could improve. One of the chief advantages is that the interviewer has an opportunity to probe and ask follow-up questions to help flesh out the underlying themes and keep the feedback constructive. Exhibit 3.4 provides an excerpt from a feedback report from an interview-based director peer review.

Exhibit 3.4.   Director Peer-Review Feedback Report Excerpt:
Interview Methodology.

Areas of greatest strength

- Your greatest strength is viewed as your strong understanding of the industry in which the company operates and your ability to apply this understanding to issues confronting the board and the company. Your fellow directors rely on you to provide this type of understanding in board discussions and consider your viewpoints on these matters with the utmost seriousness.
  - "This industry is a part of who he is. He has an understanding of this business that no other board member can come close to. I believe this is of tremendous benefit not only to the board but also to the management team. He comes up with ideas that none of the rest of us would think of."
  - "If he's not in the room and we are discussing a major strategic move, it is not even worth having the discussion. He always comes up with innovative ideas and can identify the big 'watch outs.' I don't think he realizes how much we rely on him for this."
- Another key strength is your personal integrity and willingness to avoid even the appearance of a conflict of interest. Several board members referenced the position that you took on recusing yourself from all discussions of the Company X acquisition, which they saw as demonstrating very high ethics and integrity.
  - "I was surprised when he said he wouldn't stay in the room during the Company X discussions because of the potential link to his VC firm. I don't think there was actually a conflict there—but I have to say I was impressed that he was so sensitive on this issue. I know that this is a guy who is not going to play fast and loose—and in the post-Enron world you'd better believe that's a big deal."

- "I probably shouldn't say this, but you always think of high-tech VC types as pushing the envelope on these things—so the fact that he said he shouldn't engage in conversations or the vote on the acquisition really impressed me. I would never have known his firm even had a deal with Company X in the past—and I don't think there was a real conflict—but what I thought was particularly impressive was that nobody told him he had to leave the discussions. He raised that all on his own—and I thought, say what you want about high-tech VCs, we've got one with ethics."

Opportunities for enhancement

- Board members expressed concern about your recent lack of participation in board discussions. Some of your colleagues attribute this to a loss of interest. Others believe that your participation lessened after the board off-site in January and believe it may be attributable to conflict with another board member that arose at that time. Regardless of the cause, they would like you to participate more fully in the boardroom going forward.
  - "When he first came onto the board, he was all guns blazing! Maybe some people thought he was a bit aggressive—but he had terrific ideas and brought a perspective none of the rest of us had. But I would say in the past six months, he's really pulled in his horns and I'm not sure why. I worry that maybe he's lost interest. Losing him would be a terrible blow to our board. Maybe he could have been more polished in his earlier approach, but I'd rather have that back—now, it's like he doesn't care anymore."
  - "There was a big blowup between him and Director X at the off-site. I think it was all about politics—Director X was the eminence grise, the big shooter on the board until he came along. He knew so much more about the industry, and he was making terrific points when he raised issues. I think it got Director X's nose out of joint. He was really into it at the off-site—he's terrific on strategy—and Director X just went after him. He hasn't been the same since."
  - "It's like he checked out after the off-site. I don't know exactly why. But I do know this: he's a really good director when he wants to be."

Most significant contributions

- Most of your peers reference your insights on the issue of global expansion—which led to dramatic changes in the company's global expansion strategy—as the most significant contribution you have made to the board over the past year.
  - "This is where he really shone! He had been there, done that, in this industry and knew where all the bodies were hidden on this decision. He raised stuff that I never would have thought of, and I could tell that the CEO was really helped by his contributions here. They changed the whole plan—pulled the plug on South America, started to look at some places they hadn't been looking at before."
  - "The way he got into that whole global expansion discussion—that's a perfect example of what a top-notch board member brings to the table. And the thing about it is he did it in a really good way so that he wasn't usurping the CEO or anything like that. You could see that the CEO was not put on the defensive— it was evident that he really appreciated the points that were being made. He'd walked a mile in the CEO's shoes on this stuff and it showed, not only in his insights but also in his approach. It's probably the best board discussion we've ever had, and we would not have had it without him."

SUMMARY

As board members roll up their sleeves and immerse themselves in the work that is demanded of them in today's challenging corporate climate, there's still one key area they seem hesitant to address: performance issues among their peers. The reluctance is understandable. Stepping up to these issues can involve potential embarrassment, possible political fallout, and tough face-to-face conversations. It's small wonder then that most board leaders would rather turn a blind eye and simply wring their hands over the problem. But it's shortsighted to think that a board can truly enhance its effectiveness without addressing its weak links. Despite the discomfort involved, the best board leaders recognize when director performance problems need to be tackled and address them with fairness and dignity.

Engaging all board members in defining their roles and expectations is a good place to start. Although it's important to recognize problem behavior, appropriately addressing performance issues is just as crucial. If done right, director peer assessments can be both informative and constructive. It's thorny work, to be sure, but it has the potential to enhance the accountability and effectiveness of individual directors, which can in turn help the entire board function more efficiently as a team.

CHAPTER FOUR

Board Leadership: Structures and Roles

Beverly A. Behan
David A. Nadler

W ho should lead the board?

In the ongoing debate over the future of corporate governance in the United States, few questions evoke the passionate response this one does. Many proponents of corporate reform are adamant: U.S. boards should follow the lead of their counterparts in the United Kingdom and Canada and separate the roles of chief executive and chairman of the board. Others are equally fervent about combining the roles in order to leave no doubt about ultimate corporate accountability.

ANSWERING THE LEADERSHIP QUESTION

Although we're well aware that our position borders on heresy, we have to admit that in this religious war, we are basically agnostic.

Indeed, the debate over splitting the two roles diverts attention from what we see as a more compelling—and more immediate—issue that's directly related to the board's effectiveness: the need for distinct leadership for the independent directors, who now make up the overwhelming majority on each board. If two different people fill the roles of CEO and nonexecutive chairman, then the chairman ought to lead the board as a whole, as well as the independent directors. If the roles aren't split, a lead director or presiding director should be formally appointed to lead the independent directors.

Either alternative can be effective. To be sure, the board's leadership structure is important, but which structure a board chooses is less important than how the role of the leader of the independent directors is defined. What matters most is how the leader interacts with senior management and the rest of the board. Other key considerations include determining the process that will be used to select the leader, identifying the qualifications it will take to be effective in this role, and deciding how the leader's performance will be evaluated over time.

In this chapter and the two chapters that follow, we'll be taking a close look at the role of leadership in the board-building process. This chapter focuses on the formal leadership roles and structures that have emerged as independent directors assume unprecedented influence over the work of U.S. boards. In Chapter Five, we'll examine the ways leaders shape some of the board's key work processes. Effective management of the information flow, meeting agendas, and executive sessions can improve the board's ability to operate effectively as a team by devoting their limited time to the right work and basing their decisions on appropriate information. And Chapter Six deals with the all-important issue of board culture and the unique role leaders play in shaping a social climate that's conducive to producing value-added work.

THE CONTEXT OF THE DEBATE

Traditionally, U.S. companies have combined the roles of chairman and CEO. Current surveys show that even today between 60 and 80 percent of all major corporations in the United States have the same person act as both leader of corporate management and chairman of the board. The reverse is true in Great Britain, where independent directors have historically made up a smaller percentage of directors than in the United States.

Amid the fallout from corporate scandals and the wave of regulatory reforms in the United States, many shareholder activists and governance gurus renewed their call for separating the roles of chairman and CEO. However, to date, there's little evidence that the situation is changing in any meaningful way. According to research conducted by the Corporate Library, a governance watchdog group, the number of

S&P 500 companies where the same person held both roles dropped from 394 in 2003 to 377 in 2004. But in the same period, the number of chairmen who were either former CEOs or other past or present executives of the firm rose from 74 to 87. In other words, although the percentage of companies where the CEO was also chairman dropped from 79 percent to 75 percent, the percentage where the chairman was a current or past executive of the firm only dropped from 94 percent to 93 percent—virtually no change at all.[1]

These data reflect the fact that U.S. boards are reluctant to take the chairman's title away from an incumbent who is both chairman and CEO. They are far more comfortable appointing a lead or presiding director to provide leadership to the independent directors, then reviewing their options on board leadership structure at the time of a CEO transition. In fact, U.S. boards are now more open to considering role separation when a new CEO is named, and use of this structure is likely to gain momentum.

Nevertheless, proponents of separating the roles continue to push for change. They point to the inherent circularity when one person wears two hats: as chairman, the individual is the leader of the board; as CEO, the board is his boss. This creates enormous potential for conflicts of interest, particularly when the chairman/CEO is a larger-than-life figure who surrounds himself with cronies and cowards. Moreover, leading the board and managing the company are two very different jobs; a great CEO can be a lousy chairman, and vice versa.

Although there are good arguments for separating the roles, there's no overwhelming evidence of a direct correlation between bifurcated roles and better corporate performance. To the contrary, a major study by Booz Allen Hamilton found that "splitting the roles of chief executive and chairman does not result in higher returns for shareholders. Returns to investors are lower—4.7 percentage points per year lower in Europe, and 4.1 percentage points lower in North America—when the roles are split."[2]

Anecdotally, the benefit of split roles is undermined by Enron, the poster child of corporate abuse. Kenneth Lay presided over the board and Jeffrey Skilling was CEO as the company rushed along the road to ruin. But Lay was the former CEO, not an independent chairman. More to the point is what happened at Nortel, the Canadian telecommunications giant: accounting scandals drove the company into crisis despite the oversight of Red Wilson, seasoned nonexecutive chairman. Closer to home, when George Mitchell was appointed as Disney's nonexecutive chairman to provide a counterbalance to Michael Eisner in the wake of a shareholder revolt, the move was greeted with skepticism. This suggests that a mere division of leadership roles is no automatic quick fix to deeply rooted governance concerns.

NEW APPROACHES TO GOVERNANCE

The true catalysts for driving board leadership to the forefront of U.S. corporate governance are recent requirements by both the NYSE and the Nasdaq that boards hold regular executive sessions where independent directors meet without company management. This has prompted boards to consider how to provide leadership for executive sessions, and to determine what other roles, if any, the leaders of these sessions should play.

Since the stock exchange requirements came into force two years ago, U.S. boards have been experimenting with a variety of approaches. Some have rotated leadership of the executive sessions among their independent directors on an alphabetical or seniority basis, or among committee chairs, depending on the subject to be covered at a particular meeting. Others have identified a presiding or lead director to regularly chair these sessions, and in many cases, play an expanded role in board leadership. Still others have separated the roles of chairman and CEO, along the lines of British and Canadian models, naming an independent outside director as nonexecutive chairman. Companies have also found variations on the theme that work well for them; for instance, co–lead directors at Cinergy and a vice chairman of the executive committee at Target.

The need to address board leadership structures and roles prompted the National Association of Corporate Directors (NACD) to select this as the topic for their 2004 Blue Ribbon Commission. Our leadership (with Jay Lorsch of the Harvard Business School) and deep involvement in the commission's work significantly informs the perspectives in this chapter, which discusses:

- Key findings from the NACD Blue Ribbon Commission report
- The importance of defining the roles of lead director and nonexecutive chairman
- The role of executive chairman
- Leadership of board committees

THE NACD COMMISSION: A RANGE OF OPINIONS

The fifty-one members of the Blue Ribbon Commission—board members, CEOs, chairmen, lead directors, and other thought leaders in corporate governance—were divided almost equally into three camps on the issue of separating the CEO and chairman roles.

Roughly one-third of the commissioners felt strongly that the best model for board leadership is to separate the roles of chairman and CEO, with an outside independent director acting as nonexecutive chairman. "If one of the paramount responsibilities of the board is to hire and evaluate the CEO, then it's illogical to combine the roles of chair and CEO," one commissioner pointed out. "The appearance of conflict is very, very real. I think the roles need to be separated and should be." Another noted, "I think it is critically important to split the roles because it reinforces the idea that the board is an independent entity. The CEO is charged with running the company, and the board is charged with making sure that the company is being run properly."

These commissioners dismissed the argument that having a nonexecutive chairman creates confusion about who is running the company and emphasized that the chairman and CEO roles are very different jobs that demand different skills. Many noted that a nonexecutive chairman can "unburden" the CEO from the increased demands of running a board. "Being chairman is consuming increased amounts of CEO time, and it's harder and harder to put in all that time and run the company," one commissioner said.

However, many commissioners who expressed a preference for the nonexecutive chairman model told us that a strong and capable lead director could be equally effective in providing leadership to the independent directors. "I have a 51 percent versus a 49 percent preference for the separation of roles," a commissioner said. "I can live with a good lead director as long as he or she is not the former CEO."

Roughly another third of the commissioners favored combining the roles of chairman and CEO, and naming a lead or presiding director (terms that we use interchangeably). They feel the combined role leaves no doubt as to who is accountable for the company's success or failure. "If you split the roles, you dilute company leadership and it is no longer clear where the buck stops," one commissioner explained. Another noted, "I think the combined role is better because there is no confusion about who is in charge."

There were also concerns that a division of the roles could result in bifurcated leadership and power struggles. Several commissioners pointed out that people who rise to become CEOs or chairmen don't often share power well. Others felt that the nonexecutive chairman model actually weakens the influence of the rest of the board. "I happen to like the chairman and CEO roles combined, because when they are split, some things begin to happen in the board dynamic," a commissioner said. "If the chairman represents the board, then the committee chairmen have less power. The chairman will decide things with the CEO and those two will present a united front, which is tough for a board to go up against."

The balance of the commission—also roughly one-third—felt that it is important to have someone serve as the leader of the independent directors. However, these commissioners believe it makes no difference whether a nonexecutive chairman or a lead director plays this role and/or that it depends on each situation. "I think it's a mistake to say, 'This is *the* model of board leadership,' because there are a number of factors that come into play when you're deciding if you should have a lead director or a nonexecutive chairman."

Many pointed out that neither model provides any guarantee of board effectiveness. "I don't think it's at all productive to focus too much on the different structures, because no matter how you do it, both of the structures can be easily subverted depending on who's in them," one commissioner said. Others found that both lead directors and nonexecutive chairs can provide effective leadership to the independent members of the board. "I've served on boards with both systems, and I've seen both work," a commissioner said. "I think it's wrong to be too doctrinaire about this."

The commission concluded that either the nonexecutive chairman or lead director structure could work effectively. However, they endorsed naming one individual (in either role) to provide leadership to the independent directors on an ongoing basis rather than rotating leadership of the executive sessions monthly or quarterly. The rationale for this is twofold:

First, appointing one director to an ongoing leadership role provides a "go to" person for the others in the event of any serious concern about the CEO or the company's performance.

Second, it enables one director to build an ongoing relationship with the CEO, which can enhance communication between the board and management. As one commissioner pointed out, "I don't like the idea of rotating the lead or presiding director role among every director at every meeting. The trouble is that nobody builds the kind of rapport with management that you get when someone serves in that role more permanently. And if there's a problem, who do you go to about it? The lead director of the month?"

The latest USC/Mercer Delta survey shows that U.S. boards are increasingly establishing some form of leadership structure for the independent directors. The 2004 survey found that 75 percent of respondents served on boards that had an independent director providing leadership, up from 46 percent in 2003 and 32 percent in 2001. Two-thirds of these had named an individual to this role on an ongoing basis, while the remaining one-third rotated the position among the independent directors. We predict that, over time, this balance will continue to shift as more boards recognize the benefits of appointing a single individual to serve as the leader of the independent directors.

DEFINING THE ROLES OF LEAD DIRECTOR AND NONEXECUTIVE CHAIRMAN

Regardless of the structure, it is critical for the CEO and the individual who is going to provide leadership to the independent directors (whether as lead director or nonexecutive chairman) to think through, talk about, and agree on their respective roles. All too often, off-the-shelf role guidelines are adopted, and even published on a company Web site, with little regard for the practical implications. Until, of course, a problem arises.

To quote one commissioner on this topic, "Whether it is a nonexecutive chairman or a lead director, the best way for that person to work effectively with the CEO is to be very clear about delineating the responsibilities between these two roles at the outset. Of course, there is a human element, and practically speaking, the two people need to respect their boundaries. But if you start off by putting some effort into developing a structure in which they can operate and creating a framework, that gets you off to a good start."

The main difference between the role of a lead director and that of a nonexecutive chairman is as follows: The chairman of the board (be it a chairman/CEO or a nonexecutive chairman) chairs board meetings, sets the board agenda, and oversees the premeeting information that is sent to the directors. A lead director usually provides input to the chairman/CEO on board agendas and information but does not assume this responsibility, nor does she chair meetings of the board unless the chairman/CEO is absent from the room. Both nonexecutive chairs and lead directors chair executive sessions of the independent directors and facilitate communications between board members and the CEO outside of board meetings. Neither plays any role in company operations.

Communication with external stakeholders is still a "grey area" in the United States. Usually, neither lead directors nor nonexecutive chairs play a significant role in external communications, making it clear that the CEO is the person who speaks for the company to the outside world. However, even apart from crisis situations (discussed in more detail in Chapter Ten), there are instances when nonexecutive chairs are asked by their boards and the CEO to represent the company in discussions with external stakeholders. Some lead directors also participate in meetings with key institutional investors once or twice a year.

Table 4.1, an excerpt from the Blue Ribbon Commission board leadership report, delineates the key board leadership roles.

The 2004 USC/Mercer Delta survey of directors asked about the most common activities undertaken by individuals serving in the roles of lead director, presiding director, and nonexecutive chairman. Exhibit 4.1 summarizes their responses.

Qualities of an Effective Leader of the Independent Directors

Undoubtedly, the most important quality for the leader of the independent directors is the ability to gain the trust and respect of fellow board members. Such individuals should be people who enjoy considerable influence among their peers and provide leadership their peers can clearly endorse. This is particularly important in the sensitive and challenging communications role the leader of the independent directors often plays between the CEO and the board, and among the directors themselves.

The leader should also be an independent thinker who is willing to challenge the CEO when necessary. This is not a job for a director who is either mesmerized by the CEO or unwilling to confront her. That said, absent a serious rift between the CEO and the board, the best candidate is someone who either has or can build a constructive working relationship with the CEO, one that is characterized by open communication and mutual respect. CEO wannabes and overly aggressive

Table 4.1. Roles of Leaders of the Independent Directors and of CEOs.

Areas of Responsibility	Chair/CEO Model		Nonexecutive Chair Model
	Chair/CEO Role	Lead Director Role	Nonexecutive Chair Role
Full board meetings	• Has the authority to call meetings of the board of directors. • Chairs meetings of the board of directors and the annual meeting of shareholders.	• Participates in board meetings like every other director. • Acts as an intermediary; at times, the chair may refer to the lead director for guidance or to have something taken up in executive session. • Suggests calling full board meetings to the chair when appropriate.	• Has the authority to call meetings of the board of directors. • Chairs meetings of the board of directors and the annual meeting of shareholders (although in some cases the CEO chairs in the presence of the nonexecutive chair).
Executive sessions	• Receives feedback from the executive sessions.	• Has the authority to call meetings of the independent directors. • Sets the agenda for and leads executive sessions of the independent directors. • Briefs the CEO on issues arising in the executive sessions.	• Has the authority to call meetings of the independent directors. • Sets the agenda for and leads executive sessions of the independent directors. • Briefs the CEO on issues arising in the executive sessions.
Board agendas and information	• Takes primary responsibility for shaping board agendas, consulting with the lead director to ensure that board agendas and information provide the board with what it needs to fulfill its primary responsibilities.	• Collaborates with the chair-CEO to set the board agenda and board information. • Seeks agenda input from other directors.	• Takes primary responsibility for shaping board agendas in collaboration with the CEO, consults with all directors to ensure that board agendas and information provide the board with what it needs to fulfill its primary responsibilities.

(continued)

Table 4.1. continued

Areas of Responsibility	Chair/CEO Model		Nonexecutive Chair Model
	Chair/CEO Role	Lead Director Role	Nonexecutive Chair Role
Board communications	• Communicates with all directors on key issues and concerns outside of board meetings.	• Facilitates discussion among the independent directors on key issues and concerns outside of board meetings. • Serves as a nonexecutive conduit (to the CEO) of views, concerns, and issues of the independent directors.	• Facilitates discussion among the independent directors on key issues and concerns outside of board meetings. • Serves as a nonexecutive conduit (to the CEO) of views, concerns, and issues of the independent directors.
External stakeholders	• Represents the organization to and interacts with external stakeholders and employees.	• Usually has no role in representing the organization to external stakeholders. Some boards, however, occasionally ask their lead director to participate in meetings with key institutional investors.	• Can represent the organization to and interact with external stakeholders and employees at the discretion of the board of directors.
Company operations	• Leads company operations. • Officers and employees report to him or her.	• Has no role in company operations. • Officers and employees report to CEO, not to him or her.	• Has no role in company operations. • Officers and employees report to CEO, not to him or her.

Exhibit 4.1.   Board Leader Activities.

If the board has a lead director, presiding director, or nonexecutive chair, please indicate what role this person plays:

Chairs executive sessions.	64%
Communicates with CEO between meetings.	55%
Leads the board in the event of a crisis.	41%
Mentors the CEO.	38%
Communicates with outside directors between meetings.	35%
Communicates with other company leaders between meetings.	22%
Sets the meeting agenda.	22%
Presides at board meetings.	12%
Represents the board in external communications with the media, shareholders, and so on.	9%
Other.	2%

directors with a pit bull style (discussed in greater detail in Chapter Three) are prescriptions for disaster. They can very quickly polarize a board and create disruptive political dynamics.

Because the role typically involves leading executive sessions, and in the case of a nonexecutive chair, presiding over board meetings, an ability to conduct effective meetings is essential. Good listening skills are critical; someone who dominates discussions and fails to solicit or listen to other viewpoints will quickly alienate his fellow directors. As one commissioner explained, "Ineffective board leaders are people who talk 90 percent of the time." Another noted, "If you have a domineering person who tries to drive everything to their point of view, you will increasingly have a lot of turnover on that board because directors won't put up with that, especially these days."

The individual should also know enough about the company's business and industry to determine which factors are critical to business performance and which are not. This is particularly important where board agendas and information are concerned. Someone who understands the business can make informed decisions about how the board should spend its limited time and better determine what information directors need when reviewing both corporate performance and strategy.

Selection and Performance Review

The CEO should not select the leader of the independent directors, whether a nonexecutive chairman or lead director. Instead, the independent directors should either make or ratify the selection. However, as discussed earlier, the CEO's ability to work with the individual should be taken into account when the directors make their choice. It is also important for the individual to be able to devote the necessary time to the role, which can involve numerous conversations with the CEO and with other board members outside of meetings.

Two primary methods for selecting a leader of the independent directors have emerged. One is to attach this role to the chairmanship of the nominating/governance committee. Another is for the independent directors either to hold a secret ballot or to arrive at a decision through open discussions in executive sessions. Many of the commissioners offered warnings about creating a "running-for-office" scenario. "The last thing you want is people campaigning to be lead director," one said. "It creates bad politics within the board. Too often, it's all about wanting to go to the party at the golf club and say, 'I'm the lead director of Company X.'"

Neither a lead director nor nonexecutive chairman should be appointed for life. Although some commissioners advocated term limits, an even better practice is to incorporate a performance review into the annual board assessment process. As one commissioner noted: "If you're going to have a nonexecutive chairman or a lead director, I think you need to put in another governance mechanism, which is to incorporate an evaluation of this role into the annual board assessment process and ask, 'How is the lead director or nonexecutive chairman doing?'" (Chapter Eleven discusses board assessment in greater detail.)

Working Relationship with Other Directors

"The lead director should not be the boss of the board," commissioners told us time and again, noting that the essence of the role was what one commissioner described as *primas inter paris,* first among equals. Several preferred the term *presiding director* because of its more egalitarian flavor. "I don't like the term 'lead director,'" one commissioner said. "It suggests a two-tier system where one director is more important than the others. The other directors may 'sag in the saddle' if they sense that's the case. The essence of this role is to be a facilitator; it is not a more authoritative position."

Indeed, an effective leader to the independent directors must, first and foremost, have excellent communication skills. Directors must be comfortable enough to approach the leader about issues, respecting her judgment on how to address them. Feedback that the leader conveys to the CEO from the board after executive sessions or between meetings has to be honest and candid, particularly if challenging issues are raised. Board members need to be confident that these issues are accurately passed on to the CEO. At the same time, the CEO needs to know that the lead director or nonexecutive chair is not pulling any punches. Ultimately, glossing over tricky issues with the CEO serves neither the CEO's interests nor those of the board; the CEO fails to realize that the board has a significant concern, and the other directors wonder why the CEO hasn't taken steps to respond to the problem.

From time to time, the lead director or nonexecutive chair will be asked to share feedback from the CEO with the other directors, either collectively or individually. In fact, it's beneficial for the CEO to have a lead director or nonexecutive chairman who can address director performance issues. Because the board is ultimately the CEO's boss, it can be awkward for the CEO—even with the joint title of chairman of the board—to raise performance concerns with a director. (Chapter Three discusses director performance in greater detail.)

THE EXECUTIVE CHAIRMAN

So far we have focused on the role of the leader of the independent directors—a nonexecutive chairman or lead director. In this section, we will discuss the role of executive chairman. In this model, the roles of chairman and CEO are split; however, the individual who serves as executive chairman is not an outside independent director but rather a current or former member of the company's management team.

(By the way, it's worth noting an important change in terminology that has emerged in recent years. In the past, the term *nonexecutive chairman* was often used loosely on U.S. boards to describe any chairman who wasn't the incumbent CEO. Today, U.S. boards have adopted the British and Canadian terminology; a nonexecutive chairman is an independent director with no ties to the company. Any current executive, or alternatively, a retired CEO who remains on the company payroll, is now described as an *executive chairman,* who by definition cannot be the leader of the outside directors.)

In the United States, transitioning corporate leadership has traditionally been a two-stage process where the incumbent chairman/CEO would first transfer the CEO title to his successor but stay on as executive chairman, often for a number of years. Although the former chairman/CEO was now supposed to be focusing exclusively on "running the board" as executive chairman, in fact he was often still mentoring the new company leader. The longer this situation continued, the greater the risk of bifurcated leadership as the new CEO struggled to assert her leadership while the former leader tightly held the reigns.

To prevent this from happening, current best thinking on CEO succession (discussed in detail in Chapter Nine) suggests that an outgoing CEO should either ride off into the sunset the day her successor takes the helm, or if she decides to stay on as executive chairman, the transition period when she holds the title of executive chairman should be relatively short—about eighteen months, or even less in the absence of special circumstances. This works well when the torch is being passed from one professional manager to another. However, if a founder or significant shareholder is involved, it may be better to design the role of executive chairman as a permanent rather than transitional role.

Perhaps the most noteworthy example in recent years is Bill Gates. In early 2000, Gates relinquished his title as chief executive officer and assumed the roles of chairman and chief software architect of Microsoft. Other founder CEOs followed suit: Thomas Sternberg of Staples in 2001, Allen Hassenfeld of Hasbro in 2003, and Michael Dell in 2004. As executive chairmen, these individuals not only run their company boards but also continue to be deeply involved in critical aspects of company management. Both Gates and Dell have concentrated on the development of new technology, while Sternberg has focused on entrepreneurial opportunities and strategic planning.

Similar models can also be found in family-controlled companies where a family member assumes the role of executive chairman. For example, Arthur Sulzberger Jr., executive chairman of the New York Times Company, also serves as publisher of the company's flagship newspaper, the *New York Times*. (The role of executive chairman in family-controlled companies is discussed in greater detail in Chapter Twelve.)

In all these scenarios, clarity of roles between the executive chairman and the CEO is critical, as is the working relationship between the two individuals in these positions. And the latter is no substitute for the former. A few years ago, our firm was working with a company where the chairman/CEO retired and his role split between a new executive chairman and a CEO, both of whom had worked together in the company for years. In the months leading up to the handoff, both insisted there was no need to get overly formal about specifying their respective roles, because their terrific working relationship would just continue. Less than forty-eight hours before the appointments were to be publicly announced, each produced a press release written by his own staff describing the appointments and who would be responsible for what. With the exception of board leadership, the two job descriptions were almost identical. Thus ensued two feverish days of untangling a web of sharply conflicting assumptions that should have been worked out months in advance.

Moreover, because the executive chairman and CEO are members of corporate management, a third individual often plays a board leadership role in these scenarios—namely, a lead or presiding director who provides leadership to the independent directors. Although these leadership structures may appear complex, directors who are familiar with them tell us that they can work extremely well. As one Blue Ribbon commissioner pointed out, "There has to be a good bond between the people who are playing these different roles. If there's overlap, you have to be able to say to each other, 'Hey, you're in my stuff.'"

LEADERSHIP OF BOARD COMMITTEES

The Blue Ribbon Commission suggests that effective boards have not one or two leaders but a "system of leadership" that calls on board committee chairs and other individual directors to provide leadership in various aspects of governance. Because so much of the board's most important work is done by its committees, board committee leaders in particular are a critical aspect of overall board effectiveness.

The best board committee chairs thoroughly understand the mandate and subject matter of their committees. "Effective committee chairs either should have a higher level of expertise on the topic that the committee oversees or should be willing to put in the time to really learn about that issue," one commissioner said. "In audit, you really should have someone with deep financial expertise. If you have a technology committee, you need someone who understands technology. Compensation is a bit different; there I think you can have someone who's interested in those issues and willing to devote the time to getting up the learning curve on them." Another commissioner was even more emphatic: "It is inconceivable to me that someone could chair the audit committee effectively without financial acumen. This is not a place for on-the-job training."

Committee chairs typically set committee agendas, oversee information packages sent to committee members, and chair committee meetings. They, too, must be able to conduct meetings effectively. In addition, they need to follow the processes in agenda and information management that are described in Chapter Five, "Board Work Processes."

It is critical for committee chairs to develop a constructive working relationship with the company executive who "staffs" their committee. For the audit committee this is usually the head of internal audit or the CFO, for the compensation committee it's the vice president of human resources, and for the nominating/governance committee it's the corporate secretary. In most cases, the committee chair will also manage the committee's relationship with outside advisers or consultants—external auditors, compensation consultants, executive search consultants, and so on. Recent regulatory reforms require many outside advisers who support the work of the board to report directly to a board committee. As a result, committee chairs must now take a more active role in managing relationships that used to be largely overseen by management.

Effective committee chairs are mindful of the need to safeguard their committee's independence. They not only ensure that outside advisers report directly to the committee instead of management but also allot time, when appropriate, for the committee to discuss issues without management present. Holding executive sessions of the committee at the start or end of every committee meeting can work well for this purpose.

In addition to providing effective leadership to their committees, board committee chairs also are important liaisons between the committee and the rest of the board. It is their responsibility to keep noncommittee members up to speed on committee activities, and this often requires a delicate balance. The committee chair needs to provide enough information so that nonmembers feel comfortable that they know what the committee has been doing. However, in the interest of time, the chairs also need to prevent rehashing issues discussed at the committee level during meetings of the full board. In order to step up to this challenge, committee chairs need to build the confidence of their fellow directors that their committee, under their leadership, is handling its responsibilities effectively.

SUMMARY

The debate over combining or dividing chairman and CEO roles is likely to continue as CEOs and boards experiment to determine what will work best for them. Either structure can be effective, as long as there is a process in place to provide effective leadership for the independent directors on every board. Maximizing the effectiveness of this role involves considering the qualities that would make someone excel in it, clarifying the roles and responsibilities of this role versus the role of the CEO, ensuring that the individual builds a constructive working relationship both with the CEO and his or her peers on the board, and providing a way to evaluate how the leader is doing. Moreover, we think it's critical that committee chairs—who lead much of the board's important work—also be regarded as an integral component of the board's leadership structure.

In the next two chapters we'll move beyond the formal leadership roles and structures to look at how leaders can shape both the board's work processes and its culture. These pieces, when put together, are crucial when building effective boards capable of producing value-added work.

CHAPTER FIVE

Board Work Processes

Richard Hardin
Judith A. Roland

U p to this point, our discussion of board-building has focused on assembling the right people to do the right work. Our focus over the next six chapters is on *how* those people do that work as an effective team. We begin in this chapter by taking a close look at the role of leaders in shaping three core processes that are critical to any board's successful performance:

- *Information management.* "Information is power" may be a cliché, but that's probably because it's true—particularly when it comes to the shifting balance of power between CEOs and boards. Traditionally, most CEOs have kept a firm hand on the information spigot, maintaining tight control over what their boards know and when they know it. It took some outrageous scandals to wake them up, but today most boards get the message. In the 2004 USC/Mercer Delta Corporate Board Survey, directors identified thirteen policies and practices that contribute most to board effectiveness; of those, "quality of information provided to the board" ranked first. To an enormous extent, the board's ability to provide meaningful oversight and useful advice is determined by the quality, timeliness, and credibility of the information it has. And it's clear to us that most boards have a long way to go in this area. Our in-depth interviews with the members of the NACD Blue Ribbon Commission on Board Leadership tapped into a wellspring of frustration and dissatisfaction with the content, volume, and accessibility of the information directors regularly receive. Perhaps even more disturbing, although 95 percent of the directors in our 2004 survey said their board receives sufficient information to carry out its duties, only 27 percent said they had channels independent of management through which to receive information about the company and its operations. That number was unchanged from our survey the previous year.

• *Agenda and meeting management.* It's hard to imagine a task that sounds more mundane than "agenda management." In reality, the agenda is the key to determining how productively the board spends its time together; whoever controls the agenda controls the board's ability to do useful work during the six or eight times it gathers each year. And this is an area where we're seeing significant change. In our 2003 directors survey, only 41 percent said the board had significant influence over its own agenda; just a year later, that number was up to 60 percent. The less sanguine way to look at that number, however, is that in 2004, after all the hype and hysteria about activist boards, four out of ten boards still had little or no influence on how they spent their time together.

• *Executive session management.* The requirement that the independent directors of publicly traded companies meet periodically in executive session without the CEO present has turned out to be one of the most profound changes in the way boards work. Meetings that were practically unthinkable at many companies in 2001 had become a routine and vital part of each board's work process by 2004. Their potential significance can't be overstated; they make it possible for independent directors to voice their concerns long before problems become crises. A safe, routine, and nonadversarial venue where directors can speak their minds eliminates the intrigue and suspicion that used to surround any informal meetings outside the CEO's presence. The main issue now is how boards can make the best use of executive sessions, and that boils down to some practical logistical matters: When should the meetings be held, how often, under whose leadership, using what agenda, and with what procedures for reporting the substance of the meetings back to the CEO in an accurate and impartial way?

Clearly, there's a consistent theme running through all three of these processes—a readjustment in the roles and relative power of the CEO and the board. Some CEOs have been reluctant to relinquish that power; by the same token, many boards have been hesitant to assume it. This is about shared responsibility, constructive collaboration, and a willingness on both sides of the table to step up to the challenge of working together in ways that protect and create value for the company's stakeholders.

MANAGING THE INFORMATION FLOW

Nothing is more central to the board's ability to oversee and add value to the way a company is run than information. Ira M. Millstein, senior partner at Weil, Gotshal & Manges and one of the best-known advocates of governance reform, wrote in 2003 that the failure of boards over the past three decades to be more "vigilant" could be traced to two factors: "Boards are often not helped by management to obtain needed information, and in some cases may be prevented by management from obtaining information; or the board never tries to get that information."[1]

We agree. If you examine the corporate scandals of the past few years and ask why boards didn't act sooner—or at all—to take matters in hand, the answer nearly always involves vital information that was either buried, obscured, or ignored. The blame could usually be laid on both sides of the table; management didn't volunteer it, and the board didn't ask for it—or, if it asked, was willing to accept an answer it really didn't understand.

These problems aren't new. What has changed, and dramatically, is that directors are being held personally accountable, both legally and financially, for failing to adequately exercise their "duty of care." In early 2005, WorldCom directors agreed to pay $20.2 million, and Enron directors paid $13 million—all from the directors' own pockets—to settle shareholder suits. As we write this, we're watching a proliferation of similar lawsuits by aggrieved shareholders seeking restitution from directors for alleged negligence. And in almost every case, the boards' questionable decisions, or absence of decisions, could be traced to a failure to demand or digest crucial information about management activity.

Our experience, and that of the members of the NACD Blue Ribbon Commission, is that boards must overcome several specific barriers to effective information management (see Exhibit 5.1):

- *Excessive quantity and inferior quality of information.* Directors are increasingly irritated by premeeting packets that are overstuffed with impenetrable data but short on accessible information. Some believe that management just doesn't understand

Exhibit 5.1. Overcoming Barriers to Effective Information Management.

Problem: A narrow focus on raw data or too much detail in premeeting packets	*Solution:* A streamlined combination of information and data • Summaries of the big issues • Highlights containing most important facts • Detailed appendices with supporting data
Problem: A heavy emphasis on financial and operations material	*Solution:* Information that gives a broad context and deeper understanding of company's potential risks, opportunities, and challenges • Details about marketplace, strategic issues, investor bases • Reports on internal issues such as culture, compliance, talent development • Timely updates on competitors, new technologies, market trends
Problem: Reliance on management for information the board needs to monitor management's performance	*Solution:* An independent source—the board's leadership—to manage the information flow • Sharing the responsibility with management • Gaining a clear understanding of what the board wants • Enhancing the management package through meetings with internal and external experts, company site visits

what they need; others suggest more devious intent, as the corporate secretary of a major consumer company told us. "There are two equally effective ways of keeping a board in the dark," he said. "One is to provide them with too little information. The other, ironically, is to provide too much information."

• *Nature of information.* Management has traditionally provided boards with two kinds of information: lagging indicators of operational and financial performance, and strategic outlooks framed by management's perspectives and positioned to support management's purposes. Neither provides the board with the broader foundation of information it needs on the company and the context within which it operates.

• *Information source.* There's an inherent information imbalance; managers who are immersed in the company's operations around the clock obviously know more about what's going on than the directors who meet half a dozen times a year. And yet, as we mentioned earlier, the majority of directors have no independent communication channels in the company. The result is that, by and large, boards continue to rely heavily on management for the very information they need to monitor management's performance.

Ironically, the governance reforms of 2002 are exacerbating some age-old problems. The requirement that a majority of the board, and entire committees, be made up of independent directors means that boards are populated by more people who know less about the company just when they're being held more accountable than ever for understanding what's going on. What's more, the voluminous financial disclosures mandated by Sarbanes-Oxley have raised the board's data-overload problem, and its level of frustration, to an all-time high.

The bottom line: managing information is a bigger challenge to boards than at any time in recent memory. The good news is that some boards have found successful ways to level the playing field, and many board leaders are figuring out how to make sure their members get the information they need to perform their jobs. One member of the Blue Ribbon Commission put the matter succinctly: "Defining the types and flows of information to the board is one of the most important tasks of board leadership. The basic equation is the right information at the right time from the right source."

The Right Information

Ask directors about the information they receive in their premeeting packets, and the response is almost universally negative. The real issue is the distinction between raw data and useful information that helps the board make smart decisions. There's way too much of the former and all too little of the latter; in too many cases, volume trumps value. Directors are frustrated; they know what they need, but rarely get it. "Information needs to be right in terms of volume, structure, and its focus on critical issues," said one commission member. Unfortunately, the information boards actually receive rarely meets all of those requirements, and sometimes none of them.

EXCESSIVE QUANTITY, POOR QUALITY. "There's not a board out there that's not inundated with data right now," said one commission member. "Every board is struggling with this." At the most basic level, directors feel overloaded by the sheer tonnage of material management dumps on them before each meeting and exasperated by management's apparent lack of concern about how it's received.

"Most companies don't think too much about it," a commission member explained. "A lot of people will send a package four inches thick to the board members. Well, they can't read all that stuff." Another commissioner observed, "You can really take away the energy and focus of a board if you overwhelm them with all the information rather than the right information."

And then there's Sarbanes-Oxley. As one commission member put it, the reporting requirements have resulted in board members "getting volumes—more information than they need or can do anything with—just so management can say, 'We provide the board with all this stuff.' "

It's not just the volume of material that irks directors, it's the indiscriminate way it's unloaded on them in a form that is impossible to digest. There's a real disconnect here. It's all too easy to imagine staff people pushing deadlines and pulling all-nighters prior to board meetings to compile an exhaustive report they're sure will impress the socks off the board members. But their effort to impress directors often has just the opposite effect, as one commission member explained: "Don't send out heavy, complex, technical reports that only someone working in the industry could understand. If you do that, directors come into the board meeting ticked off. They're mad at having to wade through all this stuff, and they really don't understand it, which makes it worse. Why start off a board meeting with people feeling like that? How do you think that meeting's going to go?"

Indeed, the narrow focus on raw data sometimes obscures the big picture. As a result, time and again, directors have privately admitted to us that even though they've been serving on their boards for years trying to make sense out of mountains of numbers, they don't really understand how the company "makes money." That might sound absurd until you remember the Enron board and its befuddlement over the arcane schemes and off-the-balance-sheet partnerships that resulted in a financial house of cards.

The real issue is providing information, as opposed to raw data, in a way that actually prepares directors to ask smart questions, probe the soft spots, and then make informed decisions at their next meeting. And what directors need in order to do this is a streamlined combination of information and data, summaries of the big issues to be dealt with, highlights containing the most salient facts, and detailed appendices containing the supporting data for those who have the time, expertise, or inclination to dig deeper.

Some companies already do this. A member of the Blue Ribbon Commission who is both CEO and chairman of his board explained that before each meeting, he sends out the packet with a cover letter no longer than three pages. "It says, 'Here's the information that's included in your package,' and beside each item I'll note, 'This is for information only, no discussion at the board meeting,' or 'We are seeking a decision from the board on this issue at the meeting, management's recommendation is the following.' That sets it up so that they know where to focus when they go through the reading package."

A LIMITED FOCUS. Another shortcoming of the information provided to some boards is the heavy emphasis on financial and operations reports at the expense of information that would provide directors with a broader context and deeper understanding of their company, its competitive environment, and its potential risks, opportunities, and challenges.

One commission member observed that on most boards you are given "too much operating information and a great deal of repetitive financial information, but never enough information about the marketplace and strategic issues."

Some directors are looking for more information, on a regular basis, that will keep them updated on big internal issues related to culture, compliance, talent development, and progress toward meeting strategic goals. There's also growing interest in getting timely information about competitors, new technologies, market trends, and regulatory issues.

Finally, as one commission member suggested, "We're seeing boards look for more information on their company's investor bases— for example, who's moving in and out, what are their concerns. I expect this activity to increase because boards are being held more accountable by shareholders, and board members want to know who these folks are and what they're thinking. . . . Of course, boards have always been concerned about this, but now there is a need to understand things with specificity, not generality."

THE ISSUE OF OBJECTIVITY. Many directors not only believe they're getting too much of the wrong information in a form that's hard to use but also voice concerns about objectivity. Management is positioned to decide what information to generate, what information to share with the board, and how to present that information in the most favorable light. Too often, the result is a board so dependent on management's perspective that it lacks any sufficient basis for exercising independent judgment or rigorous oversight.

"Management has the unique access and information about what issues are important," one commissioner told us. "Yet we are seeing more and more independent board leaders put in the position where they are told that part of their role is to make sure that the board is focused on the right issues."

Several years ago, our firm worked with a board that was sharply criticized for moving too slowly to fire its CEO following performance shortfalls and a huge decline in the company's value. Afterward, one director explained to us, "Six months ago, we had a very articulate CEO who made a very eloquent case about the company, and we had financial measures that indicated that we were one of the most valuable market capitalization companies in the country. How were we to know what was going on below? In fact, once we saw the problems, we acted with blinding speed, although in many ways it was too late."

Given the corporate debacles of recent years, it's not surprising that many directors—and some CEOs—believe there are still plenty of companies that intentionally manipulate information to keep their boards in the dark.

"Nothing is more tempting for a CEO than to make sure your board doesn't know anything, or they know the bare minimum," said a CEO member of the commission. "Then they can't drive you crazy with questions and take up time in the board meeting challenging you. . . . I am of the view that the more my board knows, the more their counsel increases in value. The stronger my board, the better for me. But that's not the way most CEOs think."

To some board members, both the problem and its solution are clear. "It's just human nature that the CEO is only going to want to give information about what's going well for him," said one commission member who has studied countless boards. "You have to have an independent source to make sure that the information is there." And that source is the board's leadership.

The Role of Board Leadership

There's no magic solution to all the problems we've just laid out, but one thing is clear: the only way for the board to start correcting the underlying information imbalance is for its leaders to get actively engaged in managing the flow of information to the board.

More specifically, we believe the board's leaders should:

- *Share responsibility with management.* Increasingly, more effective boards view information management, like agenda management, as a shared responsibility between the CEO and the board's independent leader. By working with management and the board, the leader can help management achieve a better balance of data and information. Leaders can also help to ensure that the premeeting packets provide a range of views and alternatives. At Best Western International, for example, the board adopted a policy in 2004 that every management recommendation forwarded to the board had to be accompanied by a discussion of the major arguments for and against it.

- *Understand what the board wants.* Although it's all too easy to lay all the blame for poor information on management's shoulders, "sometimes management just doesn't know there's a problem," said the former lead director of a major corporation. "I once went to the CEO and said I didn't like the stuff that was being sent, and he said, 'Thanks, you're the first one who ever came forward with feedback like that.'" It's the job of board leaders to constantly take their members' temperature, find out if they're getting the information they want and need, and then work with management to get it right. Some boards have formalized the process, asking their members to fill out annual questionnaires assessing the quality of the information packets and asking for specific suggestions.

• *Go beyond the management package.* Ensuring that boards receive the right kind of information from management, in the right format, and in a timely manner is important. But it's far from enough. It doesn't address the board's need for in-depth understanding of the company and its competitive market, or for unfiltered information from sources independent of management. Directors tell us they want regular information— again, from outside sources such as analyst reports and trade publications—regarding competitors, emerging technologies, and industry trends. To fill this need, more and more boards are embracing the idea of director education. This includes creating opportunities for directors to meet face-to-face with experts from both inside and outside the company and with people with different points of view who can broaden the board's thinking on critical issues. And to enhance understanding of the companies on whose boards they serve, a growing number of boards are requiring that their members make a requisite number of visits each year to the company's operating sites, though, to be sure, nearly half the directors we surveyed said their boards still had no such requirement.

Striking the Right Balance

When it comes to information management, as with so many other issues, the challenge for the board is how to strike the right balance. As one commission member described it, the board's problem is ensuring that it regularly receives information that's at "a high enough level to give a useful overview but not at such a level of detail that you end up micromanaging."

One commission member, a well-respected corporate executive who sits on several boards, explained his own misgivings: "One of the biggest issues in terms of board information is this: How do you, as a board member, stay informed without interfering with management? For example, I don't think it's appropriate for a director to be dipping down four layers in management asking questions, and I don't do it. But I see other directors do it, and guess what? They're better informed than I am, and I know they've detected some problems by doing this. But I view it as objectionable, and overstepping the line between governance and management. Consequently, however, I'm largely dependent on the CEO for my information. I don't know the answer to this, but I think it is a major issue."

He's right; it is a major issue. We suspect the answer goes back to the role of the board leaders and their responsibility to develop explicit processes that provide the board with a sufficiently clear picture of what's going on inside the organization so that individual directors don't have to operate like investigative reporters in their own companies.

MANAGING AGENDAS AND MEETINGS

If you stop and think about it, the most widely scorned symbol of the unproductive, unengaged, ceremonial board was the board meeting itself. We've all heard the derisive terms used to describe these meetings: "dog and pony shows," "Kabuki dramas," "tea ceremonies." *Question:* What device was used to strip these meetings of any consequence and exclude the board from meaningful discussion, debate, and decision making? *Answer:* The agenda.

In truth, the humble agenda constitutes the single most powerful tool for either empowering or emasculating the board. Simply stated, whoever controls the agenda controls the board's ability to do meaningful work. Traditionally, that power lay firmly in the hands of the CEO, who often exercised nearly unilateral control over how the board would spend its very limited time in the course of its very infrequent meetings.

As we noted earlier, the balance of power is quickly shifting in the board's favor, with 60 percent of the directors we surveyed in 2004 saying their boards now have significant influence over their own agendas. But the battle is far from over. "The way most boards work," said one commission member, "it's still about management reciting stuff that people should have read in advance without leaving time for discussion." Said another: "Most management views the board as another constituency to be handled and the meetings as something to get through without damage."

For meetings to be successful, the right combination of people has to determine which issues will be raised, how much time is appropriate for each item, and how best to use that time.

Sharing the Process

Those who have already tackled this issue suggest there are a variety of ways in which boards can be more involved in the agenda-building process. There's a strong and growing sentiment that board leaders should play an active role in setting the agenda; although their precise roles differ from one board to another, we're seeing some consistent themes and best practices.

Some see the independent board leader as central to the process. As one commissioner told us: "The leader is critical in setting the agenda, to make sure the board is talking about the right stuff." Although some see a trend toward lead directors actually setting the agenda, that's only the case at only a relatively small number of boards. In our 2004 directors survey, for instance, 75 percent of the respondents said their board has a lead director, but of those, only 22 percent said their lead director is responsible for developing their meeting agendas.

Clearly, many boards still believe the CEO should play a major role, and there's a good case to be made for the CEO's continued participation in agenda design. But there's also growing interest in involving the entire board in the process, rather than leaving it in the hands of one or two board leaders. One alternative is for a board leader to touch base with each director between regular meetings and ask what they all would like to see on the next agenda. Some boards end each meeting by asking the group to suggest what they'd like to see on the agenda for the next meeting. And now that executive sessions for independent directors have become common, some boards are using them as a place for candid discussion of items that perhaps should be scheduled for future meetings of the full board. Whatever process is used to solicit the directors' suggestions, it then becomes the board leader's responsibility to ensure this information is discussed with the CEO, and where appropriate, built into the agenda.

For boards interested in broadening their members' participation, it makes sense to circulate the draft agenda for comment when there's still sufficient time for directors to provide input and for leaders to make revisions. One commissioner observed, "I haven't seen many boards where the agenda is sent out enough in advance that board members can really react to it. The board leader should make an effort to get the agenda out early and ask the rest of the board, 'Are there other things you want to have us talk about?'"

Making Time for the Right Topics

More than any other type of team, the board is constrained for time. Few boards still limit themselves to four quarterly meetings per year; the norm today is between six and eight regularly scheduled meetings of the full board. But the meetings now sometimes stretch out two days or more, and there are often a host of other gatherings, either in person or over the phone: committee meetings, strategy off-sites, and special site visits, for example. Today, it's not unusual to see boards of major companies, such as General Electric, with a dozen or more meetings each year. Qwest Communications, as it tried to recover from near-collapse, reported twenty-three different meetings of board members in 2004.[2]

But there are limits. Over the years, the USC/Mercer Delta directors survey has found a 20 percent increase in the amount of time directors are devoting to their board activities; at a certain point, the combination of long hours and high risks makes the directors' job unattractive to many potential directors. Consequently, boards have to pay special attention to making the best possible use of their time together.

For one thing, boards are looking at agenda development as a two-tiered process: an annual agenda on a high level that guarantees critical topics will be covered at some point during the year, and a detailed agenda for each board meeting. There's usually some overarching framework for the annual agenda. In some cases, it's developed through discussion among the board committee chairs to ensure that major topics of concern to their respective committees are covered in at least one meeting. Target Corporation began this practice as the company was branching out from a single line of department stores; the annual agenda ensured that at least one meeting each year would focus on the strategy of each operating unit. Other companies identify the primary drivers of their corporate strategy—technology, culture, or others—and devote a meeting to each one.

In the final analysis, the critical decisions are all about which items to include in the regular meeting agendas, how much time to devote to each, and in what order. Many of the directors we interviewed complained that the routine housekeeping matters, variously described as the "minutiae" and "details," often squeeze out such substantial matters as strategic issues, potential risks, competitive threats, and reputational issues.

One commission member described what he considered to be a particularly bad example of agenda management at a board he sat on: "Somehow, we never got around to the big issues. We spent all of our time on details and perfunctory stuff. We never got a vision of where this company was going, what their competitive position was. . . . We never talked about those issues. The company was ultimately taken over." That might be an extreme example, but the underlying lesson is clear: boards that spend their meetings focused on the wrong business do so at their extreme peril.

The sequence of topics is almost as important as the selection. Directors sometimes describe board meetings as an exercise in clock-watching. As the end of the meeting draws near, people start thinking about making their flights; attention wanes and attendance dwindles. To address that reality, one commission member said, "Right after we approve the minutes of the last meeting and before we move into the financials, we go into a session of getting the important things off our chest—the meaty stuff. . . . If you save the meaty stuff for the end, you may not have everyone there to talk about it."

Conversely, administrative and housekeeping matters that are further removed from the board's chief responsibilities should be added to the agenda only if really necessary, and then, at the end, to be handled only after the most significant matters are dealt with. That way, if the board runs out of time, which it often will with an overly ambitious agenda, at least those items that require discussion and deliberation will have been addressed.

Major big-picture topics such as strategy and succession may be difficult to address adequately within the confines of a regular board meeting, requiring additional time for the in-depth exploration they deserve. Annual or semiannual board retreats and off-sites allow boards the luxury of time to devote to a substantial, complex topic and also the opportunity to stay engaged with the company's issues outside of regular meetings. The change in venue as well as the additional time can be extremely helpful in getting directors to focus properly and delve into these critical areas.

Participation Versus Presentations

As concerned as directors are about the choice of topics to be covered at their regular meetings, their greatest source of frustration is the manner in which the topics have traditionally been handled: carefully scripted, precisely orchestrated formal presentations by management, leaving little or no time for probing questions or thoughtful discussion.

"Too often, particularly in large companies with large staffs . . . the CEO calls on different members of the corporate staff to make presentations, leaving no time whatsoever for discussion," one commission member complained. "So, out of a four-hour meeting, you might have three and a half hours of presentations and thirty minutes of discussion. That is an extremely dysfunctional board meeting."

The level of frustration is finally reaching the point where board leaders are responding. We're seeing a greater emphasis on loading the prepared information in the premeeting packet and setting tighter limits on presentation time in meetings; some boards limit presentations to no more than half the time devoted to any topic. The goal, as one commission member described it, is to provide the bulk of information before the meeting, share the "information highlights" at the meeting, and spend most of the time on what the board should be doing: discussion, problem solving, and decision making.

Of course, scheduling time for discussion is no guarantee of good discussion. In too many boardrooms, discussion tends to be dominated by the most senior or the most outspoken members, while others tend to defer to their more knowledgeable—or more garrulous—colleagues. This is another area where skillful board leadership can make a world of difference; board chairs or lead directors who aren't adept at engaging the full board in discussion and debate should make a point of learning that skill.

For example, one director suggested having the chairman go around the table and ask each director for his or her opinion: "That pulls everyone into the discussion right away and gets them engaged. Also, you get the lay of the land right at the start. Perhaps most important, this technique demonstrates that everyone's opinion is valued." On the other hand, board leaders must be willing to deal with the directors who invariably hoard the "airtime," by having the gumption to say tactfully, "Let's move on." Similarly, they have to be able to get a discussion that has gone too far afield back on track. When it's time to move from discussion to decision, the chairman often has to call on another skill: consensus building. As one director we interviewed put it, "It is important to be able to provide 'pull you' leadership in the boardroom—the kind of leadership that pulls all of the directors out on an issue and fosters consensus building in a particular direction."

Perhaps the most critical rule that should govern board discussions is the simple notion that there are no dumb questions—and perhaps even more important, no dumb follow-up questions. That may sound silly, but the fact is that the corporate boardroom is a place where it's sometimes incredibly difficult for someone to say, "I don't understand. Please explain that again." After all, there's a presumption that everyone around the table is smart, experienced, and sophisticated. Nobody wants to look dumb, or to waste the board's time. The whole environment militates against admissions of ignorance or confusion. Recent corporate history might have been dramatically different if a couple of directors at Enron, Tyco, WorldCom, Qwest Communications, or any number of companies had just held up their hand and said, "Hold on. That just doesn't make sense. Explain it to me again." But it's up to the board's leadership to create an environment where members feel comfortable doing that.

Merrill Lynch: A Case in Point

As boards look for ways to put the principles of sound agenda management into practice, there are countless ways to achieve the same goals. It's instructive to look at how one company addresses the concerns we've raised, and Merrill Lynch is an interesting case. Since 2001, management has adopted many of the best practices for involving the board without relinquishing the CEO's role as the leader.

"The biggest issue is how to address all the topics that need to be on the agenda when there's a finite amount of time," says Rosemary Berkery, executive vice president and general counsel. "There are just a lot more things that have to be covered than in the past." In part, the increased workload is reflected in the proliferation of committee meetings; the audit committee, for instance, now meets ten times each year, twice as often as it did five years earlier.

But there's still the risk that mandatory housekeeping will squeeze out more substantive topics during the full board's seven regular meetings. So Merrill Lynch, like others, now creates an annual agenda. It identifies key topics to be covered—a thorough review of each of the three core businesses, discussion of major issues such as risk and liquidity—and schedules them far in advance "so we make sure we get one, two, or even three sessions of each item in the 'core curriculum' over the course of the year," Berkery says.

The meeting agendas are primarily put together by Stan O'Neal, the chairman and CEO, and Berkery, often in consultation with the chairman of the board's nominating/corporate governance committee. Any member of the board can suggest an item for the agenda, and future agendas are discussed at board meetings. With the agenda process opened to board members in recent years, Berkery says, she has noticed "a real change in the board's interest in the agenda and a lot more dialogue about the agenda."

All of the board meetings last for at least a day, with mornings devoted to committee meetings and the rest of the day to the full board. Three times a year, the meetings start late on a Sunday afternoon, and are followed by a working dinner featuring management presentations on two topics. "The Sunday sessions are great," Berkery says. "It's very informal, people are sitting at a table having dinner together. There's lots of conversation, lots of questions, a lot of depth."

During board meetings, formal presentations are generally planned for thirty-five to forty-five minutes, although certain matters are allotted significantly more time. "We've baked in a lot more time for Q&A and discussion," Berkery says. Before each meeting, presenters go through "dress rehearsals" to ensure they cover the right content in the allotted time. "We skinny down a lot of them from the initial drafts," Berkery says. "We want to make sure there's enough time for discussion, for two reasons: first, because it's important for the board to be both informed and involved, and second, because this is an opportunity for the board to see the business heads on their feet, in action fielding Q&As."

Between meetings, Berkery says, the CEO welcomes discussions between directors and members of senior management. "He really encourages that contact," Berkery says. "He doesn't think the board should just hear one voice, or have all their information funneled through the CEO."

MAKING THE MOST OF EXECUTIVE SESSIONS

Along with the rules requiring that independent directors constitute a majority of the full board and the entire membership of crucial committees, another new governance rule having a great impact on independent board oversight is the one mandating periodic executive sessions sans CEO. The timing and agendas of those meetings are still evolving, but they're already having a profound influence on the way boards operate.

Like building an agenda and information management, executive sessions, when properly organized and run, enable independent directors to function more effectively as a group and fulfill their duty as overseers of management. And once again, there are plenty of best practices to be gleaned from boards that already have a track record in holding effective executive sessions.

"Executive sessions have transformed boards," a commission member stated unequivocally. "The first time an executive session is held is often the first time ever that a board has met without management present. When we first started doing this, management was completely freaked out by the idea. The chairman/CEO would say, 'Why have a meeting without me? I'm the guy who knows everything!'"

Like some other reforms that were resisted in the beginning, executive sessions have quickly taken root in many boards and are held as a matter of course, not something that has to be planned and explained. Although the only legal requirement is that the meetings be held "periodically," many boards now hold one in conjunction with every scheduled board meeting. In practice, the more routine they become, the better for everyone involved. Rather than thinking, "I wonder what's wrong and why they decided to meet," the CEO is more likely to view the session as a routine process that helps independent directors do their job.

When boards incorporate executive sessions into their regular board meetings, they need to explore the advantages and disadvantages of holding them before or after the full-board sessions. Holding them before the actual board meeting helps ensure better attendance and provides directors with another opportunity to recommend items that should be added to the agenda for the full board to take up. The downside is that the premeeting doesn't provide an opportunity to delve into issues that came up during the board meeting. A session following the full meeting allows for that discussion, but there's likely to be attrition as members head for the airport as soon as the full board meeting is over. Some boards find that it makes sense to hold executive sessions both before and after each board meeting.

Just as there is an art to conducting efficient and effective board meetings, the same is true for executive sessions. As one director put it, "The worst thing at an executive session is for the board members to just sit and stare at each other. The first thing the leader needs to do at the start of the executive session is to set forth the agenda for what is going to be discussed in the time available and make sure that everyone is in agreement about that." Of course, as in any meeting, sometimes the most valuable discussion ensues spontaneously, rather than being agenda-driven, and there has to be some time reserved for free-flowing informal discussion that enables directors to speak their minds.

It's easy to see how CEOs could feel threatened by the sessions, particularly if they're sitting in their offices wondering what in the world is being discussed. For executive sessions to be truly valuable, there has to be an understanding that the outcome of important discussions will be communicated to the CEO quickly and accurately, employing a process that maintains the confidentiality of the private discussion while conveying the overall view of the group to the CEO.

"One of the best things about executive sessions," said one director, "is the fact that when the director who runs the session goes to the CEO with feedback, the weight of the board is behind that person. Previously, when you approached the CEO and expressed concern about an issue, it was done by an informal gang or a single individual. And the CEO often dismissed the message as a personal issue." Some boards—again, Best Western International is one example—have both the chairman and vice chairman go together to report to the CEO on the substance of meetings he didn't attend, so that the CEO isn't left wondering whether he's hearing only one point of view colored by a single director's personal agenda.

Independent directors we've spoken with who are practiced in the art of executive sessions emphasize the importance, when providing feedback to the CEO, of delivering the good news as well as the bad. We'll discuss this in greater detail in Chapter Eight in the context of using executive sessions as a routine way for independent directors to raise questions about the CEO's performance. If CEOs view the feedback from the sessions as helpful and balanced—instead of feeling that they are continually being taken to task—they are far more likely to embrace executive sessions and the information that emerges from them. Taking the process even further, some boards now hold two types of executive sessions: one with only independent directors and another with independent directors and the CEO.

SUMMARY

It has taken more than two decades for the governance reform efforts launched in earnest in the 1980s to finally shift the balance of power in U.S. boardrooms. But in the main, those governance reforms have more to do with the board's legal accountability than its operational effectiveness.

This chapter is intended to serve as a guide for boards as they search for new work processes that will provide meaning and value to their newfound activism. Those boards that have a longer track record exercising independent oversight should also benefit from the practical experience of some of the seasoned directors we interviewed for the NACD Blue Ribbon Commission. With the desire to contribute and the processes to support it, a board should be enabled to provide the sort of value long envisioned by those who have supported a healthy and constructive tension between management and independent directors on boards.

CHAPTER SIX

The Role of Leaders in Shaping Board Culture

David A. Nadler

Jack Welch's tenure as CEO of GE was, by any measure, phenomenally successful. But even the most remarkable CEOs are mere mortals, and bound to err from time to time. In Welch's case, one notable blunder was his ill-fated attempt to acquire Honeywell in 2001. It was a deal fraught with risk, undertaken with little regard for the unyielding opposition it would encounter from the European Commission. It was a classic situation where a fully engaged, high-performing board would have stepped in and cooled the CEO's acquisitive ardor. But that's not what happened.

"Jack came in with this plan," one director later told us, "and a number of us had real concerns. But we thought, 'Hell, he's Jack Welch, who are we to raise these issues?' So we didn't. There was real discomfort with his plan, but no acceptance of the idea that it was OK to challenge Jack."

The reticence to openly challenge a dominant CEO, even when his position flies in the face of common sense and prudent judgment, typifies the traditional gentlemen's club culture that still prevents so many boards from doing their jobs well. Make no mistake: it is the board's culture—the shared values and beliefs that delineate acceptable behavior—that ultimately determines how effective the board can be. You can have the right people around the table, the right items on the agenda, the right committee structure and leadership roles, but unless you have a culture that supports the active and independent participation of every director, nothing else matters.

That conviction is rooted in our belief that an effectively engaged board takes on many of the characteristics of any high-performing team. And the most important characteristic is a culture, a social climate and pattern of interactions, that enables them to work productively, both when they're together in the boardroom and when they're not.

The central question is this: What kind of culture supports effective engagement, and how do board leaders go about shaping that culture? With that in mind, this chapter will focus on four issues:

- What unique characteristics make boards so different from other teams, and as a consequence, cause their culture to be so vital to their success?

- What aspects of the traditional board culture still make it so difficult for boards to do the kind of work they should be doing?

- Assuming the traditional culture has become an anachronism, what essential attributes of the new culture should engaged boards be moving toward?

- How do boards—and more specifically their leaders—actually go about shaping a new culture and changing the old one?

Throughout this chapter, one overarching theme will emerge: the single most important factor in shaping any board's culture is the behavior of its leaders. To be sure, they need the help and support of the entire board. But in the final analysis, it is the leaders who determine the climate and dynamics of every board.

THE BOARD AS AN ANOMALY: WHAT MAKES IT DIFFERENT

The very idea that boards should operate as high-performing, work-oriented teams is relatively new, and in some ways, fairly radical. It contradicts the traditional view of boards as ceremonial appendages to the apparatus of corporate governance, and as collections of dignitaries who would assemble infrequently to place their obligatory stamp of approval on management's predetermined decisions.

That view has been changing over the past decade. We began suggesting in the 1990s that the board should transform itself from a loose aggregation of individuals into a true team, one that performs at a consistently high level.[1, 2] Over the years, we've seen growing acceptance of the idea that the board's capacity to work effectively as a team, rather than its minimal compliance with a host of new legal requirements, is what determines its ability to add value to the organization.[3] But the concept is easier to advocate than to implement. In our work with board leaders in North America and Western Europe, we find growing agreement that boards should operate as teams but considerable frustration about how to achieve that goal.

The frustration is rooted in a fundamental paradox. No team is more vital to the organization's success than the board, but at the same time no other team faces so many unique obstacles to its team performance (see Table 6.1). As we discussed in the final report of the NACD Blue Ribbon Commission on Board Leadership, certain characteristics not only make the board unique among teams but also contribute to the evolution of a social system, or culture, that diminishes the capacity for productive work. Let's consider those characteristics and the traditional board culture they've helped to shape.

Partial Affiliation

Most teams are composed of members who work for the same organization. Even if they happen to work in different disciplines, geographies, or business units, they're all employed by the same corporate entity; its work is their work. Not so for outside directors. In most cases, the board is just one of several they sit on, in addition to their regular "day job." The work of most teams is just one more aspect of each team member's job; the work of boards is wholly unrelated to how the outside directors spend the bulk of their time.

Episodic Interaction

Board members spend so little time together, and so infrequently, that it's nearly impossible for them to experience the intense personal interaction that fuels the performance of other teams. On average, boards meet between six and eight times a year. Board committees meet more often—some audit committees, in particular, get together twice as frequently as they did before Sarbanes-Oxley was adopted in

Table 6.1.   Characteristics Differentiating Boards from Other Teams.

	Typical Teams	Boards as Teams
Affiliation	Members work for the same organization.	Outside directors may be members of more than one board; this is not their "day job."
Interaction	Members spend considerable time together, experience intense personal interaction.	Directors spend little time together, making it difficult for them to build working relationships.
Time and information	Constantly immersed in company's business.	Limited time available to devote to mastering issues of complex company.
Leaders as members	Most members are not accustomed to sitting at the head of the table.	Majority of members may be CEOs, who are used to leading, not following.
Authority relationships	Members' roles on the team often reflect their status in the company.	Lines of authority complex and unclear; chairmen/CEOs both lead and report to boards.
Changing expectations	Usually created with a reasonably clear charter—such as completing a project—in mind.	Difficult to achieve consensus in a climate of unprecedented scrutiny and pressure.
Formality	High degree of formality is rare, generally reflects the culture of the company.	Physical setting and social rituals reinforce aura of power and privilege.
Meeting focus	Work of team continues between meetings.	Little time devoted to board's work between meetings.

2002—but those meetings often take place over the phone and involve only a small subset of the full board. When you add up the actual time a full board spends together in a room, usually a daylong meeting, separated by six or eight weeks of little or no contact, it's obvious that there's little opportunity for directors to build working relationships or a sense of community.

Limited Time and Information

The limited time that even the most diligent outside directors spend on board-related work severely restricts their ability to become deeply familiar with the company, its people, and its business issues. Unlike members of management, who are constantly immersed in the company's business, outside directors spend the equivalent of three to four weeks each year on board business, most of it in meetings. No matter how smart or well-intentioned a director might be, it's virtually impossible to master the issues of a complex company in that amount of time.

Preponderance of Leaders

Most outside directors have been selected because of their outstanding professional achievements. Indeed, present and former CEOs still make up the largest single source of outside directors, accounting for more than 40 percent of the total by some estimates. As a result, the board is unique among teams in that the majority of its members are more accustomed to sitting at the head of the table. For many of these individuals, it's an unusual and sometimes unsettling situation, as they each play out their own psychological needs for power, recognition, and influence.

Complex Authority Relationships

The lines of authority within a board can be complex and sometimes unclear. Board meetings aren't like management meetings, where members' roles on the team reflect their status in the corporate hierarchy. Within the board, hierarchical relationships can be fluid, even ambiguous. For instance, on more than 70 percent of the boards of publicly traded U.S. companies, the board's chairman, the CEO, also reports to the board, a perplexing power relationship if ever there was one.

Changing Expectations for Work

Most teams are created with a reasonably clear charter in mind: to provide coordination or oversight, or to complete a specified project. Today, faced with unprecedented scrutiny and pressure from every quarter, many boards are struggling to reach consensus about exactly what work they should be doing and what their role should be vis à vis senior management.

Aura of Formality

The physical setting and social rituals of board meetings reinforce the aura of power, privilege, and aristocratic civility. Even today, the format, content, and physical setting of board meetings creates a sense of formality you won't find on any other team. (If you have any doubts about the impact of the physical setting, consider what happened at Procter & Gamble in 2001. During repair work in the regular boardroom—a traditional room with dark paneling and a table so long, says retired CEO/Chairman John Pepper, "you could hardly see people at the other end"—the board temporarily relocated to another room. "The biggest difference was that it had a much smaller table, and we could actually sit around it and talk with each other," Pepper recalls. "It certainly made a difference in our interactions; there was a lot more informality, and board meetings became a lot more collegial." The board members found their temporary setting so much more conducive to productive work that they abandoned the old boardroom.)

Focus on Meetings

The work of most teams moves ahead between one meeting and the next. Again, not so with boards. As soon as the board meeting ends, directors quickly disperse and devote little time to the board's work until the next meeting rolls around. As a consequence, the quality of each meeting's design carries unusual importance.

With so many inherent limitations and unique circumstances, it's not at all surprising that traditional boards rarely thought of themselves as teams. By the same token, boards developed a unique culture that you'd be hard-pressed to find on any high-performing team, and with good reason. A traditional board that wants to become active and engaged must first bridge a cultural chasm between the old and the new.

UNDERSTANDING THE TRADITIONAL BOARD CULTURE

Let's begin, for purposes of this discussion, by agreeing on some basic terms and principles drawn from a large and learned body of work by others and our own experience in this area.

There are any number of ways to label and describe the phenomenon of culture, whether you're talking about a country or a company or a team. In our view, culture springs from shared values, a consistent view that certain things are axiomatically either good or bad in a given social context. Based on those values, people develop a set of beliefs—expectations that a particular form of behavior will inexorably lead to certain consequences, either positive or negative.

Those beliefs, in turn, give rise to *norms,* unwritten yet powerful rules that define both acceptable and unacceptable behavior. Those norms often result in *artifacts,* the observable evidence of culture at work. In the board's case, the most tangible artifact is the boardroom itself; the ornate furnishings, the chairman's seat at the head of a long table, and the engraved plaque identifying each director's designated chair all speak to the excessive formality and authoritarianism of the traditional board culture.

It's not our intention to take a deep anthropological dive into the traditional board culture. Anyone who has belonged to or been associated with the board of a major corporation is already familiar with the basics. (As John Pepper said of the old P&G boardroom, "Even if you've never seen it, you'd recognize it right away.") But even a quick backward glance will underscore that many boards still have a long way to go.

In many ways, membership on traditional boards was valued for the *status and social recognition* it implied. It was an award for meritorious achievement, public acknowledgment of your influence, knowledge, and importance. When you joined a major board, you had joined *The Club;* membership brought with it the chance to hobnob in elegant surroundings with like-minded people of similar backgrounds and accomplishments, and an opportunity to solidify and extend your network of professional, social, and civic contacts.

Indeed, the gentleman's club metaphor applies to traditional board culture in countless ways, ranging from the decor of boardrooms to the demographic homogeneity of the membership to the unspoken commitment to *civility and formality.* Good manners included appropriate loyalty to the CEO who was responsible for your appointment, who might well have retained you or your company for legal or financial guidance, and who could be counted on for generous contributions to your favorite philanthropy. Thus, one of the principle values of the traditional culture was *unswerving support for senior management.*

Another value was *service to the business community*—in the sense that you were lending your stature to another organization through membership on its board. There was also an expectation of *reciprocity;* your service on other boards created the expectation that others would answer the call and serve on your board when it was time to find another friend or ally to sit around the table.

These values were manifested in some widely held beliefs about acceptable behavior. There were a few basic assumptions: acceptance into The Club's "inner circle" resulted from supporting management, following the rules, and getting along with colleagues. And to paraphrase Woody Allen, success was mainly about "showing up"; all that was expected, in terms of your commitment to the job, was your physical presence at the table.

Those assumptions translated into the norms that dictated acceptable boardroom behavior. One simply didn't challenge management, defy the board leadership, or raise potentially embarrassing issues. And at all costs, one avoided asking questions that might lead others to doubt one's intelligence or business acumen.

That picture is neither exaggerated nor out-of-date. In the wake of Maurice "Hank" Greenberg's ouster as chairman and CEO of American International Group Inc. in March 2005, the *Wall Street Journal* pieced together a telling glimpse at a traditional board culture that persisted almost up to the moment Greenberg was fired. They described a star-studded board that included a former U.S. Secretary of Defense, a former U.S. ambassador to the United Nations, and a former chairman of the President's Council of Economic Advisers whose members were afraid to ask questions because they feared looking "ignorant" or appearing to challenge Greenberg. At one of their last meetings, when one director had the temerity to ask if it might be time to untangle some apparently conflicting ties between AIG and related companies, Greenberg's reported response was, "That would be stupid!"[4]

The tyrannical dominance by CEOs and the unquestioning acquiescence of passive boards, though less common than a few years ago, still stand in marked contrast to the culture required by boards that hope to become actively engaged.

THE CULTURE OF THE ACTIVELY ENGAGED BOARD

Here's the issue: What kind of culture supports an environment in which the board can do real work and contribute tangible value? Of course, there's no simple answer; every board operates in a particular social and business context. But most face some common challenges.

A paramount challenge in the United States, and in other countries as well, is how to manage the shifting balance of power between management and the board. That implies a second challenge: managing the balance between contention and collaboration. Given their respective roles, there should be some natural level of contention between the board and management. But in some cases we've already seen the pendulum swing wildly from board passivity all the way to interference, micromanagement, and obstructionism. Balance is the key.

The culture we're about to describe remains somewhat aspirational. The actively engaged board is a work in progress, and so too is its culture. But our own experience and observation, buttressed by the many insightful comments gathered in our interviews with the members of the NACD Blue Ribbon Commission, provide strong indications that a great many boards are striving mightily to move in this direction.

In our view, the culture of the actively engaged board builds on the foundation of five core values, and each one translates into a set of behavioral norms. The list we're about to discuss is intended to be illustrative rather than all-inclusive (see Exhibit 6.1). This is a general framework that each board should customize with its own variations.

Value #1: Independence and Integrity

"Independence is the most important factor in board effectiveness," one commissioner told us, "and the hardest thing to get."

True independence goes far beyond the legal definitions outlined in the NYSE listing requirements. Indeed, it should be apparent by now that full legal compliance provides no guarantee that a board will diligently fulfill its oversight role, much less provide any additional value to the organization. We're much more concerned with genuine emotional and intellectual independence, and not just from management, but from other directors as well. True independence is reflected in three behavioral norms:

SPIRIT OF INQUIRY. Boards get into trouble—and allow management to get their companies into trouble—by accepting management positions at face value, and by failing to ask the pointed question, dig below the surface, and doggedly pursue the truth. "All of the recent disasters—WorldCom, Enron, etc.—had boards that seemed to lack a sense of curiosity and failed to insist on full disclosure," observed one commission member.

CONSTRUCTIVE DISSENT. "Ineffective boards are characterized by an acceptance of everything that management says," asserted one commission member. "They're a pro forma body and a rubber stamp." The

Exhibit 6.1.   Core Values and Norms.

Independence and integrity	*Spirit of inquiry:* Doesn't accept management positions at face value, pursues truth by digging below the surface. *Constructive dissent:* Resists pressure to act as a rubber stamp and conform to "groupthink." *Search for relevant facts:* Demands complete and credible material, looks beyond management for information sources.
Openness	*Candid sharing of opinions:* Takes part in animated discussions, encourages debate. *Broad participation:* Discourages domination of discussions, conducts real business only when everyone is present. *Respect for common sense and intuition:* Trusts personal instincts, not afraid to ask the "stupid question."
Accountability	*Shared leadership and responsibility:* Agrees that all directors have equal responsibility to shareholders, shares the heavy lifting. *Self-management:* Accepts responsibility for managing personal behavior, speaks up, and is fully prepared. *Peer management:* Helps shape behavior of peers, raises issues, and intervenes when appropriate.
Action orientation	*Rules for resolving conflict:* Encourages guidelines that help lead to consensus and prevent deadlocks. *Development of "collective intuition":* Is diligent about helping the board develop its own form of collective intuition about the organization. *Focus on priorities:* Actively manages agenda to ensure that appropriate time is spent on the most important issues.
Mutual trust and respect	*Confidentiality inside the room, solidarity outside the room:* Fosters mutual respect and trust between directors. *Respect for expertise and diverse opinions:* Respects what new voices bring and pays attention to them. *Active and respectful listening:* Listens when other directors talk, expects them to do the same.

engaged culture encourages each director to withstand pressure, not only from management but from other board members as well. Said another commission member: "The most important thing is to make sure there is no groupthink. The leader needs to create an environment where saying 'no' and challenging is not seen as an act of disloyalty, but as an act of responsibility."

SEARCH FOR RELEVANT FACTS. Engaged boards insist on information that's both complete and credible, and refuse to become totally reliant upon management as their exclusive source of information. They find appropriate ways to obtain information directly from sources both inside and outside the organization to help them understand how well management is operating the company and addressing its strategic challenges.

Value #2: Openness

Next to independence, directors we've spoken with cite openness as the most important quality of the culture they'd like to see on their boards. They describe the value in a number of ways, including these:

CANDID SHARING OF OPINIONS. "Ineffective board leadership creates a culture where it's considered inappropriate or bad manners to engage in a vigorous debate," explained one commission member. Animated discussion should be the rule, not the exception. The director of a Fortune 100 company—one that has made more than its share of costly strategic mistakes—compared that board's gentlemanly conversation with the bare-knuckled give-and-take of another board he belongs to at a much smaller start-up company. "When you have a board made up of actual owners, venture capitalists, we argue a lot. And it's from that argument that we get the best decisions."

BROAD PARTICIPATION. On traditional boards, discussions tend to be dominated by the CEO, one or two committee chairs, and sometimes by a "superdirector," a board member whose credentials or reputation so overshadow the others that the rest of the board feels too intimidated to participate. As various directors told us, leaders of the best boards create a climate "where all members feel free to speak up," and in fact, go out of their way "to engage the more quiet directors and to bring out comments that may be controversial." Broad participation also means that the real business of the board is done at the table with everyone in attendance, rather than in huddled conversations in the hallway.

RESPECT FOR COMMON SENSE AND INTUITION. Directors are looking to their leaders, as one commission member put it, "to create a boardroom culture of openness where there are no dumb questions." If Enron directors had trusted their common sense, at least some of them would have looked at the array of agonizingly complex off-the-books schemes and asked whether management was constructing a house of cards. Intuition should have told the Tyco directors that there was simply no way to keep swallowing up one acquisition after another. Board members, by and large, are smart, experienced people, but to be effective they have to operate in an environment where they're encouraged to trust their own instincts, ask questions regardless of how "stupid" they might seem, and then ask a follow-up question if the first answer doesn't make sense.

Value #3: Accountability

As we discussed in Chapter Three, individual accountability may be the area where boards find it most difficult to embrace new beliefs and behavior. Our own surveys indicate that the practice of director peer review is still shunned by the majority of U.S. boards. But the harsh reality is that boards won't have the luxury of debating the limits of accountability much longer. The courts have seized the initiative, and in the Enron and WorldCom cases, demonstrated their willingness to hold directors individually responsible, and financially liable, for failing to exercise the requisite business judgment.

Highlighting accountability as a core value, along with independence, implies a dramatic departure from the traditional board culture. In the old culture, directors weren't expected to do much more than show up at meetings and vote "aye" at the appointed time. Today, society is imposing new and harsh demands on directors, and holding them accountable for negligent performance.

"In the most colossal corporate failures that we've seen," observed one commission member, "the members of those boards had great credentials. These were experienced, mature, and diverse boards. But what seemed to be missing was the sense of accountability."

How does accountability translate into behavior?

SHARED LEADERSHIP AND RESPONSIBILITY. It's no longer good enough for directors to sit back and leave the heavy lifting to the handful of people filling formal leadership roles. "All board members have an equal responsibility to shareholders," one commission member asserted. "No one has more responsibility or less responsibility, even if you call that person a lead director." Another put it this way: "Each and every director needs to be a leader, demonstrating expertise, meaningful ownership, and independence."

SELF-MANAGEMENT. Each director has a responsibility for managing her own behavior. At the very minimum, that involves a duty to speak up. But it's more than that; there's a responsibility to attend meetings regularly and on time, to come fully prepared, to ask probing questions, to state a point of view even when it might not be what others want to hear, to resist dominating conversations, to act with civility, and to pursue opportunities for further education about the company and the role of directors.

PEER MANAGEMENT. It's equally important for directors to take responsibility for shaping the behavior of their peers. If other directors are abusive, overbearing, inconsiderate, or in some way fail to perform their duties with diligence or integrity, then it's the responsibility of each director to raise the issue and find an appropriate way to intervene. As we've seen time and time again, it takes only the dysfunctional behavior of a single director to undermine the entire board's ability to do good work.

Value #4: Action Orientation

A board that wants to progress from ceremony and ritual to real work must create an action-oriented culture. Effective boards show little tolerance for meandering discussions sporadically punctuated by irrelevant questions. Sometimes, an airing of different views is all that's required. But at the end of the day, the board's job is to make decisions or to ensure that others are making decisions, and wisely.

We are indebted here to the work of Kathleen M. Eisenhardt of Stanford University, whose research into the decision-making processes of senior management teams offers some relevant lessons for boards.[5] Given the board's unique characteristics, not all of Eisenhardt's conclusions are directly applicable in this context. Nevertheless, there are some interesting parallels and common themes that coincide with our own experience in how boards move from deliberation to resolution.

RULES FOR RESOLVING CONFLICT. Because their meetings are infrequent and their agendas packed to overflowing, no board has the luxury of allowing discussions to drag on interminably. One particularly effective way to move from discussion to action is a two-step process that Eisenhardt calls "consensus with qualification." The initial goal is to arrive at a decision by consensus. Failing that, there should be a clear "next step." It might be to decide the issue by a simple majority vote. Or it might mean delegating the final decision to a specific individual: the CEO, or the lead director, or the chairman of whichever committee has primary jurisdiction over the matter. Whatever process is used, the important point is to have clear guidelines that prevent the board from becoming deadlocked.

DEVELOPMENT OF COLLECTIVE INTUITION. Eisenhardt and her colleagues found that effective teams can move quickly to important decisions because their members enjoy constant and intense exposure to the same information, which allows them to build what she terms *collective intuition.* Boards lack the kind of frequent and intense interaction enjoyed (or at least experienced) by other teams; nevertheless, through their diligence and active participation they can develop their own form of collective intuition about the organization's leadership, its operational strengths and weaknesses, and its strategic challenges and opportunities.

FOCUS ON PRIORITIES. One of the most frequent complaints we hear from directors is that far too much of their precious meeting time is taken up with housekeeping matters, canned presentations, and operational trivia, leaving little time for more important matters. "Part of the job of board members," one commission member suggested, "is to focus on the relevant issues and be sure that they don't spend an undue amount of time on irrelevant issues." From a cultural perspective, that requires board members to assume a much more active role in influencing their own agenda, a responsibility that traditional boards were content to leave in management's tight grip.

Value #5: Mutual Trust and Respect

One commission member provided a concise explanation of this value: "There is a chemistry in the boardroom that makes effective boards work particularly well. By good chemistry, I don't mean that it's got the atmosphere of a club; I mean an atmosphere of mutual respect between board members." In other words, it's about a sense of collegiality based on professional respect and mutual trust, rather than on social camaraderie.

In more concrete terms, this translates into:

CONFIDENTIALITY INSIDE THE ROOM, SOLIDARITY OUTSIDE. This is all about trust. As a commission member said, genuine collegiality in the boardroom requires that "you can speak freely and express your views in the meeting without worrying that you're going to read about it in the newspaper the next day." At the same time, directors have to be confident that their colleagues are committed to working through their problems with one another in the room, rather than with various stakeholders and audiences outside the board.

RESPECT FOR EXPERTISE AND DIVERSE OPINIONS. Increasingly, boards are making the effort to recruit directors who bring diverse backgrounds and specialized expertise. Bad boards use them for window dressing; good boards respect what those new voices say and pay attention to them.

ACTIVE AND RESPECTFUL LISTENING. As described in other chapters, boardrooms are rife with anecdotes about directors who sit in meetings reading reports unrelated to the board's business, doing crossword puzzles, taking calls on their cell phones, or tapping out e-mails on their PDAs. It's bad enough that they aren't participating in the board's discussions—they aren't even listening. Less egregious, but more common, is the tendency of some directors to simply stop paying attention when the speaker is a director whom they believe brings little to the discussion or is taking a contrary point of view. It seems rudimentary, but it's worth saying anyway: on effective boards, when a director talks, everybody listens.

Each of the fifteen characteristics we've just described seems almost painfully obvious. But in the aggregate, they describe a culture far different from the one most boards nurtured throughout much of the twentieth century. To a far greater extent than the Sarbanes-Oxley disclosure rules or the NYSE listing requirements, they are creating a virtual revolution in the way boards operate.

SHAPING AND CHANGING THE BOARD'S CULTURE

For boards that believe the new culture we've just described embodies the values and behavior essential to doing the kind of work they think is important, there are two basic questions: How do leaders build and shape a culture over time? And do they create a significant shift in the board's existing culture? As you begin thinking about a change in culture, there are three principles to keep in mind.

First, it takes time. The traditional board culture evolved over a period of decades; it can't be reversed overnight. A fundamental change in culture is likely to take two or three years rather than two or three months.

Second, as one commission member explained, "There is no single element but the plethora of measures that makes a difference." As discussed in previous chapters (and in others still to come), these involve an explicit definition of what work the board intends to be involved in, the board's composition, the quality and timeliness of information available to the board, the design of its agenda and decisions about how it will spend its time working together, the formal leadership structure and roles, and the processes it employs to do critical work in areas such as succession planning, CEO evaluation, and strategy development. The actions the board takes in each of those areas shape culture in important ways.

Finally, we believe the single most important factor in shaping the board's culture is its leadership. As commission members described the cultural attributes they'd like to see on their own boards, their comments invariably began with, "The leader must. . . ." or "Effective leaders always. . . ." To an enormous extent, the board's culture will be shaped by the tone leaders set and the behavior they model.

How Leaders Shape the Board's Culture

Simply put, the board's leaders shape the culture through their actions and behavior, both in and out of the boardroom. They set the tone, manage the interaction, and both clarify and reinforce the norms by rewarding behavior that's appropriate and sanctioning behavior that isn't.

In the traditional culture, the powerful CEO/chairman—a Jack Welch or Hank Greenberg or Michael Eisner—was the preeminent "culture cop." As time goes by, and the balance of power shifts from CEOs to boards, nonexecutive chairmen and lead directors are taking on a more influential role as shapers of the board's culture.

More specifically, board leaders shape the norms that are critical to the new culture we've been discussing by using effective facilitation skills to run meetings that are open, interactive, and engaging. To do that, they:

- *Stimulate discussion by encouraging participation and soliciting different points of view.* The leader actively draws directors—even the quietest ones—into the discussion, bringing out the full range of perspectives before a decision is made. The tougher the issue, the greater the need for this approach.

- *Set a tone that eliminates the ever-present fear of "asking a dumb question."* Leaders encourage directors to probe and ask for clarification.

- *Encourage directors to be persistent and ask their second and third questions if the first answer wasn't adequate.* It requires patience and skillful management of the board's time to allow all the relevant facts to come out before cutting off discussion or pushing for a vote in the interests of efficiency.

- *Encourage dissent and avoid false consensus while maintaining an atmosphere of constructive contention.* That requires knowing both when to keep probing for unspoken concerns and when to intervene to keep the discussion from veering into unproductive discussions.

- *Build real consensus.* Leaders identify and then build on widely shared points of view, rather than trying to ram through a decision that lacks genuine support. Consensus doesn't require unanimous agreement; it means that everyone can live with the decisions without harboring serious reservations.

Creating a Significant Shift in Culture

Cultures develop over time; rather than being designed, they evolve. Throughout this chapter, we've been talking about behavioral norms, and it's important to remember that the most effective, long-standing norms aren't the result of formal decrees. Instead, they represent an implicit collective understanding of what behavior is acceptable and what is not, and of what rewards or punishments are associated with each and enforced or supported by the group. These norms are passed along from one generation to the next and internalized by each new member who joins the group. Over time, cultures build up their own inertia.

Having said that, it's also clear that each board experiences certain points when the culture becomes more malleable and open to change. These might include situations in which:

- A new CEO creates significant turnover involving a majority of board members, as when Ed Breen succeeded Dennis Kozlowski in the wake of the Tyco scandal.

- A company undergoes a major crisis, such as Marsh & McLennan when the board took the lead in restructuring itself and assumed a much more activist role.

- A dominant CEO retires, such as when GE's Jack Welch was succeeded by new CEO Jeffrey Immelt, who has a markedly different view about the relative roles of the CEO and the board.

- All of the above—the kind of situation Anne Mulcahy faced when she took the reins at Xerox during a major crisis that followed the departures first of Richard Thoman and then of Paul Allaire.

Those situations, fraught with challenge, also create the opportunity for dramatic and relatively quick discontinuous change in the board's culture. Experience suggests that boards can take several steps to help maximize this kind of opportunity.

The first step is to assess the existing culture. This requires collecting data and following up with discussion to determine how people describe the culture, how they assess its effectiveness, and what problems they'd like to see addressed.

The next step is to identify the culture that's needed based on the board's definition of its work and the areas where it believes it can contribute value to the organization. The entire board needs to be involved in identifying the key gaps between the culture it has and the culture it wants.

Third, based on that *gap analysis*, the board agrees on specific changes that must be made in its composition, structure, information management, and the roles and behavior of its leaders. A sudden shift in the board's culture provides a unique opportunity for board members to reflect and agree on what kind of behavior is expected of each director. The new operating principles—the rules of the road, if you will—should be put on the table for discussion, thoroughly thrashed out by the entire board, and then codified in an explicit form that leaves no doubt as to what directors expect of each other, what kind of behavior they expect from their leaders, and what their leaders expect of them.

The fourth step is to begin implementing all the changes the board has agreed upon, instituting new work processes, initiating steps toward changing the composition, and most importantly, adhering to the new behavioral norms. As we pointed out earlier, this is where the behavior of leaders becomes so crucial; the new norms are next to meaningless unless leaders both model and enforce them.

Finally, it's essential for the board to monitor how successful it has been in making the changes and how successful the changes have been in improving the quality of its work. Initially, the board can schedule time at the conclusion of each regular meeting to step back and discuss how the change is progressing. Periodically, there ought to be more explicit assessments, such as short surveys or evaluations. Finally, culture should become a regular subject for review in the board's annual self-assessment. As we'll discuss in Chapter Eleven, boards can easily fulfill the NYSE listing requirements for annual assessment without ever discussing the health or functionality of their culture and climate. That may be legally sufficient, but it's just not good enough; culture should be a primary topic of discussion during the board's annual review of how well its members think it's operating.

Part of that formal assessment should involve peer review, an area where the majority of boards in the United States, the United Kingdom, and Canada still fear to tread. If a new culture is to survive—for new norms to take hold—there has to be a clear understanding that the group will impose sanctions on those who consciously ignore or violate the accepted rules of the road. This requires some mechanism that allows the group to express its concern to individuals who, either knowingly or not, are violating the norms and can then choose either to conform to the norms or face the consequences.

Changing the Board's Culture: Best Western International

To restate the point: a major change in any board's culture takes time and involves a wide range of actions and decisions. To illustrate, let's consider the case of Best Western International.

Best Western, the world's largest hotel chain, is also one of the most unusual. It's actually a privately held membership association, not a publicly traded company. All seven board members are association members, elected to three-year terms by the other owners and operators of the more than forty-four hundred Best Western hotels around the world.

Although some aspects of Best Western's governance system are unquestionably unique, its board faces many of the challenges you'd find at any large public corporation, including changing a board's culture.

Nayan Patel, whose family owns nine hotels, including six Best Westerns, in the Washington, D.C., area, was elected to his first term on the Best Western board in 2000. A successful young businessman who was just completing his final semester at Georgetown University Law School, he quickly discovered a culture that was deeply flawed.

"When I joined, we were absolutely a rubber-stamp board," Patel recalled years later. "The CEO back then was this incredibly charismatic guy—on a level with Bill Clinton—and he was used to the board giving him whatever he wanted."

He cited an example: "At one point, the CEO had proposed that every hotel should give every customer the choice of a hard, medium, or soft pillow in every room. Operationally, the idea was a disaster; not only would it be incredibly expensive, but in our hotels, there's just no place to store all those pillows. But he got the board to rubber-stamp it. Fortunately, when it went before the general membership for a vote, it failed miserably.

"When we voted on the board, I thought it was a bad idea, but I voted for it anyway. Why? Because I had gone against him on so many other issues that I didn't want to be branded a naysayer. From a political standpoint, I could see other members saying, 'We have this new guy on the board and he's opposing everything the CEO wants to do.' That would have made me totally ineffective. What you really want to do on a board is persuade others. When you get branded as an outsider, you lose your effectiveness."

And persuading others was hard enough on that board, Patel said. The constant clash of "big egos and strong personalities" made collaboration and compromise among board members almost impossible. "I saw a near meltdown of the decision-making process," he recalled.

In 2003, the CEO finally pushed the board too far, failing to win their approval for a plan to spin off the non-U.S. hotels as a separate, public company. He resigned, and the board gathered in Lisbon for what Patel described as "a watershed meeting": "The CEO had left. We had a 4–3 split on the board on nearly every important issue. We were literally yelling at each other. But in the end, a lot of major work came out of that meeting."

One outcome was the board's first conflict of interest–code of conduct policy, intended in part to define the appropriate relationship between board members and the CEO. "We had people on the board who liked to think of themselves as the CEO's best friend," Patel explained. "At a certain point we had to say, 'It's not appropriate to go hiking with the CEO every time you're in Phoenix [the site of BWI's headquarters] for a board meeting. It's not professional to go work out with him after every meeting. There's a professional line between the board and the CEO that shouldn't be crossed.'"

Over the next two years, including Patel's yearlong term as chairman in 2004, the board adopted a variety of policies and practices designed to make them more independent, professional, and effective:

- On a close vote, it created the position of corporate secretary to make sure the members had all the materials they needed before each meeting. "That vastly improved our decision-making process," Patel said.

- For the first time, the board retained the services of outside experts—including our colleague, David Nygren—to help them address their problems. "I can't overstate the importance of third parties," Patel said. "When you're dealing with someone from the outside with strong credentials and credibility, it forces you to think about things you perhaps didn't want to confront."

- It adopted a process for members to lodge complaints with the governance committee regarding colleagues who would habitually arrive late for meetings, leave their cell phones on throughout sessions, or engage in "some other behavior that was inappropriate or getting in the way."

- It discouraged persistent side conversations among board members by asking everyone at the beginning of each meeting if there were matters of concern that should be brought before the entire board. "It worked," Patel said. "It helped to reduce the underground tide of unexpressed feelings."

- To eliminate the confusing mixed signals management was receiving from the board, it agreed that the chairman and vice chairman, together, would brief the CEO on the substance of any board meetings he didn't attend.

- At Patel's urging, management was instructed that every proposal it sent to the board had to be accompanied by a discussion of "both the pros and cons."

- The board made director education a major priority, sending each member to a minimum of two seminars every year.

- In 2004, Patel succeeded in providing the board with detailed information on strategic initiatives, such as major marketing efforts and an Internet strategy. "We used to base decisions on hunches, not data," he explained. "Having the right data tightened up the debate, and sometimes eliminated it."

- Perhaps most importantly, the board reached what Patel called "a major turning point" in 2004 with its first peer review. "It forced board members to look at themselves in the mirror, to reevaluate who they were and what they wanted their contributions to Best Western to be. I think that had a huge effect."

Each of those initiatives played a role in transforming the Best Western board. But Patel's experience mirrored our belief that the single most important factor is leadership. "The chairman needs to lead by example," Patel said. "As a leader, I tried to demonstrate the behavior I hoped for from the members. I tried to be fair, to communicate regularly, to maintain a balanced perspective, and to adhere to basic principles while staying open-minded about particular decisions."

SUMMARY

Perhaps the most important thought we can leave with leaders intent on changing a board's culture is this: you can't mandate a culture change. You can certainly shape it, but only through a pattern of consistent and self-reinforcing decisions, actions, and behavior. That means the process you employ for changing the culture has to reflect the new culture you want to create, not the old one you want to abandon. You can't create a culture of engagement by edict; the gaping disconnect between actions and intentions simply robs the process of all credibility right from the start. To the contrary, the entire board has to be fully engaged at each step in the process and encouraged by its leaders to step up, speak out, and sign on. After all, that's what the new culture is all about.

PART TWO

Critical Areas of Work

CHAPTER SEVEN

Engaging the Board
in Corporate Strategy

David A. Nadler

W̶hat role should the board play in developing corporate strategy? At one company we worked with, the board's deep division over that seemingly simple question made it almost impossible for the management of this multi-billion-dollar global enterprise to pursue any coherent strategy at all.

The conflict had its roots four years earlier in the merger of two well-known companies, a fast-growing high-tech firm and a typical "old economy" corporation. Apart from a few newcomers, the board had basically divided itself into two factions consisting of holdovers from the two predecessor boards. One group looked like a typical Fortune 500 board—current and retired CEOs, with a sprinkling of public sector luminaries. The other was a stereotypical dot-com board—the company's senior executives, major shareholders, and a few venture capitalists.

Pursuing the right strategy was crucial to making the merger work and justifying the widely criticized cost of the deal. But as we quickly learned, there was no agreement within the board on what that strategy should be. Every time management proposed some major transaction, it touched off a new round of debate over the strategic direction. The only thing both sides agreed on was that, somehow, the strategy problem had to be fixed.

For the traditional directors, the solution was obvious: strategy was management's responsibility, so let the CEO explain it, have the board review it, and then get on with business. As one director told us, "I have confidence in management and they know the business better than I do, so I just want to hear what the strategy is so we can judge specific actions in the context of that strategy."

The dot-com directors thought the solution was just as obvious— but the complete opposite. "We need to clear the time, roll up our sleeves, sit down as a board, and figure out what the strategy of the company should be," they told us. From this group's perspective, the board's role was to design the strategy and management's job was to execute it. After all, that's the way they had grown their phenomenally successful start-up; the board would gather with the CEO at his beach house and together they would build the strategy and run the company.

Admittedly, this was an extreme case; few boards find themselves so deeply divided along philosophical lines on such a vital issue. At the same time, it illustrates the confusion and frustration that so many boards continue to face as they try to determine precisely what role they should play, and how they should be appropriately engaged, in setting their company's fundamental direction.

THE BOARD'S ROLE IN STRATEGY: PUTTING THE PIECES TOGETHER

All of our research tells us that both boards and CEOs think the board has a critical role in the general area of strategy. Precisely what that role should be is an entirely different matter. On the continuum of board engagement, from passivity at one extreme to interference at the other, where should a high-performing board position itself? How does a traditional board transcend its legacy as a rubber stamp for management's initiatives without getting "down in the weeds" and micromanaging a process that rightfully should be driven by the CEO and her team? How can the CEO and the board work together to develop a process that draws on the intelligence, insights, and experience of its directors to create and sustain a strategy that's qualitatively superior to whatever management might have come up with on its own?

If you were hoping to find the answer somewhere amid all the governance reform measures, don't bother. You can't find a better illustration of the insufficiency of legal mandates when it comes to substantially improving the quality of corporate governance. Browse through the changes imposed by Sarbanes-Oxley, regulatory agencies, and the securities exchanges, and you'll find nothing about the board's role in strategy. A board that meets every single one of the new legal requirements may have done nothing to directly enhance its ability to help management do a better job of addressing its competitive threats and opportunities.

In fact, the board's role in strategy doesn't even seem to show up on the radar screen of some self-described governance watchdogs. Take the Corporate Library, a leading force in the corporate reform movement and major clearinghouse for literature related to governance. An examination of its Web site found scores of references to recent publications, archived research, and "spotlight topics"—none of which specifically addressed the board and corporate strategy.

At the other end of the good governance spectrum, those who argue that the key to better boards is "good chemistry"—a felicitous mix of dedicated people working well together—have identified only one ingredient in the recipe for effective strategy development. To be sure, it's important for the board to include a broad range of experience and competencies, and for its members to be engaged, informed, curious, and candid. But that's not enough. Strategy planning and development involves hard work by a large number of people over an extended period of time, and it takes a deliberate structure and process to combine the brightest minds and best intentions in a way that creates outstanding output.

Few companies have successfully put all the pieces together. That should be great cause for concern for all those CEOs and boards who rate strategy near the top of the list of the board's most important responsibilities.

"Forming and implementing company strategy is the most critical role of the board," said one member of the NACD Blue Ribbon Commission on Board Leadership. "The board needs to spend a lot of time and attention, both in meetings and between meetings, assessing, shaping, agreeing to, and monitoring the strategy. By doing this, the board is focusing on essentials." Another board member described it this way: "The corporate strategy must be fully understood by the board, and the board and management have to be totally aligned about corporate strategy, because this is the foundation for all the decisions in the boardroom."

Yet many directors are clearly dissatisfied with their own boards' performance in this area, according to the USC/Mercer Delta Corporate Board Surveys conducted in 2003 and 2004. Only about one in ten directors rate their own board as "very effective" in shaping long-term strategy or identifying threats and opportunities. More than one-third described their own board as less than "effective" in this area, and in 2004 "shaping long-term strategy" was rated last on a list of ten dimensions of board effectiveness. Directors gave their boards similarly low ratings for reviewing progress on strategic goals.

What's even more disturbing is that, despite all the attention and activity in the area of corporate reform, the board's effectiveness in the critical area of strategy has barely budged in recent years. An NACD study of CEOs revealed that the board's participation in "strategic planning ranked second in importance to their companies, yet only eleventh in their board's effectiveness." That's noteworthy for two reasons. First, CEOs' ratings were almost identical to those of directors, indicating a broad consensus on how inadequately boards are performing in this area. Second, the NACD study was done in 2000, before the wave of corporate scandals and the avalanche of governance reforms. Whatever improvements those changes might have produced in board structures, composition, and reporting requirements, they have clearly had no impact on the board's effectiveness in the critical area of strategy development and oversight.

And yet, for all those whose interest in governance goes beyond legal liability to competitive viability, the board's role in influencing and approving strategy lies at the heart of its mandate. The obvious question, then, is this: Why is such a critical activity performed so ineffectively at so many companies? There are several answers, but the most obvious is: because that's the way some CEOs want it. The fact remains that there are still CEOs who view board involvement as interference, as a usurpation of traditional management prerogatives. As one member of the Blue Ribbon Commission told us, "I see a hesitancy to put both strategic issues and people issues on the board agenda. Even if the CEO says, 'OK, I know you want to talk about this, we'll talk about it,' it's always next quarter, and then something else comes up. There is a reluctance to engage on these issues, and these are very important issues."

Without question, there's a dynamic tension that invariably surrounds the board's work in the area of strategy. CEOs and boards have to walk a delicate tightrope, figuring out how to involve the board in real, roll-up-your-sleeves, hands-on work that provides tangible value without preempting essential management functions.

However, there's an even more fundamental reason why boards are frustrated. The problem is that many companies lack a clear process—the education, planning, investment of time, definition of roles and responsibilities, and so on—that enables directors to participate meaningfully in strategy development. And a real process requires real work. Just sitting around the table once a year, enduring a two-hour Power-Point presentation followed by fifteen minutes of questions, is not a process, it's window dressing. It doesn't create any real value.

In contrast, there are distinct benefits for companies that systematically and effectively involve their boards in setting strategic direction. A properly constituted, fully engaged board can provide an experienced, independent perspective that draws on broader and deeper knowledge of the overall business environment than can be found solely within the CEO's team. A board engaged in strategy development becomes better educated about the company, more committed to its chosen direction, and more supportive of management when the strategy comes under fire. A board fully immersed in the strategy is better prepared to periodically review progress against strategic goals and ask the right questions while there's still time to make midcourse corrections. Finally, the collaboration that's developed throughout the strategy process can carry over into the board's other interactions with management. There's nothing like real work to create a real working relationship.

This chapter focuses on how CEOs and boards can work together to develop a constructive and effective collaborative strategy process. After defining some basic concepts, we will:

- Examine five key elements of value-added engagement of the board in strategy.
- Provide a framework for board-management strategic decision making.
- Identify requirements for an effective participative strategy process.

UNDERSTANDING STRATEGIC ACTIVITY

The term *corporate strategy* can create some contention and confusion. To avoid such problems, this is how we define four different types of activity under the general heading of strategy:

Strategic Thinking

The first step in strategy development involves the collection, analysis, and discussion of information about the firm's business environment, the nature of its competition, and a range of alternative business designs. In this context, we're using the term *business design* to include the customer value proposition, the scope of offerings, the mechanisms for capturing profit, and the sources of competitive differentiation.[1] In multibusiness firms, strategic thinking also involves fundamental questions about the configuration of the business portfolio.

Strategic Decision Making

Strategic thinking is about scenarios and alternatives; strategic decision making is about making choices and placing strategic bets. These include basic decisions about the business portfolio and the business design, which lay the groundwork for future decisions about allocating limited resources and capabilities.

Strategic Planning

Once the strategic decisions have been made, decision makers identify priorities, set objectives, and commit the resources needed to implement their decisions. This usually results in a plan and a set of budgets. The plan evolves over time, adapting to the changing environment, new information, and the apparent impact of the strategy on the organization and its competitive situation.

Strategic Execution

Once plans and budgets are in place, the company focuses on implementation, monitoring results, and appropriate corrective action. This phase of strategy development can involve further allocation of resources and specific strategic moves, such as acquisitions or divestitures.

These are the four basic phases of strategy development. The board's role can differ dramatically from one phase to the next (see Table 7.1).

Ideally, a board that is constructively engaged in strategy is:

- Actively participating in strategic thinking
- Substantively involved in major decisions affecting the portfolio or significant investments

Table 7.1. Corporate Strategy Tasks and Roles.

Task	Description of Task	Role of the Board	Role of Senior Management
Strategic thinking	Collecting, analyzing, and discussing information about the environment of the firm, the nature of competition, and broad business design alternatives	• Bring an outside perspective and accumulated wisdom. • Test the consistency of management's thinking. • Collaborate with management.	• Initiate the process of strategic thinking. • Set the agenda—pose the questions and issues. • Actively participate with the board in discussions.
Strategic decision making	Making the fundamental set of decisions about the business portfolio and business design	• Offer input for management's decision making. • Provide ultimate review and approval on major decisions.	• Make critical decisions. • Develop proposals to the board for critical directional decisions and major resource allocation.
Strategic planning	Translating the critical strategic decisions into a set of priorities, objectives, and resource allocation actions to execute the strategy	• Review core strategic plans presented by management. • Ensure understanding of the plans and their potential risks and consequences. • Approve plans.	• Develop plans. • Review plans to ensure consistency with corporate objective and strategy. • Present plans to the board for review.
Strategic execution	Undertaking various initiatives and actions consistent with the strategic plan, including adjustments to account for environmental changes and different outcomes	• Review the process and progress of implementation of key initiatives vis à vis established milestones and objectives.	• Ensure resources and leadership for execution are in place. • Monitor progress of execution. • Make changes in either the execution or the plan, depending on outcomes.

- Providing input to the strategy implementation process, including measures and milestones necessary for strategic decisions to be turned into action within the desired time frame
- Kept apprised of strategic execution as part of its normal review of company performance

ENGAGING THE BOARD IN STRATEGY

No matter how clearly the board's role in the strategy process is distinguished from management's, many CEOs continue to harbor concerns about the board's involvement. One problem is the persistence of an all-or-nothing view of the board's role. At one extreme is cursory review, the traditional practice in which boards review the completed strategy after the management team has finished putting it together and then almost always approve it. The board has few options—either accept or reject—and little basis on which to evaluate or alter the strategy. The other extreme is for the board to lead strategy development, which most CEOs view as an infringement upon their, and management's, legitimate responsibility.

We believe there's another alternative, one we call *value-added engagement.* In this approach, the board participates in the strategic thinking and decision-making processes, adding value without overreaching. More specifically, the CEO and management lead and develop the strategic plan with directors' input, and directors have the ultimate responsibility for approving the strategy and the metrics that will be used to assess its progress. We've seen this approach used successfully, with some significant benefits.

At one company, for example, the CEO and executive team decided to engage the board in making a critical choice about the company's business portfolio and future strategic direction. There had been concern for some time that the company's widely diversified portfolio was a turnoff to potential investors. The ultimate decision was whether to divest several business units and become a pure play in the communications equipment sector, or alternatively, to concentrate resources and "turbo-charge" a small portfolio of complementary businesses.

This was a difficult choice to make in the late 1990s: the communications industry was booming and seemed certain to enjoy continued record-breaking growth. But in their work together, management and the board recognized the perils of placing all their bets on one horse. They resisted the allure of a seemingly sure thing and chose instead to pursue a balanced strategy of diversified but related businesses. As it turned out, the communications sector had cratered by early 2001, and the strategic decision to balance the portfolio was almost certainly responsible for saving the company.

Although the benefits of board participation aren't always so dramatic, the board's engagement in the strategy process can yield substantial dividends. It helps to:

- *Create deeper understanding.* As the board participates in strategic thinking, directors learn about the company and its strategic environment. Their expanded knowledge better prepares them to contribute to future strategic discussions and decisions.

- *Build ownership.* By participating in the process, the strategy becomes "our" strategy as opposed to "their" strategy. With increased ownership comes increased commitment to help the strategy succeed and to defend it when under attack.

- *Improve the quality of decisions.* Directors bring new perspectives, different points of view, and wisdom that can lead to better strategic decisions.

- *Define a more collaborative relationship between the board and management.* The board and management's collaboration on a mutual strategy enhances their ability to work as a team on other initiatives.

- *Increase board satisfaction.* Board members feel that their time, knowledge, and experience have been used constructively.

- *Prompt board members to become external company advocates.* When directors are an integral part of strategy development, they are more likely to champion and appropriately defend the company's strategy to external audiences, including analysts, customers, suppliers, and media.

To be sure, there's another side to the argument; broader board participation in strategy has its costs as well. First, board members need a comprehensive understanding of the company, and that takes time and commitment. The Conference Board explains that "in approving strategies, boards need to understand, among other things, the corporation's capital allocation, debt levels, risks and vulnerabilities, compensation strategy, and growth opportunities. Importantly, they must engage management on the central issues facing the company and have a firm grasp on the trade-offs that lie at the heart of a corporate enterprise."[2]

From management's perspective, there's also the likelihood that expanded board participation in strategy will lead to less management control. The CEO can no longer assume—in fact, should no longer expect—that the board will silently nod its assent to whatever strategic plan is laid before it. Real participation means influence, and influence means the ability to change outcomes. Nevertheless, our experience is that the benefits far outweigh the time, effort, and diminution of management control that come with a robust and collaborative process.

KEY ELEMENTS OF A VALUE-ADDED ENGAGEMENT PROCESS

Based on our work with a variety of boards, we see five elements that are critical to successfully engaging the board in strategy development.

Think of Strategy Development as a Process, Not an Event

Effective board-level strategy work usually occurs over a period of months, and ideally, continues on a regular basis. In recent years, many boards realized that their infrequent and generally jam-packed regular meetings weren't conducive to the kind of in-depth discussion necessary for a genuine understanding of the strategy and all its ramifications. The annual strategy off-site came into vogue, and it was certainly a step in the right direction. But an annual discussion, no matter how fruitful, just isn't enough. Following the initial discussion at the off-site, the board needs significant time to digest information, perform analysis, and develop insights. The strategy becomes the focus of both regular board meetings and off-sites for the ensuing six to nine months.

Design Parallel But Lagged Processes

The CEO's executive team, not just the board, should be a part of the strategy development process. That involves parallel processes, with the executive team going through the same steps and asking the same questions as the board but in more depth and detail. Usually, the activity at the board level lags a bit behind the executive team's work; that allows the CEO and executive team to pose the most pertinent questions to the board, rather than just throwing the strategy out on the table for rambling discussion and random questions. At the same time, the team shouldn't get so far out ahead of the board that it becomes deeply committed to specific positions and resists the board's input or influence. Figure 7.1 illustrates the parallel but lagged work flow process developed for one client's staff, executive team, and board.

Inform and Educate the Board

There's a limit to the value directors can provide unless they've had access to essential information. That goes beyond the mountains of financials that management is now required to regularly provide to the board. Directors tell us they want more information, particularly in the context of strategy work, on the marketplace, competitors, economic trends, and outsiders' perspectives on the company (for example, analysts' reports and relevant articles from trade publications).

Many directors also need a much deeper understanding of the business, which can be gained through briefings, training sessions, site visits, product/offering demonstrations, and so on. One board we worked with, for example, participated in a daylong working seminar on emerging technologies at one of their company's research and development centers. Others have visited manufacturing, operational, or retail sites. This immersion in a company's day-to-day operations is critical to the board's understanding of the company, its lines of business, and its strategic options.

Collect and Analyze Input from Directors

True engagement implies meaningful input. The process has to guarantee that the directors' perspectives, questions, and recommendations are accurately gathered and seriously considered. The practical problem is how to do that. Regularly scheduled board meetings probably aren't the best venue; there's usually too much work to get done in a short amount of time.

One approach we've used successfully is to interview directors individually (and in some cases, supplement those interviews with surveys) at their own offices, using a set of questions and issues related

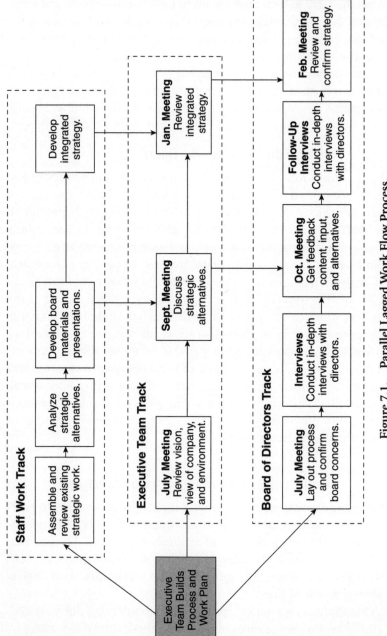

Figure 7.1. Parallel Lagged Work Flow Process.

to the current phase of the board's strategy work. Feedback is analyzed and presented to the board at its next work session as a framework that quickly guides the discussion toward the most vital issues. We've also found that in private, one-on-one conversations, directors are more likely to share concerns, observations, and questions they might be reticent to raise with the entire group. The interview-feedback cycle helps make the in-room board time more productive and ensures that the right issues are on the table.

Generate Strategic Alternatives

Real involvement comes from informed choice and the opportunity to develop strong personal commitment to the group's collective decisions. Informed choice is difficult when the only alternatives are to vote yes or no. Therefore, executive teams should develop and present to their boards a set of viable strategic alternatives involving distinctly different courses of action.

The management of the high-technology company we described earlier eventually presented its board with several variations on two themes: pure play or balanced portfolio. Neither limiting directors to a single yes-no response, nor overwhelming them with infinite possibilities, the executive team offered the board clearly differentiated business design alternatives, allowing them to compare the advantages and disadvantages of each. Directors had a real choice and were engaged with the process; they helped identify and discuss the pitfalls and opportunities they saw with each strategic alternative and worked with management to make the best choice.

A FRAMEWORK FOR STRATEGIC THINKING AND DECISION MAKING

A framework can help organize the discussions and decisions that the board will undertake and provides a useful way to implement the key elements we just discussed. Both the executive team and the board can use this framework to sequence their activities, recognizing that each situation will have its own specific requirements. (See Figure 7.2.)

This road map, which we call the Strategic Choice Process, involves six key steps:

• Agreeing on the company vision
• Viewing the opportunity space

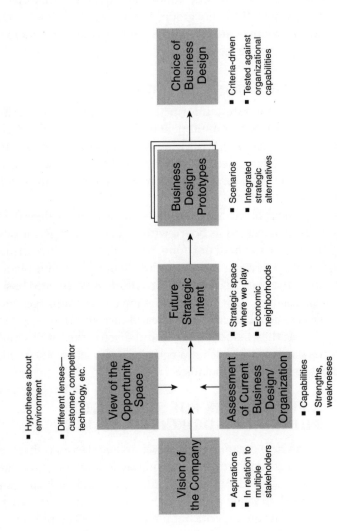

Figure 7.2. The Strategic Choice Process.

- Assessing the company's business design and internal capabilities
- Determining the company's future strategic intent
- Developing a set of business design prototypes
- Choosing the business design alternative that is deemed best

Company Vision

The work typically begins with a restatement (or confirmation) of the company vision—a description of its aspirations in relation to multiple stakeholders, including investors, customers, suppliers, employees, legislators, and communities. The vision statement should answer this question: What are we striving to become in terms of our role in the larger environment where we function?

We're well aware of the considerable cynicism regarding vision statements these days; the early infatuation with these statements sometimes resulted in shameless sloganeering and empty blather. Nevertheless, when done well, they're important and useful; indeed, the very process of sitting people down to hammer out and commit to specific principles is inherently worthwhile. That's why it's so important to revisit vision statements periodically, particularly as key players come and go, to make sure the vision is still relevant or, if not, to refine it to capture the company's commitment to a specified direction.

Some companies like to use vision statements cooked up in the marketing or public relations department and intended for a variety of external purposes. To be clear, we're talking here about vision statements that are developed specifically as an internal guide to strategy development. In this context, a vision statement is aspirational and gives a picture of what the company hopes to accomplish in the context of stakeholders but in very tangible and measurable terms. Vision statements that have "bite" talk about measures of growth, relative positions in markets or industries, or returns to shareholders. They provide a benchmark for measurement and comparison of the various strategic alternatives.

Opportunity Space

The second step in the Strategic Choice Process is to consider the potential opportunity space in which the company might compete. The starting point is a description of the environments in which the company operates, leading to some hypotheses about future conditions. In the pure-play versus balanced-portfolio case mentioned earlier, the ability of management and the board to forecast the risks of a singular focus on communications was much more than a stroke of good luck. It came from a thorough understanding of the company's business environments and a disciplined, collaborative approach to developing well-grounded hypotheses about how those environments were likely to change. Environmental analysis can be done from different perspectives, examining the environment through specific lenses such as emerging markets, new technologies, potential customers, or possible competitors.

Business Design and Internal Capabilities

The third step is to look inward—to assess the company itself, including its current business design and organization. The objective during this phase is to understand the company's current and potential capabilities in the context of the opportunity space. This assessment focuses on the relative strengths and weaknesses of the firm, including its human capital, technologies, finances, work processes, and so on. Different tools and models can be used to carry out this assessment.[3]

Future Strategic Intent

The fourth step is to bring together the vision, the view of the opportunity space, and the assessment of the current business and organization to identify a future strategic intent. The group works to identify a strategic space where the company's capabilities and the hypothesized environment come together in areas where the potential for profit is present—what could be called attractive *economic neighborhoods.* In other words, it involves determining the most attractive opportunities for the company to pursue the development of business, given its vision and its capabilities. At this point, the executive team and board can begin to identify the key criteria for evaluating a potential business design that would reflect that strategic intent. These key criteria will be used later on to make critical choices.

Business Design Prototypes

Having identified a strategic intent, the next step is to develop prototypes for each business design. Again, for this work to have real value, it's essential to develop and present a number of distinct, viable options to stretch the group's thinking and to provide the opportunity for detailed comparison and informed choice.

Best Design Choice

Ultimately, the process culminates in a single choice: the strategic alternative that is the most attractive of the feasible options. At this point, the value of engaging the board early in the process becomes abundantly clear, because they come to the table with a thorough understanding of the organizational strengths and weaknesses that will shape the company's capacity to execute each alternative. That understanding is absolutely critical. In this final stage, it's essential for reason to triumph over hope; sometimes, the prudent choice is to begin implementing a less exciting Strategy B as the company acquires the talent, technology, or capital that would be required to successfully implement the more attractive Strategy A.

The process we've just described generally takes place over a period of many months, with numerous meetings, work sessions, and rounds of data collection and feedback. From the standpoint of board-building, the Strategic Choice Process provides a concrete and constructive way to engage the board in worthwhile work. More importantly, this is where the diverse experience and expertise represented by the board can add real value. Even the best management teams can suffer from strategic tunnel vision because of their common experience in the same company or industry. Ideally, board members come at the task with a broader view and a fresh perspective that allows them to question the obvious and draw on personal insights developed over time in a wide variety of settings.

It's also important to keep in mind that the board's engagement doesn't end with the selection of a strategy and the approval of an implementation plan. The board has an important role to play in frequently revisiting the strategy, monitoring progress toward strategic goals, and reviewing the need for refinement or corrections in the strategy as the implementation unfolds.

"Boards these days—the enlightened ones—are looking at strategy not as an annual retreat," said one commission member. "They have a strategy discussion at every board meeting, and oftentimes it's right up there in front of the agenda, recognizing that strategy is not a static, built-in, concrete plan. It's one that's constantly undergoing revision, modification, and sometimes radical departures."

Whatever the cadence of meetings, their value ultimately depends on the quality of the discussion. Boards that are seriously engaged in the strategy process have little patience for what historically went on in most boardrooms—carefully rehearsed, formal presentations by management followed by perfunctory questions and uninformed discussion. One CEO on the commission described how his company has improved on that process for the format of its annual strategy retreats, which bring together his board and management team: "We provide written information in advance that talks about where we're going, what our time lines are for getting there, what's working and what's not working. Then we focus on dialogue at the session itself—not presentations with slide after slide. We have a rule that if you have twenty slides, pick three or four and put in the rest as an appendix. So what we create in the session itself is robust dialogue based on a solid foundation of information."

REQUIREMENTS FOR EFFECTIVE BOARD ENGAGEMENT IN STRATEGY

Although the elements of value-added engagement and the framework for strategic thinking and decision making can help engage the board effectively, not every board is prepared to participate. In our experience, there is a set of prerequisites to engaging a board in a value-added manner.

Balanced But Diverse Board Composition

The quality of the board's contributions will depend on the quality of its members, and several characteristics are particularly important. First, this is a situation where real independence—both financial and psychological—can pay genuine dividends. Truly independent directors can pose troubling questions or challenge sacred cows in ways that would be difficult, if not career limiting, for members of the CEO's team. But independence by itself is not enough. The other major requirement is knowledge. At least some directors need sufficient knowledge about the technologies, markets, competitors, or processes of the company to make informed contributions to strategy development. That requirement is particularly important for directors in leadership roles, as some members of the NACD Blue Ribbon Commission pointed out. As one explained, "A leader needs to understand what it would truly take for the company to move from one strategic direction to another strategic direction, to embrace a different direction."

Corporations are waking up to the benefits of a good board mix and diversifying by recruiting specific director talent, structuring new director compensation packages (to ensure independence), and increasing director pay for growing (and increasingly specific) board responsibilities.[4] Of course, board members should also possess a general wisdom, or the perspective and judgment that a director can bring as the result of her accumulated business experience. Finally, it helps to have some directors who have a long-term view of the business and a deep understanding of the company history, and others who bring fresh insight and new perspectives.

An Engaged Executive Team

Strategic thinking and decision making must involve the CEO's executive team. They need to be on a parallel track so that those responsible for leading and managing the implementation of the strategy will build understanding, ownership, and personal commitment. Ideally, the executive team's engagement should connect with the engagement of the board. Participating with the team provides the board with a tremendous opportunity to hear the leadership's multiple perspectives and also to gain insight into their capabilities as a management team.

The CEO as a Process Leader

For this approach to succeed, the CEO needs to be experienced and receptive to different ideas. Although the CEO can demonstrate this openness by serving as the leader of the strategic process with the board and by playing an active role in soliciting the directors' input, some CEOs use an outside facilitator to help guide the group through the process. This frees them to think about content and substance, without undermining the needed role of impartial and fair facilitator.

An Open and Constructive Board Culture

It's important, but less tangible, for the board to have a culture that supports constructive contention and different points of view. A board that is characterized by conformity, excessive politeness, and aversion to conflict will have a difficult time engaging in true strategic thinking and strategic decision making. On the other hand, a CEO who seeks to move the board culture toward more openness and constructive contention can use the strategy process as a catalyst to help make that happen.

Board Accountability

The board must feel that it has something at stake in the development and successful implementation of strategy. The increasing focus on board accountability and visibility helps. Other actions that can increase accountability include shaping the way the board is rewarded, using board and director assessment to motivate individuals to participate actively and constructively, and increasing the visibility of the board as spokespeople for the strategic direction.

SUMMARY

The Strategic Choice Process actively involves the board, but it doesn't mean the CEO should simply relinquish management's role in the process. To the contrary, the CEO and his executive team should lead the process, while engaging the board at every step. The important message we've tried to convey is that this can work—and work well—without the CEO giving up management's prerogative to manage and run the company. In the Strategic Choice Process and steps we outlined for value-added board engagement, the CEO and the executive team lead the way.

There are specific and tangible benefits to this approach. First, the process yields better strategic decisions, leading to the creation of a more thoughtful strategy than would have been developed otherwise. Second, the satisfaction of the directors increases significantly. They feel they have made a contribution, they feel their capabilities have been employed, they feel they have been listened to, and ultimately, they feel they've been able to add value. Third, the process results in a profound understanding of the company, and this degree of understanding affects how the board will work in the future. Specific proposals for investments, capital, acquisitions, and so on, are now considered in the context of a strategy that everyone around the table owns, rather than as isolated, one-off transactions. This typically results in more thoughtful discussion of and stronger support for proposals that are consistent with the strategic direction. Finally, the process results in strong ownership and support, and these are particularly useful when the company hits a difficult period or a crisis. The board that has been engaged is much more likely to support management and urge them to "stay the course" rather than cut and run.

CHAPTER EIGHT

CEO Performance Evaluation

J. Carlos Rivero
Mark B. Nadler

David Pottruck, the CEO of Charles Schwab Corp., showed up at the company's board meeting on July 19, 2004, ready to deliver a presentation on corporate strategy. Almost as soon as the meeting started, he was asked to leave the room so the board could meet in executive session. An hour and a half went by before Pottruck was summoned back to the boardroom and given the bad news. Just fourteen months into his tenure as the sole CEO (after sharing the job for five years with founder Charles Schwab), Pottruck was being asked to resign.

The next day, Pottruck told the *Wall Street Journal* he had been "totally surprised" by the board's action. "I was really focused on running and growing the company," he told a reporter, "and I didn't realize how unhappy the board was."[1]

The board might have been justified in its decision, which reportedly stemmed from concern over declining financial results and dissatisfaction that Pottruck had neglected to tell the board of his plans to sell off a recent acquisition. But setting aside the substance of the decision, something was seriously amiss in a process that resulted in a CEO being caught so completely off guard by the level of disaffection on his own board that he apparently hadn't a clue that his job was in jeopardy. That kind of shock to the system does a disservice not only to a CEO—particularly one like Pottruck, who had been hailed as a superstar earlier in his tenure—but to the organization and its stakeholders as well.

In recent years, formal appraisals of the CEO's performance have become a requirement for publicly traded U.S. companies. But this is another situation in which mere compliance with minimal standards is no guarantee of better, or even good, governance. In the Schwab case, the appraisal process clearly lacked essential features that should have provided Pottruck with early warnings of his board's concerns and a chance to address them long before they reached crisis proportions. And periodic assessment and continuing communication are only two elements of the kind of rigorous CEO appraisal process that requires the board to do much more than just grade the CEO at the end of each year on a narrow list of financial goals.

In our interviews with the NACD Blue Ribbon Commission on Board Leadership, many of the commission members cited CEO evaluation as "the most critical element of board activity." Yet as recently as 2004, only 40 percent of the directors who responded to the USC/Mercer Delta Corporate Board Survey rated their own board's CEO evaluation process as "very effective." That was a significant improvement over the previous year's 26 percent, but a clear indication that most boards could still be doing much better.

As one commission member stated, "Assessing the CEO is one of the most critical functions, but it is also among the most difficult." Difficult, yes—but doable. In this chapter, we'll explore the essential steps each board should take as it designs its own CEO evaluation process:

- Creating a shared understanding of the purpose of CEO appraisal
- Designing a sequenced process for identifying goals, monitoring progress, and assessing year-end performance, then agreeing on who should play which roles
- Identifying the appropriate areas on which to rate the CEO's performance
- Deciding the best way to gather data on the difficult-to-measure nonfinancial performance dimensions
- Communicating effectively with the CEO on performance-related issues

Designing and implementing a full-scale appraisal process requires hard work and tough decisions. As one director on the commission told us, "The problem with a really good evaluation is that it takes an enormous amount of time and knowledge, and it's not easily based on quantifiable things." Beyond that, there's a very human dimension to the process, a potential clash of egos and interests that goes to the very heart of the changing relationship and the shifting balance of power between CEOs and boards.

Indeed, CEO appraisal is the starkest example of the performance appraisal paradox we find in so many organizations: the more senior the executive, and the greater his impact on the organization's performance, the less rigorous the evaluation process. In many companies, front-line supervisors are subjected to yearly painstaking reviews in which they're systematically graded on a detailed set of performance goals. As you go up the ladder, the reviews become more conversational, informal, and sometimes, downright perfunctory. Before the recent requirements were put in place, countless CEOs had gone for years without a formal performance review. Having reached the pinnacle of the organization, it comes as something of a shock to be suddenly subjected to the kind of rigorous appraisal that is usually reserved for junior managers.

In addition, many CEOs—particularly those who also held the title of chairman—may have viewed the board as their boss strictly in an abstract legal sense. The annual appraisal process makes that reporting relationship absolutely explicit; it's a tangible reminder that the age of the imperial CEO is drawing to a close. That's a dramatic role change that some CEOs are reluctant to accept and some directors are hesitant to assume.

Finally, there's the distinctly personal dimension of assessing CEOs—usually strong, powerful people who, by nature, find it emotionally difficult to accept critical feedback. Many chief executives believe that no one, including board members, can possibly appreciate the complexity of their jobs or accurately judge their performance. And some directors who traditionally played passive, or even subservient, roles are intimidated by the prospect of personally delivering a tough appraisal. One CEO who served on the commission put it this way: "So many CEOs are prima donnas, and nobody wants to tell them anything but that they got all A's on their performance."

Nevertheless, given the unique role of the CEO in today's corporate world, and the board's growing responsibility to provide both oversight and assistance to the CEO, high-performing boards have little choice but to address the challenge head-on.

THE CONTEXT: CEO PERFORMANCE AND ACCOUNTABILITY

Never in recent memory has CEO performance been the subject of such intense scrutiny or broad concern as it is today. Little wonder, then, that the board's role in overseeing CEO performance has emerged as a significant component of governance reform.

Regulations that require boards to perform periodic, formal CEO performance evaluations have partially resolved what used to be a sticky issue at many companies. CEOs no longer have the option of digging in their heels and resisting regular reviews. Today, they have three choices. One, they can sit back and watch as the board develops a process on its own. Two, they can try to dilute the process by steering the board toward a superficial checklist that satisfies the legal requirements. We strongly recommend a third option: a collaborative effort by the CEO and the board to design an evaluation process that is serious, deliberate, helpful to the CEO, and beneficial to the company and its stakeholders.

The overall process is fairly straightforward, but it will vary from one company to the next, shaped by personalities, history, and strategic context; there is no one-size-fits-all solution. You'll never find a better illustration of the notion that "the devil is in the details."

Here's one more thought to keep in mind: this process is fragile. At several critical stages, it can easily fall apart. For everyone involved, each step requires a sincere intention to collaborate and a firm commitment to communicate. Without ongoing cooperation and steadfast determination by all parties to make it work, the best-designed evaluation process will fail.

CLARIFYING THE PURPOSE OF THE PROCESS

The first step in designing an effective CEO evaluation process is to establish clear objectives. Just like performance appraisal processes at lower levels of the organization, a CEO evaluation process can serve three distinct but closely related objectives:

- It enables the board, its leaders, and its appropriate committees—usually compensation and/or governance—to work with the

CEO to establish a clear focus on the company's future direction by specifying strategic objectives and performance metrics for the year ahead.

- It gives the board an opportunity to support the CEO's development by setting goals and providing ongoing feedback in areas where the CEO needs to change behavior, learn new skills, or focus additional attention.

- It provides useful ways for the board and its committees to collect and interpret the data that informs their assessment of the CEO's past performance, leading to decisions about the CEO's compensation and continued employment.

All three elements are essential in order for the process to create the maximum value. Realistically, any board that embraces all three is committing itself to go far beyond the legal requirements, which mandate nothing more than a mechanical accounting exercise focused exclusively on determining compensation for past performance. In the strictest sense, the board's oversight role doesn't require any attention to whether the CEO possesses the vision, strategy, and personal capabilities to achieve the performance objectives. The broader perspective we recommend requires the board to assess the degree of "fit" between the CEO's leadership qualities and the demands imposed by the organization's strategic objectives.

As we've listed them here, the three evaluation objectives seem to be distinct. In practice, they are frequently bundled into the same process. Time constraints may force the board to evaluate the CEO's performance over the previous year while simultaneously making compensation decisions, setting next year's targets, and discussing specific areas for improvement—often in a single meeting.

However, in the absence of a process that clearly delineates and recognizes the importance of all three objectives, what often happens is that the review of past performance for compensation purposes takes on disproportionate weight and dominates the discussion. It's easy to see why; it not only satisfies the regulatory requirements but is also a "safer place to go"—a mathematical exercise rather than a probing assessment of the CEO's personal strengths and weaknesses. When time is short, some CEOs and boards dispense with developmental discussion altogether, using the compensation review to set the CEO's future objectives.

In contrast, some boards make sure that developmental discussions don't get short shrift. Honeywell once scheduled separate meetings focusing on past and future performance to ensure adequate attention to each objective. In mid-January, the CEO sent the board his self-assessment on past performance and his plan for the coming year, including his personal leadership objectives. The board followed up during its January meeting with a discussion of the coming year's objectives, and in February with a review of the CEO's performance over the past year.

The specific structure and timing of the meetings are less important than the board's commitment to fully address all the evaluation objectives. For instance, Target Corporation, a company with a reputation for excellence in corporate governance, determined evaluation objectives could be well served in a single meeting because of the board's and CEO's commitment to a detailed review of past performance as well as an open discussion of future performance expectations and developmental needs.[2]

IMPLEMENTING THE CEO EVALUATION PROCESS: CRITICAL ROLES AND ACTIVITIES

Over the course of our work with the NACD Blue Ribbon Commission, no particular model for structuring the CEO evaluation process emerged as the clear favorite. A variety of models seem to work, but they all share two key elements. First, they involve a fairly detailed, formal process with a sequenced calendar of events; important activities aren't squeezed in at the last minute or abandoned for lack of time. Second, the best processes are characterized by careful attention to who should be involved, and in what roles, at every stage.

Defining Objectives

The assessment process usually begins before the start of the fiscal year, when the CEO works with board leaders to establish the key business objectives for the coming year, ensuring they are consistent with the company's strategic plan. Using the strategy as a starting point, the CEO formulates an initial set of personal performance targets, specifying how progress against each target will be measured, and submits the plan to the board.

As boards design their appraisal processes, the first decision is to determine who should be involved in reviewing and approving the

CEO's goals. Historically, that's been the job of the compensation committee, and its chairman has led the process. But our interviews detected an emerging view that all directors should be taking a more active role in this process, rather than leaving all of the responsibility in the hands of committees or their leaders.

"Some people keep CEO assessment a closed process within the compensation committee," said one commission member. "I believe it should be an exercise for the full board. The compensation committee can begin or design the process, but they need to engage with the full board on it."

Commission members agreed that there is an absolute need for a specific director—either the chairman of the compensation committee, the lead director, or the nonexecutive chairman—to clearly assume the lead role for the assessment process, starting with a very explicit conversation with the CEO that results in a shared understanding of the board's expectations.

"The entire board should contribute to assessing the performance of the CEO," said one commission member, "but it's important to have someone primarily responsible for the process in order to make sure that expectations are clearly conveyed and that the appraisal is entirely consistent with those up-front expectations."

The clarity of those conversations is critical and shouldn't be taken for granted. One former CEO on the commission explained: "Regardless of the conversation at the start of the year about objectives and measures, very often at the end of the year the CEO will go to the board leader who is doing the evaluation and say, 'This has been a really tough year.' When that happens, you have to say, 'Hey, I hear you, but that's not what we decided on.' Again, the more time you take with this at the beginning, the less trouble you're going to have when this comes up at the end."

Ongoing Assessment

Some boards finalize the CEO's performance goals and then decide their work is done until it's time for the year-end review. They're wrong. At the very least, the compensation committee and the board should sit down six months into the year and take time to review the targets and progress against them. Although many boards skip this midyear review or do it informally, it can provide great value for two reasons. First, it helps the board and the CEO make sure they share a common understanding of how the year is going and of any issues that require closer attention. Second, it provides an opportunity for mid-course corrections based on changes in the economy or competitive environment.

Beyond that, periodic check-ins are essential to the CEO's personal development, particularly during a CEO's first year or two.

"The most important decision any board makes is choosing and firing the CEO," one commission member observed. "In between, it is equally important that they focus on retaining and developing the CEO. Boards have a tendency not to pay much attention to CEO development, but especially for new CEOs there is a need for a development process, and the CEO evaluation should be an integral component to that process."

Periodic assessment can provide a means for ensuring that the CEO and the board stay on the same page and deal with problems before they've reached the breaking point, as in the Schwab situation described earlier. As one commission member explained: "It is critical to have a midyear or regular review of the CEO, and to provide a forum for that. If you don't have something like that, when a performance issue arises, there is a tendency to say, 'Let's just wait and see if he or she is still doing that by the end of the year.' Often, by then, what began as a more minor problem has grown into a significant issue that could have been avoided if it were addressed earlier."

Increasingly, these discussions are taking place in executive sessions, which boards are now required to hold periodically in the CEO's absence. These meetings are turning out to be a great boon to the evaluation process; they create not only the opportunity but also the expectation that the board will routinely discuss the CEO's performance, eliminating much of the drama and intrigue that inevitably used to surround any informal gathering of disgruntled independent directors. But at the end of the day, the value of the process is determined by each board's candor and courage.

"The most important thing is for the board to be honest and address CEO performance issues when there are early signs of real trouble," said one commission member. "Don't put it off and hope that it's going to get better; it probably won't, and you'll end up taking action much later than you should have. Executive sessions are the key to this; they are the forum for these issues to come up, and the director debriefing with the CEO afterwards can raise these issues."

Year-End Assessment

As was the case with the design of the CEO's annual goals, there are various models for arriving at the year-end appraisal of the CEO's performance. Once again, our research has surfaced growing support for involving the entire board in substantive discussions of the CEO's performance, rather than leaving the heavy lifting to the compensation and governance committees, or to private discussions among the lead director and committee chairs.

On one point, however, there was practically unanimous agreement: the most difficult element of the year-end assessment is the actual communication of its content to the CEO. That involves everything from who assembles the performance data to who delivers that information, how, in what setting, and with whom in attendance. These issues require meticulous planning and execution in order to ensure that the right messages are delivered, and heard, in the right context. Indeed, many directors view communication with the CEO as by far the most difficult part of the entire appraisal process. We'll return to that issue as the final topic in this chapter.

The entire process we've just described—starting with the development of a shared understanding of the purpose of the appraisal—should be repeated each year. As part of its own annual performance evaluation, the board should include a review of the CEO evaluation process and seek ways to improve it. Figure 8.1 illustrates the steps identified here as a recurring cycle. This type of tool is useful for managing the pacing and timing of each step.

Exhibit 8.1 provides a worksheet that can help stimulate thinking about the objectives and implementation of the process we just discussed. It also applies to other areas we will cover in more depth in the rest of this chapter: identifying the dimensions the CEO will be rated on, determining the best way to measure performance, and communicating with the CEO.

DEFINING PERFORMANCE DIMENSIONS AND MEASURES

The defining element of any component of the appraisal process—whether for compensation decisions, goal setting, or developmental feedback—is the specific set of dimensions on which the CEO will be evaluated. These form the basis of all the measures, objectives, and

Figure 8.1.   CEO Evaluation Time Line.

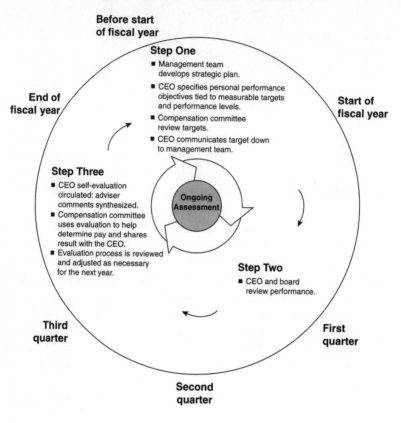

Exhibit 8.1.   CEO Evaluation Process Review.

Purpose: This worksheet is designed to assess the quality and comprehensiveness of a CEO evaluation process. The questions are derived from best practices in three areas: the process of evaluation, relevant roles during the process, and the content of the evaluation itself.

Instructions: Enter Yes, No, or N/A (Not Applicable) in the rating column.

PROCEDURAL ELEMENTS

Criteria	Rating	Comments
1. Is there an explicit description of the CEO evaluation process with articulated goals, roles, and responsibilities?		
2. Is there an explicit process calendar with detailed deadlines and milestones?		

Criteria	Rating	Comments
3. Is the process calendar aligned with the corporate calendar (i.e., do CEO evaluation events fit with pre-existing governance and management schedules)?		
4. Does the process include a midyear check-in on CEO performance?		
5. Does the process include a focus on CEO development and opportunities for developmental feedback?		
6. Is the process consistent with the company's values and culture?		
7. Does the process include quality assurance mechanisms that allow it to be revised as needed?		

ROLES AND RESPONSIBILITIES

Criteria	Rating	Comments
8. Does the process have a clearly defined leader?		
9. Is the process sufficiently controlled (led and managed) by outside directors to preserve the integrity of the evaluation?		
10. Is there a clearly defined role (or external consultant) for the collecting and compiling of performance data, ratings, etc.?		
11. Is the CEO considered a partner at each stage of the process, with ample opportunity for input?		
12. Are the people with the most valid information about the CEO's actions and leadership impact given the opportunity to provide feedback?		
13. Has the feedback deliverer been identified? Does this person have the skills required to effectively deliver CEO performance feedback?		

CONTENT AND MEASURES

Criteria	Rating	Comments
14. Have performance standards and criteria for evaluating the CEO been identified and made explicit?		
15. Are all relevant aspects of CEO performance included in the performance criteria?		
16. Do performance criteria encompass both CEO and chairman roles?		
17. Is there a clear link between the performance criteria that make up the evaluation and the company's strategic objectives and business requirements?		
18. Can the business rationale be articulated for each performance criterion?		
19. Is there a valid, feasible measure identified for each relevant performance criterion?		
20. Are statistically sound methods used to gather and interpret performance data?		

targets used in the process. Among all the decisions that must be made throughout the process, the selection of performance dimensions, and the relative weighting given to each, is probably the most challenging because it forces the board to sort through the complex relationship between the CEO's personal effectiveness and the organization's collective performance.

"Typically, CEO evaluation consists of assessing the CEO based on financial measures established at the start of the year and linked to the compensation plans, but that's not enough," said one CEO on the Blue Ribbon Commission. "A CEO evaluation should be much broader than that to be effective."

Indeed, many commission members were emphatic in their belief that assessment has to involve a variety of both hard and soft measures. "Hitting the metrics around financials is not a complete review," one commission member stated. "These metrics are just the entry point. There needs to be more emphasis on character issues, so meeting metrics is not taken to mean that the assessment is complete. The board needs to dive into issues of developing a bench, integrity, leadership strength, and building a coffer for the long haul."

When you step back and look at the totality of the CEO's complex role, the job of coming up with a comprehensive yet manageable set of goals seems daunting. But there are ways to organize the board's thinking about the CEO's role that can simplify the task. One useful approach is to consider how effectively the CEO behaves as a leader, distinct from the organizational impact of the leader's actions. Further, the impact of the CEO's actions can be assessed in terms of both the organization's operational effectiveness and its bottom-line performance. In other words, there are three generic classes of CEO performance: bottom-line impact, operational impact, and leadership effectiveness.

Bottom-Line Impact

Over the years, the inherent irony of CEO performance appraisal is that it has placed the greatest emphasis on the set of measures over which the CEO exerts the least direct influence: short-term financial performance. There's no escaping the critical importance of the bottom line and market valuation, and they should certainly constitute an essential part of the appraisal mix. Yet, the underlying assumption of many CEO evaluation and "pay-for-performance" plans is the highly questionable proposition that a CEO's actions have a direct, immediate, and significant impact on the company's financial performance and stock price.

In the absence of brilliant decisions or egregious mistakes, it's incredibly difficult to accurately measure the CEO's short-term impact on the financial performance of a complex organization—but that doesn't stop boards from trying. (Figure 8.2 shows the types of bottom-line metrics used to evaluate the effectiveness of one CEO. The compensation and personnel committee measures the company's actual performance, then compares this performance against the CEO's projections in his or her annual plan.) These bottom-line measures have severe deficiencies as sole indicators of CEO performance. As the person at the top supposedly "pulling all the levers," CEOs are acutely aware that the impact of their own personal actions on the company's bottom line is far from direct, rarely immediate, and seldom dramatic.

Figure 8.3 provides an example of why this is the case in the area of customer relationship management (CRM). In this example, the CEO engaged in direct action to improve customer relations, personally intervening with key customers and sponsoring organizational programs to build CRM capabilities. The impact of these actions on the strength of the customer relationship (in this case measured by customer satisfaction) can be quite strong, and diminished or enhanced by only a handful of extraneous factors. However, the impact of the CEO's actions on the bottom line (in this case defined as growth in earnings from existing customers) is moderated by a bewildering array of external factors. The farther removed the desired impact is from the CEO's direct action, the greater the likelihood that the actual results are influenced by factors beyond the CEO's control.

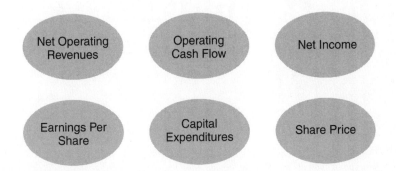

Figure 8.2. Bottom-Line Impact Dimensions Used in CEO Evaluation.

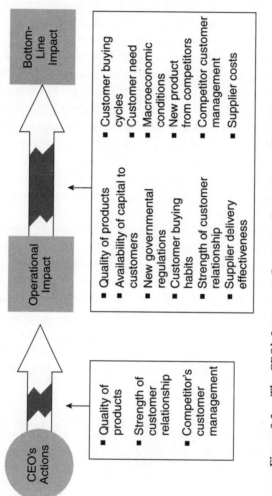

Figure 8.3.   The CEO's Impact on Company Operations and the Bottom Line.

Operational Impact

The second category of performance issues involves operational impact—the CEO's personal effect on the company's operational and organizational effectiveness. Taken together, these actions answer the question, "Has the CEO made changes that either improve or diminish the organization's ability to function and perform effectively?" Measures of operational impact include indicators of organizational functioning (for example, retention rates, employee satisfaction scores), operational effectiveness (quality ratings of products, time to market, productivity), and strategic implementation (number of acquisitions, total head-count reduction, growth in market share).

Figure 8.4 shows the operational impact dimensions identified as "most important in evaluating CEO performance" by almost 350 directors.[3] As the Conference Board report on CEO compensation suggests, "These measures may give a better indication of a company's underlying potential to create value, rather than looking to the immediate stock price, which is subject to marketwide volatility."[4] Although still subject to a variety of forces beyond the CEO's immediate control, this type of performance is more closely related than bottom-line impact to the CEO's personal actions.

Leadership Effectiveness

As a class of performance, leadership effectiveness involves the CEO's personal behavior and actions, which in turn influence operational

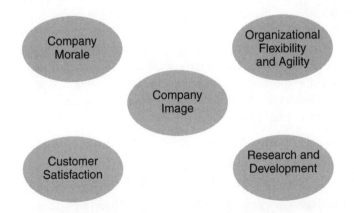

Figure 8.4. Most Important Dimensions of Operational Impact, per Corporate Directors Survey.

impact, and ultimately, bottom-line impact. Accordingly, this category is quite different from the other two in that it assesses impact that is entirely under the CEO's control rather than diffused and indirect organizational outcomes.

This area involves an assessment of the CEO's personal interactions with the entire range of internal and external constituencies. Internally, it relates to the CEO's effectiveness in developing strategy, talent, and culture. Externally, it measures the CEO's performance as the organization's face to the world and the key player in shaping its reputation and relationships with key stakeholders. Leadership effectiveness is clearly a growing concern for board members in an era of continuing corporate scandals, intense regulatory scrutiny, mishandled CEO succession, and pervasive cynicism about business ethics.

"I don't believe that the CEO's assessment should be based 100 percent on earnings," said a former chairman and CEO of a major corporation who served on the Blue Ribbon Commission. "At least 20 to 30 percent should involve some soft measures. For example, if the CEO is sixty-three and there is no apparent successor, 25 percent of it might relate to developing succession candidates. Or, if the company has developed a bad reputation for something, there should be a percentage of the CEO's evaluation linked to improving the company's reputation in that area, and that should be measured."

Many commission members zeroed in on the importance of succession planning and corporate reputation as key aspects of effective leadership. They also placed a high priority on the CEO's leadership of the executive team, retention and development of key talent, interactions with the financial community, ability to energize employees, and demonstration of personal integrity. In short, there's a growing awareness that the CEO should be held accountable for a broad range of personal behaviors that have significant, though not necessarily short-term, impact on the organization's success. Figure 8.5 identifies three key leadership effectiveness dimensions used to evaluate the CEO of Prudential Insurance.[5]

SELECTING OBJECTIVES AND SPECIFYING MEASURES

The three categories just identified—bottom-line impact, operational impact, and leadership effectiveness—simply describe the waterfront of CEO performance in generic terms. The specific dimensions and

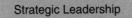

Strategic Leadership

Leads the development of appropriate strategies for the enterprise; achieves support and commitment for the strategies from management and the board.

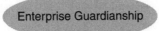

Enterprise Guardianship

Sets the "tone at the top" in such matters as enterprise reputation, ethics, legal compliance, customer relations, and ensuring results.

Board Relationship

Works collaboratively with board members and committees, communicates information in a timely manner to ensure full and informed consent about matters of enterprise governance.

Figure 8.5. Leadership Effectiveness Dimensions at Prudential Insurance.

objectives used in a particular evaluation process will vary for each company, and in fact, ought to vary to a certain extent from one year to the next in response to specific problems or opportunities. Nonetheless, there are some general principles that leading companies follow in selecting CEO performance objectives.[6]

- *Be sure to look beyond bottom-line performance.* It's worth stating one more time, because this principle captures the most dramatic difference between traditional CEO evaluations and the emerging model. To ensure a full picture of the CEO's performance and to compensate for the limitations inherent in bottom-line measures, the evaluation must include objectives covering leadership effectiveness and operational impact.

- *Limit the objectives to a manageable number.* An exhaustive list that tries to address every aspect of a CEO's performance in detail can quickly get out of hand. It's vital to get the number of dimensions right: too few and the process is likely to be dominated by short-term financial objectives, too many and the CEO and her management team risk losing focus. There's no magic number, but best-practice companies usually have between four and ten.[7] The presiding director of one global firm told us, "Typically, you want the CEO to be focused on a set of four to six major strategic items. Boards do struggle with the objective-setting process, but those who stay with it get better over time. What I've observed is that their list of goals for the CEO starts off too general, and then evolves into something more specific and more effective."

- *When the same person is both chairman and CEO, include separate objectives for each role.* In reality, there are two ways to handle these situations. One is to create distinct goals and performance measures for each role but within a single appraisal process. The other is to evaluate the CEO's performance as chairman in the context of the board's self-assessment process. Either way, it's crucial to use the appraisal process to underscore both the importance of the chairman's role and its substantive differences from the CEO's management roles.

- *Define measures for each objective.* Each objective must be coupled with explicit measures that will be used to track performance. This is simple enough for all bottom-line and most operational impact objectives, which easily lend themselves to quantitative measurement. Where boards assume they'll run into trouble is in devising similarly robust measures of the "soft stuff"—but those measures do, indeed, exist. For instance, leadership behaviors can be measured through ratings that ask board members to indicate the frequency with which the CEO engages in desired behaviors and with what perceived effect.

- *Clearly relate performance to rewards.* As one former CEO on the commission explained, "The more you have a pre-understanding about what the pay opportunities and measures are, the fewer problems you will have later on. For instance, 'If you get an A, you will get a bonus of twice your salary, a B is one times your salary, and a C or a D is nothing.' That should be spelled out right at the beginning. That way, the CEO's not surprised at the end." That kind of specificity, though still all too rare, is essential to building a shared understanding of performance expectations.

GATHERING ASSESSMENT FEEDBACK

Though the independent directors who make up the compensation committee and hold leadership positions bear the principal responsibility for the CEO evaluation process, many boards and CEOs have found it useful to involve others in the process, either as sources of information or as facilitators of the process. With appropriate participation, these outside parties can substantially increase the amount of information and quality of decision making.

One increasingly popular practice in CEO evaluation is *multisource feedback*. In this process, the CEO is evaluated on a range of behaviors by a variety of groups or individuals—the board, the executive team, customers, and so on. When done well, a multisource assessment can provide both the CEO and the board with a clear picture of which actions and behaviors are having the desired impact, and which need some refinement. Figure 8.6 illustrates how one chemical company structured a multisource feedback process for its CEO.

Here's how one member of the commission, a current CEO, described his own appraisal process: "Our CEO evaluation is a 360. The directors all rate me and the direct reports rate me, and the direct reports' ratings all go to the board. I write up a seven- or eight-page document for the board; that is how I evaluate myself. This covers financial measures, milestones that have been accomplished, and then issues of leadership that relate to the ratings of the board and of my

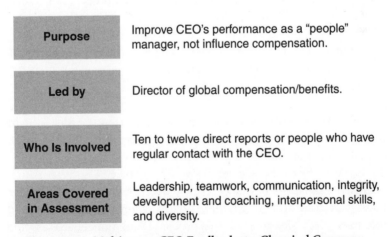

Purpose	Improve CEO's performance as a "people" manager, not influence compensation.
Led by	Director of global compensation/benefits.
Who Is Involved	Ten to twelve direct reports or people who have regular contact with the CEO.
Areas Covered in Assessment	Leadership, teamwork, communication, integrity, development and coaching, interpersonal skills, and diversity.

Figure 8.6.   Multisource CEO Feedback at a Chemical Company.

direct reports. The board discusses this in executive sessions and the head of the compensation and head of the governance committees jointly give me feedback."

Despite its potential benefits, the decision to include additional people in the CEO evaluation process is not without risks. It increases the complexity of the process and introduces a tricky set of political and interpersonal dynamics that have to be managed. In the end, for the feedback to be viewed as constructive and credible, both the board and the CEO have to be comfortable with the source. We suggest three criteria to consider before involving additional "voices" in the feedback process:

- Does the individual or group have a valuable and informed point of view based on firsthand experience and observation?

- Are there collateral benefits to involving certain groups or individuals in the process? For example, a potential benefit of soliciting feedback from customers might be a stronger relationship and increased sense of ownership in the company's success.

- Does the feedback process have integrity—is it objective, and does it safeguard the confidentiality of those who are willing to be critical of the CEO? Here's how one CEO member of the commission discussed the issue: "It's critically important that the CEO performance assessment provide useful information to the CEO. To do that, it has to be well thought out, fair, and objective, and it has to protect the confidentiality of participants. One board I am on has used a third party to gather the input so that it's seen as objective and also protects confidentiality. You may not want to use a third party every year, but every so often as a bit of a reality check."

A number of commission members supported the idea of using independent third parties to help with this very complex task. In the past, that kind of outside help was not only rare but also problematic, because outside advisers generally were hired by CEOs rather than by boards; the situation inevitably resulted in blurred and sometimes conflicting loyalties. Today, with more boards retaining their own outside resources, that's becoming less of a problem. And more boards are finding value in that approach. As one director on the Blue Ribbon Commission explained it, "What really helps in assessing the CEO in a rigorous and complete way is to have the information gathered, distilled, and fed back in a high-quality way. Using independent third parties really helps in this regard, as do the use of 360-degree approaches with defined criteria. The consultant doing the assessment also needs to be reporting to the board."

COMMUNICATING WITH THE CEO

As we said earlier, there are several critical junctures at which the entire appraisal process can fall apart, and the final communication of the assessment may be the most fragile of all. No matter how meticulous the board has been about each preceding step in the process, its ultimate success hinges on whether the appraisal is communicated in a way that ensures that the CEO will hear, and take to heart, the messages the board intends to send.

"The toughest part of the CEO assessment process is talking to the CEO about his or her performance," observed one commission member. "Often, the CEO ends up hating the individual who has to deliver the feedback. Or, the board feels that individual has not delivered the message to the CEO effectively because the CEO doesn't change what he or she is doing. . . . This is a very difficult thing."

In any performance appraisal, how the messages are conveyed is as important as the messages themselves. That's particularly true of CEO appraisals. Giving tough feedback to a powerful CEO requires a combination of tact, toughness, and in-depth knowledge of the company. Beyond that, the CEO has multiple "bosses" on the board, and sometimes wonders whether the feedback reflects a true consensus or just the personal opinions of the director sitting across the table. Consequently, the CEO appraisal, more than any other, requires careful planning regarding not only the content but also who will deliver the messages and how.

"In providing feedback to the CEO after his or her assessment, it's important to spend meaningful time in executive session talking about how the key messages will be communicated to the CEO," explained a commission member. "Everyone always agrees on the strengths and weaknesses, but frequently they don't spend time on how to communicate the feedback. That's an essential part of the process and one that needs to be discussed, so that the CEO understands the messages." More specifically, another commission member said, "The key point is that thought is given by board members on who should do the review, how, and when, given the nature of the feedback and the circumstances."

Our interviews made it clear that boards employ practically every possible permutation when it comes to deciding who will deliver the appraisal to the CEO. In some companies, that task is delegated to the board leader, be it the nonexecutive chairman, lead director, or presiding director. On other boards, the chair of the compensation or governance committee sits down alone with the CEO. Some commissioners were adamant in their belief that the appraisal is delivered most effectively in a one-on-one conversation, whereas others argued just as vehemently that "it should never be just one director."

Regardless of which individuals are chosen to provide the feedback, commission members were very specific about the qualifications those people need in order to do the job well. Clearly, they must have the trust and respect of both the CEO and the board. In particular, said one CEO on the commission, "The director in this role needs to understand the company and its environment and not just rely on the financial numbers in providing feedback to the CEO. A lead director numb to a company's situation won't have the respect of the CEO." Just as important, said another commission member, is that whoever delivers the feedback "needs to be honest and candid . . . and needs to be someone who will not be cowed by a strong CEO."

Interestingly, a number of CEOs on the commission expressed a strong preference for having the feedback delivered by the entire board, rather than by one or two individuals.

"As a CEO, I like getting my assessment review with all the board members in the room, rather than just the chair of the compensation committee sitting down with me," said one of the CEOs. "With everyone in the room, you are not just hearing one person's interpretation of what was said by the group, and you can make sure that the feedback hasn't been screened the wrong way—for example, spending more time on what's important to the person delivering the feedback may not have been the most important issue in the minds of everyone on the board."

One final concern raised by a number of commission members is the need to ensure that the delivery of the appraisal is a rigorous and "more formal process, rather than 'between you and me.'" To that end, they strongly recommended that the face-to-face discussion with the CEO be followed up with a written document, approved in advance by the board, that not only reiterates the board's appraisal of past performance but also spells out the developmental goals for the year to come.

SUMMARY

The rigorous, systematic approach to CEO appraisal set forth in this chapter is emblematic of the changing nature of corporate governance. For much of the twentieth century, the notion that the board would undertake a serious, periodic assessment of the CEO's performance was practically unheard of at many companies. Gradually, the idea of pay for performance began to take hold—but for the most part, "performance" was narrowly measured in terms of short-term financial performance.

Our survey research and interviews with dozens of members of the NACD Blue Ribbon Commission reinforce our own observations in boardrooms across the United States, revealing a growing interest in a rigorous appraisal process that takes into account the complexity of the CEO's job and the variety of ways in which the CEO's behavior and decisions influence the organization's overall performance. In our view, this development is long overdue, but a welcome step toward enabling high-performing boards to add real and significant value to the governance process.

CHAPTER NINE

The Board's New Roles in CEO Succession

William A. Pasmore
Roselinde Torres

The handoff of leadership from one CEO to another is an important event in the life of any enterprise. "Passing the baton," as it has been called, is a critical challenge made all the more complicated by the interplay of corporate politics and personal emotion. In addition, as difficult as the succession process has always been, it has become infinitely more complex in the current corporate environment where the performances of the CEO and the company have become inexorably intertwined. Meanwhile, tectonic shifts have reshaped the topography of corporate governance: for boards, what used to be a spectator event is now a close contact sport.

This chapter is intended to provide guidance to CEOs and boards as they navigate the succession process in this new environment. Although we have worked with CEOs on succession for more than two decades, over the past five years an increasing amount of this work has included boards as well.[1] That experience has provided us with some valuable lessons about the factors that are critical to managing succession in this new environment.

We will begin by setting the scene with some chilling examples of how easily the succession process can go awry. Then, we'll discuss the new environment and context for succession, including the changing role of the board. Next, we'll examine three distinctly different approaches to the CEO succession process and identify the factors critical to the success of a collaborative process involving the board and the incumbent CEO. We will explain why the new work of the board goes far beyond what many boards are currently doing, and requires reaching down into the organization to assess executive bench strength and planning the series of moves that inevitably accompany CEO succession. We will conclude with some advice for CEOs and boards who are rethinking the board's role in the succession process.

SUCCESSION GONE WRONG

Let's start with some actual examples of succession failures in otherwise well-run companies.

Case 1: Board Regrets Rubber Stamp

The long-term, trusted CEO of a $25-billion manufacturing company approached his transition confidently, knowing that he had the board's full support for his plan to promote the single internal candidate who was clearly the best choice to succeed him. A year later, the retired CEO wondered how things could have gone so terribly wrong in such a short time. His replacement seemed to be a different person after he became the chief executive. He made poor decisions unilaterally, snubbed the board's advice, and walled himself off from his own team as things quickly went from bad to worse. The new CEO was fired, the retired CEO was pressed back into service, and the transition process started all over again. This time, however, the board vowed to be much more involved in selecting the next CEO.

Case 2: Lack of Planning Leaves a Void

In his third year as CEO, the highly successful, almost luminary leader of a $15-billion diversified services firm reassured his board that things were under control, even as the press reported continued investigations of his company. When the evidence could no longer be denied, the board acted swiftly to remove the CEO. Unfortunately, the youthful CEO, who believed he was years away from retirement, hadn't done any succession planning. The board had previously inquired about succession plans but had been reluctant to force the "celebrity" CEO to name a successor. Consequently, the board was left without a clear candidate to fill the void left by the CEO's sudden departure, even as the company struggled to regain its reputation.

Case 3: Failure to Act Is Costly

The board knew that replacing the founder of the $2-billion electronics firm wouldn't be easy. They also knew that the founder had stayed too long and was becoming a liability; despite constant changes in the competitive landscape, he refused to consider new business models. Using back channels, the board sent messages to the founder suggesting that he groom a successor. He would hear nothing of it and retained power even as the fortunes of the company declined. By the time the board finally removed him, the company was worth only a fraction of its former value.

THE NEW ENVIRONMENT OF CEO SUCCESSION

As these vignettes illustrate, a board's action—or inaction—regarding succession can have a tremendous impact on the company it is obligated to protect. Over the past ten years, we have seen pressure on the CEOs of major public corporations grow. Increased demands for performance and shareholder return and a growing view that the CEO is ultimately accountable for corporate performance have added significantly to the already substantial pressures of the job. Today, CEOs operate in an environment of dynamic global markets, constant changes in technology, continuing economic uncertainty, and the dramatically increased role and influence of external constituencies (interest groups, regulators, and so on).

Another important change in the succession environment is the role of the board. As a result of the significant corporate scandals early in this decade, and a subsequent stream of regulations and guidelines (for example, Sarbanes-Oxley, the SEC, and the NYSE), the rules of the game have changed. The fact is that in North America (and to a lesser extent in much of Western Europe) boards have become more independent and more accountable. When CEOs run into trouble, the blame is shared by the boards that appointed and supported them as performance faltered. Beyond that, boards have come to realize that even though the departing CEO has traditionally led the way on succession decisions, the board must ultimately live with the consequences long after the CEO is gone.

In conjunction with these changes in recent years, we have observed some key trends involving boards and the succession process:

- The best boards are quickly moving toward becoming full partners in the process.

- Boards want to see a larger slate of potential candidates, and they want to see them earlier in the selection process.

- Boards want more exposure to candidates in informal settings that allow for substantial personal interaction, rather than just seeing how they handle themselves during formal presentations at board meetings.

- Boards want to see long-term succession planning, involving one or two generations out, to ensure that the leadership pipeline is being developed and managed.

- Boards are becoming more focused on factors that contribute to CEO failure and want better information to help predict the performance of potential candidates.

- Boards are taking more interest in what happens after succession, including the choices made about the new senior team and the backups to individuals who are promoted. Failures during the transition period have caused boards to become more involved in planning multiple moves and monitoring the early performance of CEOs.

Taken together, these trends signal a dramatic shift in the respective roles of the board and the incumbent CEO in the selection process.

EVOLVING MODELS OF THE CEO SUCCESSION PROCESS

For years, the normal approach to CEO succession looked something like this: At some point in his tenure, the CEO starts to identify potential candidates, and often with the help of internal or external advisers, gradually develops and tests them. In the best cases, the CEO periodically updates the board on the potential successors, how they're coming along, and what's being done to manage their development. As the CEO's tenure begins to draw to a close—usually this happens sometime in the final two years—the CEO selects a successor and informs the board. In most cases, the board gives its assent. At that point, the new CEO is left to select a team and run the company.

In the traditional process we've just described, the guiding principle is board concurrence. The CEO manages the process, makes the decisions, occasionally keeps the board informed, and finally seeks a vote ratifying the CEO's choice of a successor. We describe that approach as a *concurrence model* of CEO succession.

During the 1990s, as boards became more active and engaged, they also got more involved in CEO succession, usually by becoming more assertive in the final stage of the process. Even through that period, however, many boards continued to be passive observers of the process, as we found through a recent survey of directors conducted by the University of Southern California and Mercer Delta. In a surprising number of cases, directors reported that the CEO managed the CEO succession process alone and informed the board only after a choice had been made. Fully 40 percent of the directors surveyed reported that their involvement in the succession process was less than optimal, despite acknowledging the critical importance of this role for the board.[2]

Now, we're seeing the emergence of two new and different models that reflect the board's changing role in succession (see Figure 9.1). The first is a *collaborative model* in which the board actively partners with the incumbent CEO. The CEO still drives the process, but the board participates fully and makes the final decision. In most cases, an independent director—it might be the lead director or one of the committee chairs—plays an active role in structuring and overseeing the process.

The collaborative model assumes that there is an incumbent CEO who is performing effectively and has credibility with the board. Obviously, that's not always the case, and other situations call for a different approach—for example, a CEO may become ill, incapacitated, or die. CEOs may be removed because of either external factors (scandals, investigations, and so on), or internal problems (poor company performance, ineffective leadership), or a combination of both. In any of these situations, the CEO is no longer capable of being a credible driver of the process, or even a participant. The result is a *crisis model* in which the board must assume the active management of the succession process. (In Chapter Ten, we'll take a much more detailed look at the board's role in CEO-related crises.)

The crisis model can evolve in very different ways, but one constant is that the time frame for making the selection decision is dramatically compressed. One obvious implication is that boards that are

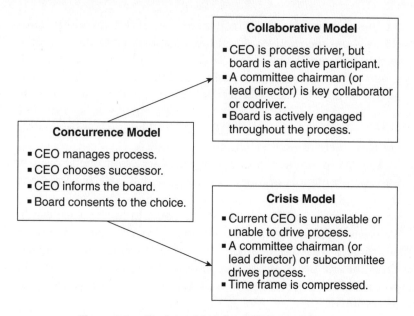

Figure 9.1. Evolving Models of CEO Succession.

actively involved in the succession process on a continuing basis are much less likely to find themselves caught without reasonable options if and when a crisis occurs. That underscores the importance of the collaborative model for developing succession alternatives and developing the pipeline of leadership talent.

In both the collaborative and crisis models, boards are increasingly likely to broaden the scope of their involvement during the succession process. Because the leadership of key units is so important to any company's success, boards are more likely now than a decade ago to review decisions affecting talent at the top few layers of the organization. They are also more likely to take an active role in monitoring CEO performance during the transition period in order to provide directional guidance, support, and even active intervention if required.

CRITICAL SUCCESS FACTORS IN COLLABORATIVE SUCCESSION MANAGEMENT

The concurrence model typically involves a fairly informal succession process. The CEO, often acting alone, uses largely intuitive criteria to sort through the potential candidates. The collaborative model, in contrast, employs a much more explicit approach, and its success rests on several critical factors. It requires a clear set of steps and absolute clarity about the relative roles of the incumbent CEO and the board members. Figure 9.2 provides a suggested template for the process. It begins with the discussion of context and then moves to the creation of criteria and the identification of the talent pool. It then moves to successive rounds of assessment, using a variety of appropriate methodologies. The board and the CEO build shared understanding and agreement through iteration.

The cycle of discussion, development, observation, and assessment is repeated a number of times. At the end of each cycle, the board and the CEO should step back and ask several questions: Who are our potential choices? What should we be doing to further each candidate's development? What additional information would help us make our choice? What are the trade-offs among the different candidates? Given the amount of time required to work through each step in the process, ideally it should start as early as five years in advance of the succession date.

Context

The incumbent CEO and the board have to develop a shared perspective regarding the environment in which the next CEO will operate. They must agree on the most significant strategic challenges the company is likely to face and the leadership capabilities the next CEO will need in order to meet them successfully; for example, as the CEO and board of a health services company worked on succession plans, they agreed that they were nearing the end of a long period of growth through aggressive acquisitions. As a result, the next CEO would require more technical expertise and deep familiarity with the company's core activities in order to grow the company "organically."

This context is a collection of predictions and hypotheses about the company's future. These ideas ought to be revisited periodically to make sure they remain consistent with inevitable changes in the company, its strategy, and its business environment.

Criteria

Based on that shared understanding of the context, the CEO and board must identify the specific dimensions that will be used to assess and select the candidates. Traditionally, the intuitive approach to succession

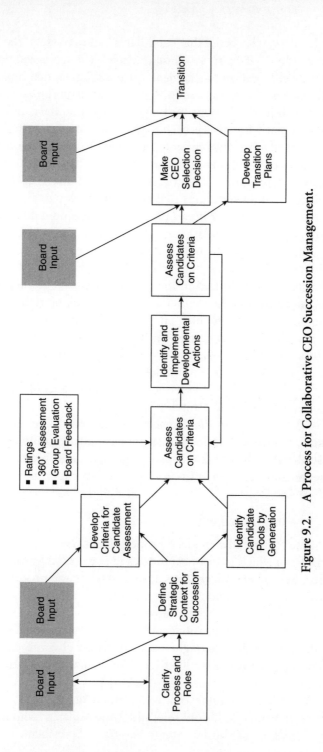

Figure 9.2. A Process for Collaborative CEO Succession Management.

has boiled down to a belief that candidates had to possess "the right stuff," even though it wasn't specifically defined. The succession process was a single elimination tournament; once candidates demonstrated through poor performance, a serious mistake, or inappropriate behavior that they lacked "the right stuff," they were out of the game.

Contrast that with an approach that employs explicit criteria and assumes that all candidates either (a) have gaps that come from a lack of experience or capability or (b) have not had the chance to test or demonstrate capabilities. The process assesses candidates against criteria, places them in situations that can help develop or further test them, and over time, produces a picture of each candidate's relative strengths and weaknesses. Although the criteria are mixed—some are generic, others are specific to the situation—they should be observable and measurable. They should reflect the required leadership capabilities that were identified in the development of the succession context, meaning that they should be forward-looking rather than a reflection of past requirements. They should involve those aspects of each candidate's behavior that are fairly well in place—what we might think of as "character"—as well as those capabilities that can be enhanced through further knowledge and skill. Exhibit 9.1 provides an example from our work with one of our clients, a set of CEO succession criteria used by a technology company.

In collaborative succession management, the board is an active participant in this work. The board may not have full exposure to all the candidates, but it can and should play a significant role in determining the assessment criteria and ranking their relative importance.

Candidate Pool

A key to the collaborative model is properly identifying the broad pool of talent from which to draw candidates. It is essential for the board and the CEO to have alternatives at each stage in the process; at all costs, they must avoid finding themselves captive to a single candidate who knows that she is the only viable choice.

The initial pool must be sufficiently broad for two reasons. For one thing, the best candidates might not be the most obvious. Consider the situation at Xerox in May 2000. Rick Thoman, who had been hired away from IBM just thirteen months earlier, was removed by the board. Paul Allaire, the nonexecutive chairman and former CEO, was asked to step back into his old role, and Anne Mulcahy, who headed one of Xerox's smaller business units, was named president. Mulcahy

Exhibit 9.1.   Sample Set of CEO Candidate Assessment Criteria.

Strategic criteria

Strategic vision: Creates and articulates a future shared vision for the company based on the financial, political, and technical aspects of the business and industry.

Intellectual capacity: Demonstrates intellectual depth, agility, and guts. Encourages initiative and innovation.

Technological competence: Understands and leads the development of technology and makes that a significant part of the vision for the next generation of the company.

Personal criteria

Inspirational leadership: Motivates others through his excitement and enthusiasm about the future direction of the company.

Ethics and values: Conveys high personal standards in how she behaves. Has a sense of social responsibility and social justice.

Respect for the company's heritage: Personally demonstrates the values, beliefs, and philosophy of the company.

Interpersonal criteria

Constituency relationship management: Seeks out opportunities to represent the company and its leadership in order to develop positive relationships with important external and internal constituency groups.

Team builder: Shares information openly and freely with those who have a need to know. Focuses on the development of people and recognizes team accomplishments.

Operational criteria

Breadth of management experience: Demonstrates sufficient knowledge of a wide range of functional areas of the business, including finance, marketing, and customer service.

Execution and operational excellence: Translates vision and strategic intentions into concrete objectives and plans.

Focus and delegation: Focuses time and energy on the most important priorities. Grants sufficient authority to direct reports to enable them to make significant decisions within their areas of responsibility.

---

subsequently became CEO in 2001, and a very effective one; she is widely credited with leading the company's successful turnaround. However, at the time Thoman was hired, Mulcahy wasn't considered CEO material. Years later, Xerox directors began to wonder whether there might be "other Anne Mulcahys" out there—talented but overlooked individuals who ought to be included in a broader talent pool.

There's another reason why the CEO and the board should develop a broad talent pool that looks beyond the current generation. Ultimately, the board is doing more than selecting the next CEO; it is also responsible for ensuring that the company has a strong array of talent on the executive team. A broader pool gives the board a more complete view of the executive bench's strengths and weaknesses, and gives them an understanding of which executives can help complement the shortcomings that any CEO is sure to have.

Assessment Methodology

Given sufficient time, another critical factor is to ensure that the CEO and the board have a process for generating the data they need to measure the candidates against the selection criteria. As you read in Chapter Eight, there are a variety of methods for generating this kind of information.

Regardless of the methodology, a sound assessment has four objectives. It should:

- Generate *understanding* of the candidate, particularly her relative strengths and weaknesses on the specific selection criteria.

- Identify *data gaps* through structured assessment, which forces raters to confront what they don't know about the candidate and helps identify experiences and activities that may fill in the blanks.

- Enable *prediction* and provide some basis for anticipating how a candidate might perform in a particular situation.

- Identify *developmental priorities* for each candidate by determining areas of weakness, which should guide the design of assignments, experiences, or activities that might help the candidate to develop his capabilities.

Development Plans

Few candidates emerge from the process fully formed, with all the capabilities in place to become an effective CEO. Even the best candidates usually have areas they need to develop: specific skills, knowledge, or experience they need to round out the profile. Therefore, another element of the CEO succession process is the design and implementation of development plans. Again, this is an area where the board should play an active role. If the directors have a clear set of criteria, a stream of assessment data, and firsthand experience with the candidates, they should be capable of actively contributing ideas about how to develop candidates, based on their experiences in their own companies and others.

PLANNING A SUCCESSFUL TRANSITION

Ultimately, a choice is made, and the focus turns to "passing the baton," a time when it's essential to have a plan to bridge the gap between the period when the incumbent CEO is clearly still in charge and when the new CEO is operating effectively in the eyes of the board. The objective is to move the leading candidate into the CEO job in stages, while continuing to develop and assess that candidate. It's crucial for the board to leave itself some room to maneuver—to allow board members to change their minds if new information or insights suggest that their first choice might actually be a disastrous one. The board should also be concerned about retaining key players who might be disappointed about not getting the top job but will be sorely needed on the new executive team.

Successful transitions rarely just happen; they require careful planning. There are usually five phases, as indicated in Figure 9.3. First, the lead candidate is placed in a role, such as chief operating officer or head of a core business unit, which will test his ability to lead at a more senior level. The second phase is the confidential designation of the new CEO, who uses this time to think through the structure of the company and the composition of her new executive team. The next phase, which may be short, is the official announcement of the heir apparent. The fourth phase is the overlap period, in which the new CEO runs the company, but the departing CEO continues in some

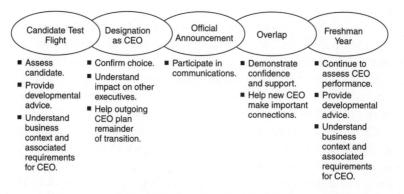

Figure 9.3. Key Roles for the Board in CEO Transitions.

other role, such as chairman of the board. Again, there are different approaches to this phase, ranging from the incumbent's immediate departure to an overlap lasting several years. The fifth phase occurs when the incumbent CEO is gone and the new CEO is fully in place and working through a "freshman year."

It's difficult for the outgoing CEO and the leading candidate or candidates to think very far beyond the transition itself or to think dispassionately about the politics and emotions that inevitably surround a change in leadership. The great danger in discussing succession as a systematic process is the risk of overlooking the powerful emotions that permeate the entire process. For the CEO relinquishing the job and the new CEO assuming it, this is an intensely personal experience that can drain emotions and strain long-standing relationships, even in the best situations. The board bears a tremendous responsibility to recognize and rise above the emotional issues, to view the players objectively, and to provide continuity. It's critical for the board to maintain the long-term view and institutional perspective that become increasingly difficult for the departing and incoming CEOs to retain as they get deeper into the handoff and transition.

Phase 1: Candidate Test Flight

Borrowing a metaphor from aviation, the first phase of the transition process begins with a "test flight" of the final candidate or candidates under conditions that simulate the running of the enterprise. Typically, the formal position is that of the head of the largest business unit, vice president, CFO, or COO. By this time, many people are aware that the candidate is being groomed for the top job and that it is "hers to lose."

Boards must remain vigilant during this phase for warning signs of future problems. Like airplane test flights, this is the time for corrective action, before the passengers are onboard. The board needs frequent and direct access to the candidate, both during and outside of formal board meetings. Without its own "test data," the board is forced to rely on secondhand assessments of the candidate's performance.

Boards that play a more active role during the test flight stand to gain several benefits. First, they are in a better position to certify their choice of successor. Second, they have more data on which to base developmental and transition plans. Third, they begin to develop a stronger relationship with the heir apparent sooner, leading to a smoother transition. Fourth, they can provide mentoring that will help prepare the candidate to assume the full responsibilities of her new role. Finally, they can understand more fully the context within which the transition will take place, so they can be better prepared to attend to business and leadership issues that the new CEO must confront.

Phase 2: Designation as CEO

The second transition phase begins when the new CEO is appointed and lasts until the new executive team is in place. If there is one phase that has received insufficient board attention in most successions, this is it.

During this phase, three things are happening simultaneously. First, the old CEO is leaving. The board and the outgoing CEO must decide when the actual transition will occur. If they determine there should be an overlap period between the designation of the new CEO and the stepping aside of the outgoing CEO, they need to decide how long it will be. The board must decide whether the new CEO would benefit from the old CEO's guiding hand or whether a clean break is better. This decision has huge consequences; it directly influences the latitude afforded the new CEO to address business issues or even to be recognized as the company's leader.

To the extent that boards in the United States are separating the CEO and chairman roles—and that trend is still far from a groundswell—most are inclined to disconnect the roles during the succession process, rather than asking a sitting CEO to relinquish the chairman role. In our view, there is no universally right or wrong answer to whether the roles should be split; each board should decide what is best based on due consideration of the company's business circumstances and the new CEO's qualifications. But any board that has not engaged in this situation should be forewarned that it can easily emerge as a major point of contention with a new CEO, particularly a successor chosen from inside the company, who feels personally insulted by not being granted the same title and power as his predecessor.

The second thing that happens during the designation phase is that the new CEO assembles the new executive team. The extent of change is usually dictated by the company's success; the weaker the business performance, the greater the expectation of wholesale changes in the top team.

Boards that assume a more active role during this phase of the transition need enough knowledge of the capabilities and relationships among potential senior team members to help the incoming CEO make the best choices. Clearly, boards that have been on top of the talent development issues all along will be in a better position to provide real assistance.

Boards differ on the roles they play during this important phase. Intervening boards will insist on approving the slate of senior team members. Engaged boards will work hand in hand with the new CEO to review choices and provide advice when necessary, while leaving the ultimate decisions to the new CEO. Disengaged boards will do neither, trusting that the CEO will make appropriate choices and deal with the consequences.

This brings us to the third thing that is happening in the designation phase. During this crucial time, the new CEO is forming his relationship with the board. Until now, the board held the power to decide the candidate's fate, making it less likely that the candidate would challenge the board on its advice, decisions, or composition. As a full partner, the new CEO must be willing to engage the board on equal footing and call for reforms in board processes that she views as important. The new CEO may even need to call for reformulation of the board to provide greater independence, expertise on emerging business issues, or stronger financial oversight.

During the relationship-forming phase, the new CEO is also learning which board members to trust as her closest advisers and how to influence members of the board who disagree with her point of view. Finally, from a tactical standpoint, new CEOs must learn the ins and outs of managing the board, including such things as how much information to provide prior to board meetings, how to handle communications between board meetings, and how to set the agenda for meetings.

Phase 3: Official Announcement

During the official announcement, the new CEO is signaling his intentions about running the company to employees and external stakeholders. As Franklin D. Roosevelt discovered, the "first hundred days" are critical in establishing the tone and tenor of a leader's tenure.[3] From the board's perspective, it's important that the candidate has a plan and has shared it with the board to get feedback and support. As part of that plan, the CEO and the board should agree on the actions the board will take during the first hundred days to help solidify the new CEO's leadership of the company.

During the official announcement phase, the board should be visible and supportive of the new CEO. Just as the CEO should have a detailed communication plan for the first hundred days—and beyond—the board should develop its own communication plan to ensure that the new CEO receives the required public support.

Phase 4: Overlap

Although overlap with their predecessors can be extremely beneficial to fledgling new CEOs, boards should be aware that strong CEOs may create roles for themselves that are impediments to the success of the new CEO. Some outgoing CEOs have created conditions that made it impossible for their successors to operate. Micromanaging decisions and raising doubts with the board about the new CEO's abilities are signs that the old CEO is having trouble letting go. It's up to the board to provide an objective assessment of what's best for the company and then make the right choice regarding the outgoing CEO's role.

Phase 5: Freshman Year

The first year of any CEO's tenure is a strong predictor of her ultimate success in running the company. In fact, success in the first year is so critical that many CEOs never see a second year.

During the freshman year, there is intense pressure to improve business performance, declare a strategic direction for the company that reflects the latest developments in the market, forge relationships with key customers and external stakeholders, build an effective executive team, be the spokesperson for the company, meet employees, influence the culture, sponsor executive development, and at a minimum, gain the confidence of the board. Clearly, doing all these things well requires talent and superhuman effort.

In times past, boards could afford to be patient with CEOs who were learning their craft. There was a degree of tolerance for on-the-job learning. Not anymore; today, the margin for error and tolerance for mistakes are a fraction of what they once were. Even "celebrity" CEOs have limited time to prove their worth in a world that is dominated by quarterly reports, unprecedented transparency, and relentless second-guessing. Boards feel pressure to consider removing new CEOs who fail to measure up in the eyes of important publications or analysts. Shareholder wealth, though difficult to create, can be wiped out overnight by unfavorable reports concerning the CEO or his board.

Although it seems early in a new CEO's tenure to raise the subject, it's important that the board and the new CEO agree on a process to assess the CEO's performance. The new CEO has a right to know where he stands with his board and what his options are for dealing with issues that arise. The new CEO should meet with board members individually to understand their feedback and advice. Beyond that, though, the CEO and the board should design a more formal process for data gathering and feedback that provides the new CEO with an up-to-date "report card" on his performance.

Some boards feel that assessing the performance of the new CEO in his first year is simply too early and may convey a lack of trust in the new CEO's capabilities. CEOs who have run into problems in their first year would strongly disagree. They would say that it's much better to be involved in ongoing dialogue with the board about performance issues than to discover that private conversations have been taking place among board members or the entire board behind closed doors. As we discussed in Chapter Eight, the recently mandated executive sessions are providing a long-overdue venue for boards to regularly discuss the CEO's performance and provide feedback on areas of concern before they evolve into major problems, or even full-blown crises.

It's important that the evaluation criteria for the CEO be consistent with the selection criteria. Boards sometimes surprise CEOs by introducing entirely different performance criteria once the CEO is in office. For example, the governance committee of a retail company asked us to conduct an evaluation of the CEO because of a downturn in the company's performance and an alarming turnover rate of senior leaders. When we asked about the dimensions and process used to evaluate the CEO's performance, we were told that the board held one executive session a year where they discussed the CEO's strengths and areas for development. We learned that in selecting the CEO, the board had developed specific criteria and a set of possible risks that could cause the CEO to derail. However, these criteria and risks never surfaced as part of any of the CEO's annual evaluations. Instead, the governance committee and board relied on general impressions because the company had been performing well in the first years of the CEO's tenure. Ultimately, the CEO was removed from his job and the board had to resort to a crisis succession scenario. Had the board used its original CEO selection criteria, it might have seen early indicators of the CEO's troubles and intervened to avoid the significant loss of shareholder value and the resulting feeding frenzy by competitors once the CEO was removed.

The flip side of the CEO assessment story is that the new CEO and board should agree on how the board will work and be evaluated as well. Agendas for board meetings need to be set, processes for conducting meetings reviewed, and criteria for assessing individual board members and the board as a whole put in place. Although such matters seem mundane, they are extremely influential in determining the character of the relationship between the board and the CEO. It's in the interest of both parties to treat these discussions seriously, considering a range of options before settling on solutions that are right for the company and board in question. The CEO will find it difficult to change these arrangements as they become set over time. The best opportunity to shape board dynamics and governance processes is at the beginning of the CEO's tenure.

A UNIQUE CASE: REPLACING THE FOUNDER

Some firms face the additional challenge during succession of replacing the founder of the firm with a "professional" CEO for the first time. Founder CEO leadership transitions are always complex and challenging and can often be a defining moment for an organization. The founder's succession is often an undiscussable subject; the board doesn't want to offend the founder, and the founder is in no particular hurry to find a replacement.

The founder CEO of one pharmaceutical company continuously put off discussions about his succession. Finally, when pushed by an influential board member during a private session, the founder revealed that in his desk drawer there was an envelope containing the name of his successor. But it wasn't to be read until he died—because that was the only time someone else would run his company.

The board is in a unique position to prepare the founder and the organization for the future. What's more, it has a duty to guarantee a CEO succession process that ensures the institution's viability. Framing the succession process as a fiduciary responsibility helps make the board's intervention less personal. Although every situation has its unique requirements based on the founder's personality and other circumstances, there are some ways in which boards can help the succession process along:

- Engage the founder in imagining the organization without him by talking about the company in five, ten, or twenty years under various scenarios.

- Institutionalize the founder's legacy by having him articulate core values and incorporating them into the selection criteria for the new CEO.

- Support the founder's emotional process of letting go by helping him consider other contributions he could make to society, public policy, his community, family, favored charities, and so on.

- Strengthen the board's effectiveness as a team so it becomes capable of having constructive and candid conversations, both with and without the founder in the room.

- Build consensus among influential board members and help them overcome their reticence to address thorny issues with the founder, either collectively or in on-on-one conversations.

- Stay close to the new CEO who succeeds the founder. The successor faces an inevitable mourning period following the founder's departure and will have the difficult task of balancing the old with the new. It will be at least a year before the uncertainty over the change in leadership subsides.

In the end, the board's greatest challenge is to act responsibly, and to resist being intimidated or granting undue deference to a figure of legendary proportions in their company.

SUMMARY

Our bias is clear: we firmly believe that the collaborative model of managing the succession process will provide results superior to either the concurrence or the crisis model. The collaborative model requires time, investment, and the ability of the board and the CEO to work together effectively. It also implies several imperatives.

First, the process must start early. Too often, succession is left to the final year or two of the incumbent CEO's term. Although it may seem very early and even premature, this approach requires the CEO and the board to begin the process early enough to provide time for engagement in assessment, development, and selection.

The second imperative is to develop talent. The best collaborative succession process in the world will be severely hampered if, five years from the transition, the board and the CEO realize the company lacks sufficient talent. To succeed, this approach requires a long-term strategy for developing the right talent to fill the leadership pipeline.[4]

A third imperative is to clarify the process and the role of the board and individual directors. There are many places for the board to be engaged: in the description of context, in the development of criteria, in reviewing and discussing assessments, in exposure to candidates, in participation in the choice process, and in planning and overseeing the transition. This requires a continuity of engagement, with constant updates. The collaboration is created through a continuing discussion over time, one that allows for constructive contention and helps create a shared understanding and common point of view.

Fourth, transition is important. Frequently, there is a temptation to view the process as finished when the choice is made. However, how the baton is passed and what happens during the overlap period are critical to the initial success of the new CEO. The board has an absolutely crucial role to play as third party to the handoff.

Fifth, although it is difficult to contemplate, the board should always be preparing for a sudden departure. It can happen at any time in a CEO's tenure, and it frequently occurs when least expected. Changes in the nature of companies, the demands on leadership, and the shape of corporate governance have all contributed to a new environment for CEO succession. Those factors have combined, we believe, to create the need for a new approach to the succession task, one characterized by collaboration, engagement, and clarity. The shape of that new process is beginning to emerge.

CHAPTER TEN

The Board's Role in Corporate Crises

Mark B. Nadler

⟶∿⟵ **K**enneth W. Freeman, the chairman and CEO of Quest Diagnostics Inc., was flying back to New Jersey from meetings in Mexico City the afternoon of February 14, 2002, when his assistant reached him aboard the corporate jet. Could Mr. Freeman, who also served as chairman of the compensation committee at TRW Inc., meet right away to discuss a "time-sensitive matter" with David M. Cote, TRW's chairman and chief executive?

At 3:45 P.M., the jet landed at Teterboro Airport, and Freeman walked across the street to Quest Diagnostics' corporate headquarters for his unscheduled meeting with Cote. This wasn't how Freeman had planned to spend the afternoon; his attention was focused on the final round of negotiations involving a major acquisition on the West Coast. But Cote's message had sounded urgent.

At 4 P.M., the two men sat down in the conference room adjoining Freeman's office, and Cote delivered the news: after just one year as head of TRW, Cote had agreed to succeed Larry Bossidy as CEO of Honeywell. The Honeywell board had approved the decision, and wanted to make a public announcement the next morning.

Freeman was stunned. Up until that moment, no one at TRW had any idea that Cote was thinking about leaving. The timing couldn't have been worse. TRW, after a long slump, was just beginning to benefit from the streamlining of its automotive and aerospace businesses, but its success was far from certain. What's more, just one year into Cote's tenure, there was no designated successor to fill the suddenly vacant CEO slot.

After Cote left, Freeman's first calls were to TRW's corporate secretary and senior vice president for HR. He asked them to call the board members, tell them the news, and arrange for a board conference call early the next afternoon; then he asked the two men to requisition a TRW plane and fly from Cleveland to Teterboro for an 8 A.M. meeting the following day.

At 9 the next morning, Freeman reached Larry Bossidy and persuaded him to delay Honeywell's announcement until the following week. He worked with the two TRW staff people until 1 P.M., when he got on the call with the board, and presented them with several alternatives for an interim CEO. The board agreed with Freeman's recommendation for the job, and then named Freeman—who had been on the board for less than a year, and chairman of the compensation committee for only two months—to be lead director.

Honeywell and TRW made their announcements on February 19. Freeman and the interim CEO met with TRW's senior executives to explain the situation. TRW's share price plunged 30 percent on the news of Cote's departure, but for the moment, it seemed, the board's quick action had averted almost certain chaos.

Unfortunately, students of corporate crises are well aware of a cruel fact: the first crisis is almost always followed by a second. In TRW's case, it was a genuine double whammy. Just three days later, Northrop Grumman Corp. announced a tender offer for TRW—an offer that, after being rebuffed by the board, turned into a prolonged hostile takeover bid. After maneuvering by the TRW board resulted in a much sweetened offer, TRW was acquired by Northrop in December 2002.

"In the end, everybody was happy with the way it turned out, including the shareholders," Freeman said two years later. (Freeman retired from Quest Diagnostics in 2004 and joined venture capital firm KKR as a managing director the following year.)

THE BOARD'S INDISPENSABLE ROLE

Looking at the TRW crisis, it's impossible to fathom how the situation could have been managed as well if the board and its leaders hadn't played such a central role. And yet, if you were to search through the existing library of standard "bibles" on crisis management, you'd be hard-pressed to find any serious discussion of the board's role. At best, there's some obligatory reference to the board on the list of stakeholders that the CEO should touch base with during a lull in the real action.

Indeed, conventional thinking on crisis management closely mirrors the traditional views of the CEO and the board. There's an implicit assumption that crisis management is all about the CEO donning a Superman cape and single-handedly defending the corporation. That view was always simplistic; in today's world, it's irrelevant.

As we'll discuss in this chapter, there are several reasons why empowered boards and smart CEOs are coming to realize that boards have such an important role to play, not just when a crisis erupts but during the preparation and recovery stages as well (see Figure 10.1).

To begin with, the board can add real value in the emerging area of *enterprise risk management,* the essential first steps toward identifying the potential sources of crises and taking action to either prevent them or mitigate their consequences. "The upsurge in compliance reminded us of our risk management responsibilities—that is, how are we doing managing risk from all sources," explained a member of the NACD Blue Ribbon Commission on Board Leadership. "A more effective board today has a broader radar screen, and they look at things sooner rather than later."

Second, the old CEO-centric approach to crisis management overlooked the reality that in many situations—TRW is just one example— the CEO, far from providing the cure, is actually the cause. A CEO's disastrous performance, illegal activities, or sudden departure, due to resignation, poor health, or even death, automatically casts the board in a lead role that needs to be understood, thoroughly planned, and carefully executed.

Third, even during crises when the CEO remains fully in charge, the board has an important role to play. It exercises oversight in reviewing and influencing the CEO's crisis management plans. It also provides the CEO with a sounding board, a source of support, and a wealth of insight and guidance based on the directors' personal experiences with crises and expertise in specialized areas—investment banking, legal issues, or investor relations, for example—that might be particularly relevant in a given situation.

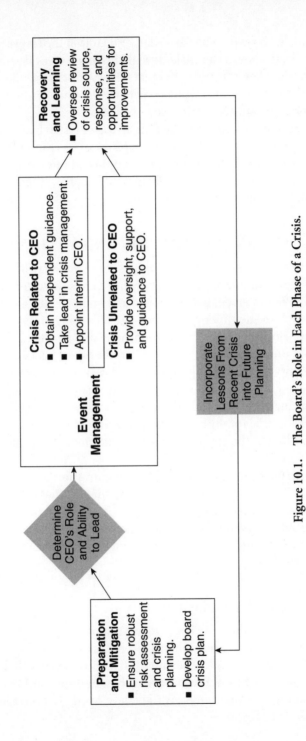

Figure 10.1.   The Board's Role in Each Phase of a Crisis.

Fourth, the board can be particularly valuable in the recovery stage. Specifically, the board can make sure that management doesn't miss the limited window of opportunity that follows any crisis to thoroughly explore any organizational weaknesses that might have caused the crisis or hampered efforts to effectively manage it.

After examining each of those four areas, we'll step back and consider the implications for the board in terms of its composition and leadership. Just saying the board has an important role to play in each of the four areas won't automatically make it happen without the right mix of skills, experience, and leadership.

CRISIS PREPARATION AND MITIGATION

The board's crisis-related responsibilities come into play long before a crisis erupts. An important aspect of the board's fiduciary role is to ensure that management has developed and implemented a robust set of processes for identifying potential risks, flagging and addressing problems before they reach crisis proportions, and managing unavoidable crises once they occur. Beyond that, the board bears particular responsibility for developing its own crisis management procedures. And together, the CEO and the board share responsibility for fostering a working relationship that will serve them well during a crisis.

First, it's crucial for the board and management to develop a shared understanding of the appropriate scope and intensity of the board's involvement.

"In both boards that I'm on," said one commission member, "there is some form of a matrix of issues, with a sense of what is the probability of the issues occurring and what are the potential consequences of that event. . . . Even there, however, we recognize that the board's job is not to manage these issues but to make sure that management is effectively dealing with them."

Risk Management

Without question, the CEO has primary responsibility for enterprise risk management, a comprehensive process for identifying and addressing the full range of seriously disruptive events that could threaten the institution. But the board has an important oversight role—making sure the process is fully developed, well thought out, and regularly updated.

Increasingly, boards are getting actively involved in the risk identification process. As one commission member described it, that process requires the board to ask, "What is the worst thing that could happen to us as an organization and what are we doing to prepare for that? What is management doing to prepare for that, and what kind of oversight strategies and processes will the board follow?"

Boards can contribute real value by prodding management to stretch its thinking about the potential sources of corporate crisis. "Risk management today has gone way beyond 'the CEO may have a heart attack,'" said one commission member. "It requires that we look on an ongoing basis at our exposure on a number of fronts, such as human resources, products, operating parameters, reputational risk, environmental risk, and so on."

Risk management, much like CEO evaluation, succession planning, and strategy development, is an area where "appropriate engagement" by the board translates into "real work" rather than perfunctory approval. To be effective, the board has to roll up its sleeves and understand the nuts and bolts of the business it oversees.

For example, said one commission member, "In one of my companies, products are being made in China. So we have had to pay attention to the longshoreman issues on the West Coast, because developments there can very negatively impact the ability of the business to deliver. We need to anticipate contingency plans. This means good boards are probing deeper into the businesses their company runs, and developing a deeper understanding of how they operate."

Differentiating Types of Crises

Several members of the Blue Ribbon Commission took the tough stance, as one put it, that "once there is a crisis, the board has already failed." That's true in some cases, but not always.

The fact is, there are all sorts of crises; some are preventable, some aren't. To be sure, many crises are of a company's own making, resulting from sins of commission or omission. In those cases, the board certainly has a role to play in crisis prevention and clear accountability for failing to faithfully execute its fiduciary duties. A good many crises are "slow boils," developing gradually, over time, with plenty of opportunities for an alert board to step in and take corrective action.

"Apart from something like the Tylenol scandal," said a commission member, "most crises don't start as crises, they start as problems. A problem that isn't dealt with immediately can become a crisis. It's like that saying, 'Problems are like ice cream cones—if you don't lick them, they can become a real mess.'" But sometimes the ice cream doesn't melt; it just falls out of the cone without any warning.

Based on Mercer Delta's study of corporate crises, we tend to view them in four categories, depending on whether they originated inside or outside the company, and whether they developed gradually or abruptly (see Figure 10.2):

- *Gradual emergence, external origin:* These might involve economic downturns, the emergence of new competitive threats such as breakthrough technologies, new go-to-market strategies, alliances of major competitors, or regulatory changes that limit business practices or expand competition.

- *Gradual emergence, internal origin:* Examples range from strategic mistakes (such as a poorly conceived or executed merger or acquisition) to failed product launches, the loss of key talent to competitors, and employee discrimination suits. We also put many, but not all, CEO succession crises into this category,

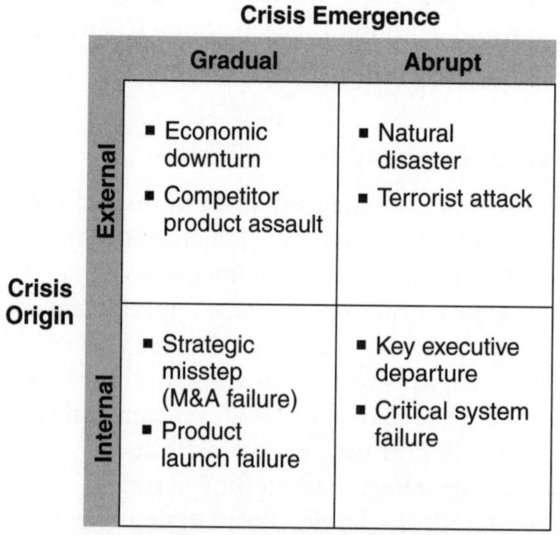

Crisis Emergence

		Gradual	Abrupt
Crisis Origin	External	■ Economic downturn ■ Competitor product assault	■ Natural disaster ■ Terrorist attack
	Internal	■ Strategic misstep (M&A failure) ■ Product launch failure	■ Key executive departure ■ Critical system failure

Figure 10.2.   Crisis Types.

since the absence of strong internal candidates usually results from years of inattention.

- *Abrupt emergence, external origin:* Some of the most obvious examples are natural disasters, terrorist attacks, and product tampering.

- *Abrupt emergence, internal origin:* This can include the sudden death or resignation of one or more key executives, failure of critical technology, production, or delivery systems, or workplace violence.

These categories provide CEOs and boards with a simple framework for understanding and preparing for vastly different categories of crises, because, in fact, different types of crises require very different types of preparation and response. For instance, in the case of a gradually emerging crisis, a robust risk management process would send up red flags in plenty of time for the company either to avoid the problem entirely or to take corrective action before it develops into a full-blown crisis. The abrupt crises are more problematic—there's nothing companies could have done to stop the 9/11 attacks. No one can predict a terrorist attack, or for that matter, an earthquake, plane crash, shooting spree by a disgruntled employee, or a CEO's sudden decision to quit and go to work for a competitor. But sound planning can help the company mitigate the consequences and speed the recovery.

The board's oversight duty doesn't end with the development of a risk identification process and a crisis management plan. It's not enough to have a good plan that sits on a shelf collecting dust. One lesson from 9/11 is that when disaster struck, many companies dug out their crisis management plans and quickly realized they were hopelessly out-of-date. Emergency calling trees were filled with names of people who hadn't been with the company for years. Technology backup plans were designed for obsolete systems. Important phone numbers had been changed. At one major newspaper, back in the 1980s, editors gathered early one Sunday morning for a crisis drill at the site of an underground emergency newsroom, only to find that no one could remember who was supposed to have the key.

The board has an obligation to ensure that management regularly reviews, updates, and practices all aspects of crisis planning, everything from risk assessment to emergency succession plans to departmental calling trees. "Board leadership is not crisis management. That's more management's job," said one commission member. "It's what comes before a crisis occurs."

The Board's Crisis Management Plan

One of the board's unique responsibilities is putting together its own crisis management plan; no one else can do that. And that begins with an understanding of the different roles the board might be called on to play depending on management's role in the crisis. One former CEO on the commission summarized it this way: "There are two types of corporate crises: The first is a corporate crisis where the CEO is clearly the person handling the situation—such as a hostile takeover, a product issue, etc. In that situation, the role of the board is to be there to help the CEO behind the scenes and not to get in front of the public or usurp the CEO's ability to manage. The second is a corporate crisis where the CEO is the problem, such as a fraud scandal. In the latter situation, the board has to get out in front of the issues. The role of the board leadership in that type of situation is to keep the board together, hire the outside advisers you need, and play a more visible public role."

As we'll discuss in more detail, the board faces a particularly complex situation—and has an especially critical role to play—when the CEO is the source of the crisis. That requires detailed planning about the specific role of board leaders and individual directors. It requires frequently updated lists of outside resources the board can call on for independent guidance on legal, financial, or public relations issues. It requires a clear understanding of who is authorized to speak publicly on the board's behalf, and under what circumstances.

The board's planning for its own crisis role is just as important as management's. It demands the same attention to detail, periodic review, and occasional practice—for instance, to ensure that every director can be reached at a moment's notice. The board needs to be absolutely clear about how it will be organized during a crisis, which members have particular expertise that might be of use in various crisis situations, and who will take the lead in dealing with management. Ideally, all of this should be planned well in advance.

"The issue is being ready as a board to respond to a crisis because you don't know what it will be," said a commission member. "Leaders must take their boards through steps to prepare and establish clear ground rules about what board members should and should not do when a crisis comes."

Building on Existing Relationships

The final aspect of crisis preparation has less to do with creating plans and more to do with building relationships.

A basic tenet of crisis management is that it's crucial, long before a crisis happens, for the company to build strong relationships with key groups because the crisis will inevitably strain those relationships. For example, if a company hasn't established its credibility with the press or government regulators or community leaders, there's no reservoir of trust or goodwill to draw on during a crisis and the ensuing rush to judgment.

The same is true of the relationship between the CEO and the board. Unless they've already built a solid working relationship based on trust and open communications, they'll quickly find that it's impossible to suddenly create that relationship in a crisis atmosphere.

"If you've been sensitive and open with your board and laid that sort of foundation in working with them, it will particularly help you in the way they'll respond and support you through a crisis situation," said one board chairman on the commission. "If you haven't built that kind of relationship with them and a corporate crisis occurs, then it's too late."

One commission member recalled sitting on the board of a successful company: "At the board meetings management basically numbed us with detail, and then rolled us out. But when they stumbled, everyone on the board had a lot of pent-up desire to jump on them. I think it was because they had never given us, the board members, a chance to really feel that we were a part of it. The board made them pay for it when the crisis came."

CRISES INVOLVING THE CEO

In most crisis situations, the board has an important but clearly secondary role to play; the CEO is the chief crisis manager and communicator, and the board operates in the background to provide oversight, advice, and support.

But when the CEO is the cause of the crisis, it's a whole different ball game. That's when the board takes center stage and assumes the full burden of safeguarding the interests of the institution and its shareholders. More than at any other time, said one commission member, "that's when you need an independent board member to take a leadership role in addressing the situation."

That situation can arise for a host of reasons. The most obvious is the CEO's death or sudden departure for health reasons; in 2004, McDonald's had the misfortune to experience both situations in rapid succession. The CEO might resign without any warning, as we saw in the TRW case. Or, as seems to be happening with increasing frequency, a CEO accused of malfeasance might give up the job, as in the case of Martha Stewart, or be forced out, like Conrad Black, the newspaper tycoon accused of looting the coffers of Hollinger International.

But things aren't always so clear-cut, and sometimes the board's first duty is to determine whether the crisis creates a real or potential conflict between management's interests and the company's.

One example might be a hostile takeover bid that could cost top executives their jobs but still be in the shareholders' best interests. Another might be the kind of situation our parent company, Marsh & McLennan, experienced in 2004. (The Mercer family of consulting firms, to which Mercer Delta belongs, is part of Marsh & McLennan, along with the Marsh insurance brokerage business and Putnam investment funds.) Eliot Spitzer, the New York State attorney general, filed a civil suit accusing the company of illegal business practices and clearly signaled his refusal to engage in any settlement discussions until the company replaced its top leaders. That placed the board squarely between a rock and a hard place. It had to choose between abandoning a CEO who hadn't been accused, let alone convicted, of any personal wrongdoing, or standing aside while Spitzer filed criminal charges against the corporation, which, for all intents and purposes, would have resulted in the company's immediate collapse and put nearly sixty thousand employees out of work.

What followed was a textbook case on how a board should handle a crisis involving the CEO. First, the board retained its own legal counsel, separate from management's. It launched an independent internal investigation into the charges contained in Spitzer's civil suit. As reported in the *Wall Street Journal*, a small group of independent directors met with Spitzer to gauge the seriousness of the situation, a meeting quickly followed by CEO Jeffrey Greenberg's decision to resign and the board's appointment of a new CEO.[1] The board quickly reorganized, with the resignation of all management directors except the CEO. Robert Erburu, chairman of the directors and governance committee, was formally named to the lead director role he had been filling on an informal basis and ultimately was appointed nonexecutive chairman. With new management in place, the company was eventually able to reach a settlement with Spitzer and begin to put the crisis behind it.

In such situations, only the board can exercise the leadership so essential to maintaining the stability of the company and retaining the confidence of employees, customers, and the financial markets. It's hard to imagine any other situation in which the board plays such an essential role.

Every board should have a detailed plan for dealing with the sudden and unexpected loss of the CEO that answers questions such as these:

- Within the current leadership team, is there an obvious choice for interim or permanent CEO, and if so, who would fill that executive's current role?

- If the CEO also serves as chairman, has one of the directors been designated to serve as interim chairman?

- Is there a plan to deal with the sudden loss of the company's top three executives? Are there policies in place that prevent the top officers from traveling together?

- Are there emergency succession plans for other top officers, such as the chief finance officer and chief operating officer, and has the board had an opportunity to become familiar with those who would step into those roles in an emergency?

Once emergency succession plans for the CEO and other top officers have been developed and agreed on by the board and the CEO, they should be reviewed and updated at least once a year, or at any other time when a change in top management would affect such plans.

SUPPORTING AND ADVISING THE CEO

Most corporate crises are not about the CEO, allowing the chief executive to shoulder the primary responsibility for leading the institution, marshaling the company's internal resources, maintaining continuity and morale, and communicating both inside and outside the company.

That doesn't mean the board's role is to step aside and hope for the best. The board still has an obligation to stay involved in a number of ways: approving key decisions, providing the CEO with a confidential sounding board, giving informed advice based on directors' previous crisis experience or special expertise, and demonstrating confidence in the CEO and support for management's efforts to navigate the crisis.

Of course, once a crisis hits, nothing is neat and clean; the path to successful crisis management inevitably involves trade-offs. It requires a good-faith effort on the part of both management and the board, balancing sometimes conflicting needs for speed and decisiveness as well as collaboration and consensus. "In a crisis like an environmental disaster, things are occurring so fast that you need split-second decision making, and the CEO doesn't have time to call a board meeting," said one commission member. "In that situation, the CEO, as leader, has to move as fast as possible, but then keep the board informed about what happened, what was done, etc."

One reality of a corporate crisis is that the need for communication between the CEO and the board is most intense just when the time available is most limited. It generally makes sense for the board to designate a small number of directors to be the primary touch point with the CEO. In some cases, it might be the lead director and the chair of a board committee directly involved with the substance of the crisis. Or there might be a mechanism in place for leaders to quickly create a special crisis group within the board. Whatever the specifics, this is an area where the value of precrisis planning becomes readily apparent; these aren't issues the board should be thinking about for the first time in the chaotic hours after a crisis has erupted.

Having said that, it remains important for the CEO to communicate as frequently as possible with the entire board, either collectively or individually. Throughout the crisis, the CEO has to take the lead, but without getting so far out in front that the board loses sight of what the CEO is planning or doing. One commission member who led his company through a major crisis described his own experience:

"In a crisis situation we went through, we made a real effort to bring the board into how we were addressing it so that they quickly became convinced that management was all over this situation. We laid out the various things we were looking at that we had to deal with it. We had telephonic board meetings to keep the lines of communication open, and the chairman also reached out to individual board members. We were all surprised when the crisis arose, but after the initial shock of the situation, the board was never surprised by anything that happened after that because we kept them well-informed all along. They were incredibly supportive of management and what they were going through."

The constant communication between the CEO and the board serves several purposes. At the most basic level, the CEO has to keep the board informed as events unfold. Beyond that, the CEO should be discussing with the board the alternative courses of action, some of which might require the board's formal approval—or at the very least, its informal support. "The leader should be on the phone with the board or sending them e-mails all the time—hour-by-hour, day-by-day updates," said one commission member. "That does two things: it gives board members the confidence that things are being addressed, and it also conveys that the board has an important role to play, that they are intimately involved."

That involvement provides value in another way: it gives the CEO the benefit of the board's collective experience with crises at other companies. That experience is more valuable than you might think. Companies are rarely hit with the same kind of crisis more than once over a short period of time, for two reasons. First, most crises are, by definition, aberrations, sharp departures from normal circumstances; second, after the first incidence of a particular kind of crisis, the company takes preventive measures that lessen the odds of that crisis recurring any time soon. The result is that most crises involve a set of circumstances that the current management team has never encountered before, at least in the same company.

If the board's membership is sufficiently diverse, with collective experience in a broad range of companies and industries, the odds are good that they bring to the table a set of relevant experiences that go beyond those of the CEO and the management team. For example, one commission member cited the actions of the CEO of a major utility company that experienced an equipment malfunction that resulted in the death of an employee in public view. "He got on the phone with all of the directors immediately," he recalled. "That way, they're not only informed, but if you make this round of ten calls, as CEO you'll get the benefit of their experience in solving problems like this one and getting advice."

There was a broad consensus among commission members that the key element of communication during crisis periods is absolute candor. "Don't put your head in the sand when a problem arises; get it out with truth and honesty and don't mince your words," said one commission member. "Your board is there to advise you—they may have seen something similar to this before and can give you some ideas on how to deal with it."

RECOVERY AND LEARNING

One of the timeworn clichés of crisis management is that the Chinese word for "crisis" incorporates two characters—one meaning "threats," the other "opportunities." This observation gets trotted out to support the notion that the recovery phase of a crisis presents a unique opportunity for the organization to learn from its mistakes.

If only it were true.

Yes, that window of opportunity for learning and change does open in the wake of a crisis. But experience and research tell us that the window stays open for just a brief time, and usually slams shut before the important lessons have been learned and the most essential changes have been made. So, before the crisis fades into the hazy mists of corporate memory, the board has one final role to play: working with the CEO to ensure that the lessons have been learned, and most importantly, translated into action.

"After the immediate crisis has passed," one commission member recommended, "board leadership needs to raise and see that the board discusses the long-term implications of the crisis. What created the failure that caused this problem to occur? What is the long-term impact of this problem? These things need to get on the board agenda."

Not only that, they also need to get on the board agenda quickly. Here's why.

As illustrated in Figure 10.3, each phase of a crisis—from preparation through event management and recovery—is characterized by distinctly different time frames that either expand or limit the range of options available for consideration. For example, during the earliest stages of preparation, there are no time constraints; planners have the luxury of considering the widest possible range of alternatives under stable conditions conducive to expansive thinking. During a gradually emerging crisis, the list of options inevitably narrows as the disruptive event draws closer. And when a sudden crisis erupts, the available options—and, very literally, our capacity to think creatively—become severely limited in the face of imminent disaster.

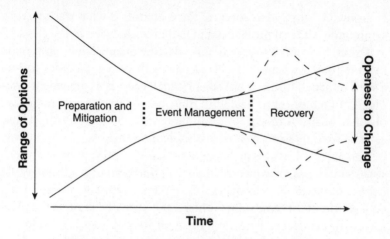

Figure 10.3. Options and Openness to Change.

The same holds true for the recovery phase. The conventional thinking is that this is an ideal time for an organization to learn from experience. In reality, the opportunity for collective introspection and improvement is surprisingly brief. The organization quickly loses its appetite for Big Questions and Big Answers. Why? Because there is an inevitable organizational imperative to regain normalcy, calm, and control. People—and management in particular—share an intense desire to put the crisis behind them. Left uncontrolled, that drive to normalcy will overwhelm all but the most diligent efforts to dig deep into the root causes of the crisis or to learn how the organization might function differently.

Case in point: on March 27, 1987, a ferry crossing the English Channel from Belgium to Dover capsized just moments after leaving the port of Zeebrugge, drowning 273 passengers and crew. The owner, P&O Ltd., quickly concluded that the cause was obvious: a crewman was sleeping on duty and had failed to close the loading doors through which vehicles drove from the dock onto the ferry. However, a more thorough examination by outsiders turned up nearly a dozen other contributing causes, ranging from excessively long work shifts to high turnover among officers to instability inherent in the ferry's design. Over time, researchers deepened their analysis, finding that the ferocious competition among Channel ferry operators had forced companies to cut costs by reducing crew sizes, stretching their passenger capacity, and speeding the loading and unloading processes. In other words, the official crisis review stopped as soon as it had identified what was merely a symptom of the real problems that had inexorably led to the crisis.[2]

Driven by a desire to regain normalcy, the organization seizes upon the most obvious causes of a crisis, paving the way for a quick fix and a swift return to business as usual. Human error is a convenient finding; it's much easier to deal with than system error, bad strategy, an obsolete business model, or a fundamentally flawed culture. Those can't be fixed by firing a worker who slept on the job.

The potential lessons go beyond the cause or prevention of the crisis; in some cases, they involve important things an organization could learn about itself from its own crisis response. Typically, a crisis brings on a period of "organizational unfreezing"; for a brief time, the place is run differently. Leaders might be more accessible and communicative than they were before, on-site managers might have unusual freedom to make decisions, bureaucratic procedures might be bypassed in the interest of speed and efficiency, and so on. After the immediate danger has passed, it's common for people to step back and say, "You know, this could be a very different place. We don't have to go back to the way we were."

But they almost always do. It takes a powerful countervailing force—like the board—to withstand the organization's powerful drive to regain equilibrium at any cost. This is a time when the board can demonstrate its independence, leadership, and value to the organization by resisting the rush to normalcy and insisting that management stop and learn the most important lessons from its recent brush with disaster.

IMPLICATIONS FOR THE BOARD

In the final analysis, thorough risk assessment and a well-thought-out crisis management plan are essential but not enough to ensure the board will play its proper role. The final ingredient is board composition and leadership—the right mix of skills, experience, and availability. In its periodic self-assessments, the board should always be looking at its composition through the prism of crisis planning and asking whether it has the right people in the right roles.

The First Requirement: Availability

Many commission members expressed a very practical concern: when a major crisis erupts, board members—or at least some of them—have to be willing to drop everything and wade knee-deep into crisis management. And for some on the commission, that raises a concern about how many seats on each board should be filled by active CEOs, who might be unable to ignore their "day jobs" when a board they sit on becomes embroiled in a major crisis.

"When a crisis comes up, the most important factor is time," said one commission member. "Active CEOs make great directors, but they seldom have the time to really get involved in a crisis situation. So you have to make sure there are people on the board who can devote the time if something like that happens." Another commission member cited a particularly extreme example: "A crisis arose at a company where the board members were all CEOs of other companies and did not have the time to deal directly with the problem, so they all resigned to make room for others. A lot of knowledge and history of the company was lost right at a time when you needed it."

A closely related issue involves membership on multiple boards. "One of the reasons you really need to limit the number of boards you serve on is because of the demands on a board member in a crisis situation," suggested one commission member. "One board I was on that had a crisis had weekly meetings, then scaled back to monthly meetings, but those were in addition to regular board meetings. You really have to roll up your sleeves in that situation and you have to devote a lot of time."

Crisis Leadership for the Board

One phenomenon that makes crisis management so difficult is that crises often require executives and managers to behave in unaccustomed ways, or to demonstrate skills they don't normally need. The same is true of the board's leadership. As one commission member succinctly put it, "There is a big difference between being a board leader in good times and in bad times, such as a corporate crisis."

One result, for both management and boards, is that during crises, leaders sometimes emerge from unexpected places; certain people, due to a combination of skills, experience, and temperament, step up to the plate and emerge as natural leaders regardless of their normal place in the hierarchy. It's hard to predict with total accuracy who those people might be, but you can certainly increase the odds that they will be there when you need them by purposefully seeding board leadership positions with directors who fit the basic requirements for crisis leadership.

Many times, directors are chosen for leadership positions because of their skills as facilitators and consensus builders. That works fine until a crisis comes along—particularly one involving a CEO who is also chairman. Suddenly, there's a gaping vacuum that must be filled by a board leader whose strengths are speed, decisiveness, courage, and the ability to both analyze and explain a complex situation. The person you'd want leading the board in a crisis, said one commission member, "is not always the person you would have picked to be the board leader in good times." Consequently, the board's leaders should collectively possess a range of leadership styles and skills, including those that might be needed most during a crisis.

A second important requirement is crisis experience. There's nothing like a crisis to prepare you for a crisis. Board leaders who have been there before "can draw on their experience and they know some of the challenges you are going to face," one commission member explained.

The third requirement is psychological independence, which goes far beyond the legal definition of an "independent director." As a crisis develops—or erupts—someone on the board has to be ready to call the question as to whether management is the cause of the problem or whether management has an inherent conflict that requires the board to step in and take the lead. And someone has to ask whether it's time for the board to retain its own professional advisers, rather than relying on guidance from the same in-house and external resources that management would normally place at the board's disposal. As one commission member explained, "A crisis situation really tests your independence as a board member, formulating an independent view on the situation rather than just relying on management."

The final requirement is experience in senior corporate management. This brings us back to the question of CEOs on the board. We fully agree that a board overloaded with active CEOs will find itself at a disadvantage. Nevertheless, in crisis situations there's no substitute for having directors in leadership positions who have had CEO experience. Consider two of the crisis situations we've already discussed, TRW and Marsh & McLennan. In the first, it was a sitting CEO—the chair of TRW's compensation committee—who quickly assumed a leading role in guiding TRW through its dual crises. In the Marsh & McLennan situation, it was the retired CEO of Times Mirror Corp.—the chair of the MMC's directors and governance committee—who took the initiative when it became clear that management would be unable to resolve the crisis.

"You need somebody with operational experience," says Ken Freeman of his TRW crisis experience. "It requires a sense of urgency, and an appreciation of the risk and potential damage. Without thinking about it, I treated TRW as if it were my own company; I guess I acted like a CEO. But at the same time, I had to be careful about how I presented things to the board, and was careful to get their approval before I acted. If it had looked like I was taking over the company, there would have been a mutiny."

All of that suggests how important it is for the board, as a key element of its own crisis preparedness, to make every effort to have at least one person with CEO experience in a leadership role, ready to step forward should a crisis occur.

SUMMARY

From one perspective, nearly all of the board's "normal" duties involving the oversight of the company's financial performance and the CEO's personal performance have the underlying intent of helping the organization to avoid a wide range of preventable crises. So many of the corporate scandals of recent years came to pass because boards were "asleep at the switch." In some cases, they simply failed to take the time or effort to understand the financials, business models, and strategies that should have raised red flags and caused them to ask management some serious questions. And a board that's actively engaged in the work discussed in three other chapters—CEO succession, corporate strategy, and CEO appraisal—will have achieved a sufficient level of familiarity with the business to help the CEO address problems before they become crises, and to have a succession plan in place should the CEO's position suddenly become vacant.

Nevertheless, the board has a number of very specific roles to play in the areas of risk assessment, crisis planning, and organizational recovery. When it comes to crises, the quality of the board's involvement can literally make the difference between the organization's ultimate failure or success.

CHAPTER ELEVEN

Board Assessment

Beverly A. Behan

oard assessment is both a critical opening step and concluding phase of the board-building framework. Done well, it provides a fantastic opportunity for boards to monitor their progress and renew their commitment to doing good work. Done badly, as we're about to see, it can turn into a mechanical exercise that tests the board's patience and creates little or no value.

One of America's best CEOs was ready to call it quits. He was widely recognized for leading a dramatic turnaround, which in less than a decade took a sleepy consumer goods company from the brink of bankruptcy to an enviable position at the top of its industry. Yet, just when he should have been basking at the pinnacle of his career, he was seriously thinking about cleaning out his desk. Why? Because his board was driving him crazy.

Let's be clear—this wasn't the case of an imperial CEO feeling stymied by an engaged board. On the contrary, he was bothered by the board's persistent "off-the-wall" questions, lack of understanding of the industry, and chronic micromanagement. In fact, one of his biggest concerns, and the reason he called us for help, involved his successor. "I cannot in good conscience leave Susan this board," he said. "They'll drive her nuts. But more importantly, I want to leave her a board that can really help her when she becomes CEO, a top-notch team that gives her solid advice, tells her when she's on shaky ground, and challenges her thinking. If I don't do that, I'll have done her a disservice."

We quickly recommended conducting a board assessment—and just as quickly, were almost shown the door. "A board assessment?" the CEO roared. "We've been doing that! Give me a minute and I'll show you the long form that everybody fills out once a year. Guess what it tells us? It says everything with our board is just fine and dandy."

His frustration was well-founded, and by no means unique. Since the NYSE made annual board assessment a listing requirement in 2002, just about every board of a publicly traded U.S. company has complied with the requirement. But this issue, perhaps more than any other, illustrates that minimum compliance with the technical requirements of good governance has little to do with substantively improving a board's effectiveness.

Rather than a robust and rigorous process that helps boards figure out whether they're doing the right work in the right way, we far too often see a mechanical exercise in ticking off the boxes on a formulaic checklist often borrowed from another company. A board can certainly get away with that and confidently report one more area where it complies with the NYSE rules. However, it will waste an opportunity if it does nothing to increase its effectiveness or value to the company and its stakeholders. As one member of the NACD Blue Ribbon Commission on Board Leadership stated, "The whole point of a board assessment is that your focus has to be on improvement of the board, rather than giving them a report card."

In reality, almost every board could find ways to do its job better. Investing the necessary time and effort for continuous improvement is in fact a hallmark of an effective board.

When we finally reviewed the assessment form of the board we were just describing, we saw that it consisted mainly of a stock list of questions (rated on a five-point scale), such as whether the board's committees were in compliance with their charters. The thrust and format did nothing to raise any fundamental concerns about how the board spent its time, how effectively it took action or made decisions, or how constructively its members interacted with each other or with management.

To be sure, the checklist satisfied the NYSE requirements. But as we explained to the CEO, it was a totally inadequate tool for identifying and addressing the obstacles that prevent a good board from becoming great. Assessment can be a starting point for board improvement, but only if the board is prepared to design it appropriately and spend substantial time reviewing the findings and addressing the key issues that will make a real difference.

Too frequently we see board assessments that produce the same results that were driving this CEO to distraction—the conclusion that "we have no issues." More often than not, that result is a clear signal either that the assessment was designed badly or that the board has become so disengaged that it simply has no interest in talking about how to raise its game. Fortunately, if you fix the first problem, you can start to address the second. Most boards are composed of high achievers; continuous improvement is their mantra. Given a constructive forum in which to express their views and a reasonable expectation that their participation will yield results, they will almost always dig in and suggest ways to make their board better.

We started our work with this board by conducting confidential interviews with each director, covering all the key aspects of how a board works together and focusing on critical issues the board had addressed during the past year. As is almost always the case, the directors enjoyed the interviews. They, too, had concerns about how the board was working and its relationship with the CEO. And their point of view came across loud and clear: this wasn't a bad board, but rather a board that had developed some bad habits that were preventing it from being as good as it could be.

Our interviews unearthed three primary themes, which were addressed at a meeting of the full board, including the CEO. The first issue was board composition: no one, apart from the CEO, had any significant experience in this industry, nor were they planning to fill the gap by recruiting new members. To the contrary, since the board was already fairly large at thirteen directors, they were planning to use two impending retirements to shrink their membership. However, because the assessment identified the lack of industry expertise as a critical shortcoming, they put the issue back on the table.

The second issue was the vicious cycle the CEO and the board were caught up in. Directors complained that they weren't given enough information or education about the industry. The financial reports they regularly received were adequate as far as they went, but they included little information about competitors, market trends, or emerging technologies. Moreover, the board's involvement in corporate strategy was superficial at best. Generally, the CEO would come to the board with a finished strategic plan, give a forty-five-minute overview, and then ask the directors for their approval. The CEO pleaded guilty, explaining that the board was so ill-informed about the industry that he was leery of engaging them at any depth in strategy work. The assessment helped both sides understand there were things they could do to break the cycle.

The third issue was micromanagement, and this time it was the board's turn to plead guilty. They attributed this tendency to their rocky relationship with the previous CEO, who had driven the company into Chapter 11. They had little trust in his abilities and were forced to probe relentlessly to grasp the magnitude of the company's problems. Even though the current CEO had been on the job for seven years and had proved himself to be an extraordinarily successful manager, the board had become so locked into a micromanaging operating style that even new directors had adopted it because that was "the way this board seems to work." The assessment provoked an open discussion of the issue and an understanding that it was long past time for a change.

The discussions we just described led to real action; the CEO and the board prioritized the points of contention and mapped a plan for dealing with each one. We've gone into so much detail about them because they clearly illustrate our belief that board assessment, when done well, can accomplish much more than mere compliance with stock exchange listing requirements. It can be used as a platform to enhance the board's effectiveness both in their work together and with senior management.

In this chapter, we will consider the following issues, which can help maximize the impact of your annual board assessment and make it a fundamental part of your board-building:

- The role of board assessment in the context of board-building
- Three board assessment methodologies
- Assessing board committees
- Assessing the chairman or lead director
- Integrating management's perspective into board assessment

BOARD ASSESSMENT IN THE CONTEXT OF BOARD-BUILDING

Let's start by positioning board assessment in the larger context of building an effective board. If you think back to the board-building framework we presented in Chapter One, board assessment plays a vital role in two phases of this process: taking stock of the board and assessing quality of engagement (see Figure 11.1).

Taking Stock of the Board

The natural starting point in board-building is a board assessment. It should consist of an intense diagnosis of how individual directors— and frequently senior executives—perceive the board and how they feel about its working dynamics, the relationship between the board and management, and the board's ability to do productive and value-added work. As we suggested in Chapter One, it's impossible for any board to know which aspects of board-building to focus on without this initial snapshot of where the board stands today. This assessment will help answer two key questions: What are this board's acknowledged strengths? And where are there opportunities for improvement?

Assessing Quality of Engagement

Board assessment is also a critical component of the concluding phase of the board-building framework. Early on, the board uses an intensive diagnostic process to map the work it should be doing and to be explicit about what work is primarily the board's, what is primarily management's responsibility, and what ought to be shared by both. This initial board assessment provides the baseline for the annual assessment and generates the feedback the board can use to figure out how closely it has stuck to its original road map—and what value resulted from that work. Have the changes led to more effective board engagement on strategic issues, for example, or have they created another set of concerns? Are there other gaps appearing in board composition now that there are new directors with industry knowledge? This feedback allows the board to make necessary adjustments as it implements changes and learns from experience.

It can be burdensome—and frankly, unnecessary—to do an in-depth analysis every year. The objective at this concluding stage of assessing the quality of engagement is a "pulse check," not an intensive assessment. For example, the board that undertook the interview process outlined in the opening paragraphs conducted a short survey a year after its initial assessment. Even more informal processes, such as incorporating a "How are we doing?" discussion at the end of every executive session, can work well.

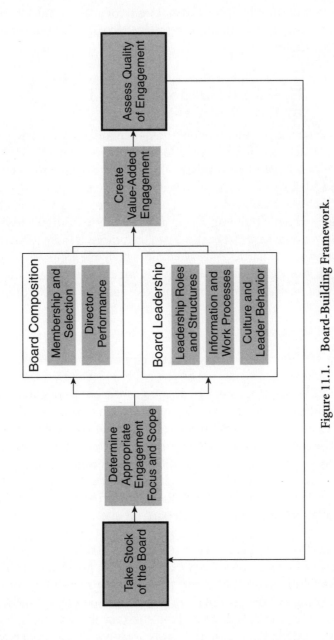

Figure 11.1. Board-Building Framework.

When designing a board assessment process and selecting an appropriate methodology, be aware of where you are in the board-boarding context. What you need and want for a taking-stock process is far different from what will be helpful when you close the feedback loop by assessing the quality of engagement.

THREE BOARD ASSESSMENT METHODOLOGIES

Three methodologies are commonly used to conduct board assessments: surveys, structured interviews, and focus groups (see Table 11.1). Each provides a different lens through which to view the board's performance and effectiveness. As already discussed, one methodology may be preferable to another depending on the goal of the assessment and the stage of board-building. Using a combination of these methodologies over time has two benefits. First, the process is more robust and interesting for the participants when more than one approach is used. Second, it also yields a richer data source, which is particularly important if your goal is to continuously enhance your board's effectiveness.

Surveys

Most boards use a survey to conduct their first board assessment.

HOW THEY WORK. With surveys, directors are asked to rate the board on a number of dimensions using a graded scale, and when appropriate, to provide a sentence or two in response to open-ended questions. The completed surveys are tabulated, analyzed, and summarized in a report by either an outside consultant or someone inside the organization, often the corporate secretary or general counsel. The summary report is usually shared with the full board and discussed either at a regular board meeting or at a board off-site.

ILLUSTRATION OF A SURVEY FEEDBACK REPORT. Exhibit 11.1 provides an excerpt of a board assessment feedback report for a bank that used a survey questionnaire. The report provides both an average score for each question and the percentage of favorable responses—namely, the number of respondents that rated the question either a four or a five on a five-point scale. It also highlights areas where directors have a wide range of views and where they are more cohesive. Written comments are summarized at the bottom of the page.

Table 11.1.   Board Assessment Methodologies.

	Quantitative: Survey	Qualitative: Structured Interviews	Qualitative: Focus Group
Description	Board members complete a written survey rating board performance on a numeric scale; results are discussed by full board in feedback session.	One-on-one interviews are conducted with each board member; results are discussed by full board in feedback session.	Trained consultants lead a group discussion of the full board; sessions are summarized in report for future use.
Strengths	• Participants are familiar with this straightforward, standard practice. • Can be completed at participants' convenience. • Can track a board's progress over time. • Feedback sessions often focus on generating additional information and insights to supplement the survey data. • Anonymity can be ensured.	• Participants become engaged in the interview process; most find it interesting and even enjoyable. • Information tends to be more detailed and complete than with a survey; is helpful in fully understanding the issues, setting priorities, and developing plans to address them. • Feedback sessions tend to be highly engaging. • Anonymity can be ensured.	• Participants find the process energizing, engaging. • Critical thinking is heightened because views are shared with everyone and participants can question each other. • Generates consensus on priorities and support for plans to address them. • Requires no preparation by participants. • Serves as a team-building exercise. • Most effective when there is a high degree of trust and openness among board members.

In this case, one major area for improvement emerged: the need for a better balance of presentation and discussion time in board meetings. Two other areas also required attention: whether the right items were getting onto board agendas, and whether board members were encouraged to raise different viewpoints.

PROS AND CONS. Surveys are ideal pulse-check tools to discern whether there is a need for course correction or further modifications to changes that may have been initiated as a result of a more comprehensive assessment.

Exhibit 11.1.   Illustration of Survey Feedback Report.

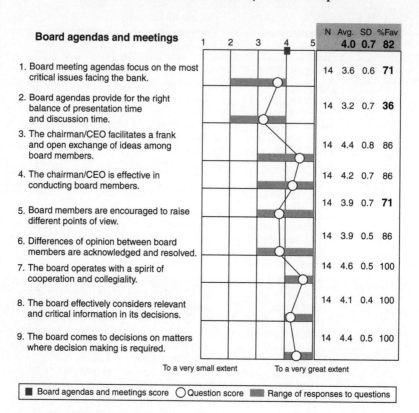

Board agendas and meetings

	N	Avg.	SD	%Fav
		4.0	**0.7**	**82**
1. Board meeting agendas focus on the most critical issues facing the bank.	14	3.6	0.6	**71**
2. Board agendas provide for the right balance of presentation time and discussion time.	14	3.2	0.7	**36**
3. The chairman/CEO facilitates a frank and open exchange of ideas among board members.	14	4.4	0.8	86
4. The chairman/CEO is effective in conducting board members.	14	4.2	0.7	86
5. Board members are encouraged to raise different points of view.	14	3.9	0.7	**71**
6. Differences of opinion between board members are acknowledged and resolved.	14	3.9	0.5	86
7. The board operates with a spirit of cooperation and collegiality.	14	4.6	0.5	100
8. The board effectively considers relevant and critical information in its decisions.	14	4.1	0.4	100
9. The board comes to decisions on matters where decision making is required.	14	4.4	0.5	100

To a very small extent   To a very great extent

■ Board agendas and meetings score   ○ Question score   ▬ Range of responses to questions

Comments on board agendas and meetings

- Board agenda planning needs more attention; more accurate agenda item time allotment and management by chairman may help. Use of vote master to identify action items on priorities may help flow.
- Chair and lead director should review draft agendas and ensure items and time frames are appropriate, including time needed for executive sessions.
- Board meetings are too long given activity level of committees. Should be more efficient. Board members need to read committee minutes.
- Chair must truncate routine items to ensure that strategic discussion items can be addressed without rushing or allowing meeting time to extend beyond planned time frame.
- Lack of adherence to meeting time frames on a routine basis is an issue for directors who are working in full-time positions. This will increase in importance as we attempt to recruit acting public company CEOs. The entire board must force itself to deal with matters efficiently and effectively and support the chair's efforts to keep us on track and on time.

Their main drawback, however, is that although they can focus attention on one or two major areas that received low ratings, they fail to unearth the underlying issues. For example, in Exhibit 11.1 there is a low score on the mix of presentation and discussion time, but it's unclear what's really going on. Do presentations eat up too much time rehashing material in the board books? Is agenda management the culprit? Does the quality of the presentations contribute to the problem? And what about the premeeting reading material? Unless directors are given the appropriate background material, it's not likely that presentation time in the boardroom can be significantly reduced. All of these issues would have to be explored at the board meeting where the assessment is reviewed in order to determine the real problems and how best to address them.

Supplementing or even replacing a board survey with another format that provides richer qualitative feedback, such as structured interviews or focus groups, can yield more useful insights into the underlying issues at the outset, producing better discussion and action planning when the full board meets to discuss the assessment results.

Structured Interviews

Confidential interviews with directors typically yield in-depth insights about the board's performance and key issues the board is working on.

HOW THEY WORK. One-on-one interviews are conducted in person or by phone and last about an hour. The interview questions are generally shared with the board members beforehand so they have time to reflect on the issues before they are asked to express their views. Although the interviews are structured to ensure that the core set of topics is covered with everyone, directors also have the opportunity to raise additional concerns. The interview format also allows for probes and follow-ups. After the interviews are completed, notes are compiled and analyzed by key themes. A summary report is shared with the full board before a working session where the feedback is discussed, either as part of a regular board meeting or at an off-site.

It can be useful to have a third party conduct the interviews—as was the case in the example outlined at the beginning of this chapter—at least occasionally. Board members are inevitably more candid when talking to third parties and are more apt to bring up unpleasant but unspoken issues. Moreover, capturing, summarizing, analyzing, and ultimately creating a detailed report of the interview comments is a tremendous amount of work. Few directors have the time—or the software—to do this well. Finally, if the interview process is used to "take stock" in a board-building process, experienced third parties can be helpful in many ways, including serving as a resource on how other boards have dealt with some of the issues that emerge from the assessment feedback.

ILLUSTRATION OF AN INTERVIEW SUMMARY FEEDBACK REPORT. Table 11.2 provides an excerpt from a board assessment feedback report for a financial services company that used confidential one-on-one interviews with each board member. The comments collected from the interviews were analyzed by key themes. Representative comments (without attribution) provide the flavor of the issues underlying each theme. This format also shows consistency of views by illustrating how prevalent each view is among the twelve directors.

PROS AND CONS. Confidential, one-on-one, structured interviews yield a rich mine of data. Most directors appreciate the added dimension that discussion provides, and the board sessions to discuss the feedback from the interviews tend to be highly engaging and interactive. There is a downside: interviews are time-consuming, and if an outside third party is used, usually more expensive. But more than any other process, confidential one-on-one interviews will yield the kinds of deep insights that are the catalyst for discussing real problems and searching for real solutions.

Table 11.2. Illustration of Interview Summary Feedback Report.

Areas for Improvement	Consistency	Illustrative Comments from Interviews
There is a lack of consensus about corporate strategy.	◗	I don't think there's a consensus on the board about where the company should go strategically. Some directors aren't convinced that the diversification strategy is the best one for the company. We need to talk more about this.
		I'm not completely sold on our strategic mission. Growth or diversification for the sake of diversification doesn't give you anything. Our diversification strategy has not really been that successful.

Areas for Improvement	Consistency	Illustrative Comments from Interviews
		I don't think the board really buys into the current strategy. The process that was used last time to try to get everyone on the same page around strategy was superb. At the end of that, the board members were all nodding their heads in the room, which suggested agreement with the strategy. After some time had elapsed, people started to stray from what they'd said at that session, but they didn't step up to the issue and dissent or express their views in the session. They just nodded as if in agreement.
		The board and management all have to get on the same page in terms of strategic direction for the company because otherwise we just use up a lot of energy unproductively. If management is unsure of where the board stands, they can be reluctant to apply the resources that are needed to move forward with the strategy.
Board information has somewhat improved but could be more succinct.	◗	In the past we have had a problem with board information being everything but the kitchen sink. I think efforts have been made to address that. The CFO has tried to get competitive comparisons and provides us with summary financial information and information on trends. There's still an awful lot of information, though, like 47 pages of statistical data for the investment committee, none of which is very meaningful. We need narrative highlights and summaries to make this material more manageable.
		The board information is getting better. We get quarterly results against plan and discuss the variances. Similar on the balance sheet. You still have to wade through them a bit. We get more than we need in terms of detail; we could use an executive summary.
		The type, format, and amount of information that the board receives before meetings has been changed, and I think, improved. There is a boatload of information, including analysts' reports and a lot of competitor information. The only criticism might be that there is too much raw data, and it could be synthesized more.

● 10 or more respondents   ◗ 6–9 respondents   ◖ 5 or fewer respondents

Board Focus Groups

As with structured interviews, the board focus-group methodology is driven by discussion.

HOW THEY WORK. An experienced facilitator, usually an outsider, leads a structured discussion of the board following a protocol consisting of questions specifically designed to focus on key parameters of board performance.

Depending on the size of the board, the session, which usually lasts sixty to ninety minutes, can be held with the whole board or two smaller groups. If the board has been subdivided, which is recommended for groups of eight or more, a feedback session consolidating the key themes of each group discussion is subsequently held with all the directors. When the full board meets, it prioritizes the issues that surfaced in the group session (or sessions), discusses alternatives to address the priority items, and agrees on how to move forward and in what time frame.

Board focus groups can be used effectively in conjunction with a survey, essentially adding a qualitative element that is more robust than write-in questions. Alternatively, the focus group methodology can be used as a stand-alone process.

Focus groups are the "new kid on the block" when it comes to board assessments. We first used this process in 2003 with two New York–based not-for-profit boards: Green Chimneys, a children's charity in Brewster, and Nyack Hospital in Nyack.[1]

Green Chimneys had used a survey-style board assessment in prior years. At the conclusion of the assessment process using a focus group, Rick MacRae, Green Chimneys' board president said, "Where the survey disclosed two areas that needed attention, it did not present solutions or a mechanism to arrive at a solution. The discussion that resulted after using the focus group approach yielded a direction and a process for solutions in a very time-efficient way."

Frank Borelli, chairman of the board of trustees of Nyack Hospital, also found the focus group approach far superior to a survey. "It gave each board member an opportunity to interact with their colleagues on a real-time basis and jointly build a prioritized agenda for the board to act on in the future," he said. "Within a year from the time we completed the process, we had already covered, in some form, most of the items on our priority list. It is clear to me that we wouldn't have made this kind of progress if we had relied solely on a survey. Further, the matters deliberated on by the board in these discussions and the outcomes developed have had a profound, positive effect on the operations of the hospital."

Since then, we have used board focus groups in both public and private company settings with equally positive results.

ILLUSTRATION OF ACTION PLAN RESULTING FROM A BOARD FOCUS GROUP. Exhibit 11.2 provides an excerpt of a board action plan that resulted from a group assessment. The plan was prepared to summarize

Exhibit 11.2.   Board of Trustees: Focus Group Action Plan.

Overview

At the November board meeting, the board discussed the summary report from the board assessment focus groups and prioritized key issues surfaced in the assessment discussions, namely, fundraising expectations for board members and the interface between the foundation board and the main board. The following is a summary of action plans developed in relation to these items at the November meeting.

Action plans

1. *Creating board member expectations*
   It was recommended that the executive committee put together a one- or two-page document outlining expectations for directors, including both attendance expectations and fundraising expectations. In developing expectations around fundraising, there seemed to be consensus that requiring a minimum contribution would not be an appropriate policy. Instead, the direction seemed to be an expectation that the foundation be one of the significant charities on the board members' list of charities to which they donate, that there be an expectation that board members attend one or two foundation functions every year, and that they participate in fundraising activities, leaving some discretion to individuals as to how they fulfill that fundraising expectation.
2. *Providing training, support, and alternatives to meet fundraising expectations*
   It was recommended that the fund development committee develop a training course-program for board members to provide them with some education about fundraising so that they are better able and better supported in their efforts. In addition, the fund development committee should provide board members with various ideas and alternatives for their participation in fundraising so that board members can choose to do their fundraising in a format that they are most comfortable with, whether that be selling advertising in a foundation publication or a table at the annual gala.
3. *Interface between the foundation board and the fund development committee*
   The executive director and the board chair have had conversations with legal counsel relative to the structuring and interface of the main board (and its fund development committee) with the foundation board and have determined that it is possible to have some overlapping membership so as to enhance the degree of alignment and communication between these two entities. The fund development committee will take the lead in working with the foundation board on creating these linkage points as well as alignment of the activities of the foundation board with the overall approach and objectives for fundraising.

discussions in the board meeting where results of the assessment focus groups were prioritized, discussed, and addressed.

PROS AND CONS. Focus groups require limited or no preparation by board members before the group meets. The group discussion—in which participants either build on each other's views or offer a contrary perspective—tends to foster consensus-building. This creates a common ground for setting board priorities and action plans, or at the very least generates a common understanding of different viewpoints. As a result, there is a stronger team-building element inherent in focus group assessments than in the survey and interview processes.

One drawback of the focus group approach compared with structured interviews is that directors are typically more candid about highly sensitive issues in confidential interviews. Interviews also allow more time to fully explore each director's view on key issues than is possible when six board members, for example, are all chiming in during a sixty-minute group session. Nevertheless, because of the collective nature of the dialogue, a focus group may yield better overall data about the board than a summary of individual interpretations, whether collected through surveys or interviews.

BOARD ASSESSMENT FEEDBACK SESSIONS

"Too many board assessments just result in pages of junk and charts that everybody just sticks into a folder at the end of the day and ignores," said one of the NACD Blue Ribbon commissioners. "The value of a board assessment is in the discussion, and however you do it, you need to design your board assessment in a way that can generate good discussions." These sentiments sum up one of the most critical aspects of an effective board assessment: an engaged discussion of the assessment results by the full board that leads to a prioritization of key issues and an action plan to address them.

Notably, in the 2003 USC/Mercer Delta Corporate Board Survey, only 25 percent of respondents indicated that their boards included action planning as a step in their assessment process. This suggests that the review of board assessment results—arguably the single most important aspect of the board assessment process—is cursory at best in many boardrooms. The outcome of the board discussion should be an action plan similar to the example shown in Exhibit 11.2, which outlines the key items the board plans to address. In addition, the plan needs to indicate how the issues will be addressed, who will assume responsibility for them, and what the time frame for achieving them will be. Once completed, the action plan should be reviewed either during executive sessions or perhaps quarterly by the board to monitor progress. As a Blue Ribbon commissioner said, "At every board meeting you say 'Here are the things we wanted to improve. Now, here's where we stand.'"

ASSESSMENT OF BOARD COMMITTEES

NYSE rules require not only an annual self-assessment of the board's performance but also an assessment of its key committees. The three methodologies previously outlined can be readily adapted for committee assessments; for example, if interviews are being conducted, questions on each board committee can be included. Similarly, if a survey is used for the board assessment, the questionnaire can include ratings on each board committee.

Focus groups work particularly well for board committees, which usually consist of three to five members, an ideal number for a structured discussion about performance. In a forty-five- to sixty-minute session, a board committee can generally cover all of the key parameters of its own operations in detail and still have time to prioritize areas for improvement and create an action plan. This discussion can be an excellent team-building exercise. It can be particularly effective with new or recently recomposed committees in which there is an emphasis on looking forward (for instance, How will we work together? What are our priorities?), rather than looking backward to assess past performance.

It's helpful to get perspectives on the committee's performance from both members and nonmembers. Clearly, the questions will vary, depending on whether or not a director serves as a committee member:

- For committee members, questions tend to focus on the effectiveness of committee meetings, the information provided to committee members, whether the committee is spending its time on the right things, the relationship between the committee and its independent advisers (such as auditors or executive compensation consultants) and with the company executive who usually interfaces with the committee (such as the vice president of human resources for the compensation committee or the internal auditor and CFO for the audit committee).

- For nonmembers, questions tend to focus on the information and updates they are receiving from the committee. Do they feel fully informed about the committee's activities? Or are they too informed, bogged down by issues the committee should have dealt with instead of rehashing at board meetings? Have they generally agreed with the recommendations or decisions of the committee?

A few years back, we worked with a board whose compensation committee had just tackled a host of tough issues. They had to put a contract in place for a new CEO and review contracts for several other new members of the executive team. In addition, they overhauled the annual bonus plan and put in a restricted stock plan. Feeling satisfied with all they had accomplished, the committee was shocked when their fellow directors expressed concerns during an assessment.

Nonmembers recognized that the compensation committee had been working hard, but they felt they hadn't been kept in the loop on why certain decisions had been made. As one nonmember noted, "If someone asked me why we changed the bonus plan and what the impact of those changes were, I couldn't tell you. I can't even remember if we talked about the golden parachute we gave Roger when he became CEO." Once this shortcoming was pointed out, the compensation committee held a special session the night before a board meeting to update nonmembers on all of their activities.

ASSESSING THE CHAIRMAN OR LEAD DIRECTOR

No regulatory requirements dictate annual assessments of the chairman or lead director. However, as discussed in Chapter Three, a feedback process for these roles is critical in order to optimize their effectiveness. As one Blue Ribbon commissioner noted, "If you're going to have a nonexecutive chair or a lead director, I think you need another governance mechanism, which is to incorporate an evaluation of that nonexecutive chair or lead director into the annual board assessment process and ask, 'How is the nonexecutive chair or lead director doing?'" To encourage candor, it is generally a good idea to provide some assurance of confidentiality to the respondents.

One of the first questions to address: Who will lead the process, review the data, and provide feedback? If the chairman and CEO roles are combined, the lead director frequently leads the process of assessing the chairman/CEO in her role as chairman. It gets a little trickier with a nonexecutive chairman or a lead director. If that individual does not chair the nominating/governance committee, this committee's chair often shoulders the responsibility.

Another key decision is whether the full board will receive the feedback report provided to the nonexecutive chairman or lead director. Many feel that because this assessment involves individual feedback, it is best not to share the full report with the entire board to prevent any embarrassment or defensiveness in front of the group. When this practice is adopted, the individual who leads the review process or the lead director or nonexecutive chair will usually update the board verbally on some of the themes surfaced in the assessment and any relevant action plans.

Assessment topics for a lead director or nonexecutive chair include how effective that individual is in the following areas: chairing board meetings or executive sessions (depending on the role), providing input into board agendas or information, working with the CEO, and communicating with fellow directors. As with the board assessment itself, it is critical to tailor the questions to a particular individual; for example, if a lead director had to address a director performance issue (which is discussed in greater detail in Chapter Three), it may be appropriate to gather some feedback on how the other directors felt this was handled. Similarly, if a nonexecutive chair plays a significant role in orienting or mentoring new directors, effectiveness in this area should be explored.

INTEGRATING MANAGEMENT'S PERSPECTIVE INTO THE BOARD ASSESSMENT

A number of boards are beginning to incorporate feedback from management about the board's performance into their assessment process in order to gain another measure of its effectiveness. One member of the Blue Ribbon Commission who sits on a board that has adopted this practice noted, "I think board assessment needs to go beyond just soliciting the board's views of its performance and has to also involve senior management in assessing the board. Otherwise, the board doesn't fully understand how effective they are in adding value for the company."

Such feedback can help identify differences and even uncover issues in the working relationship between the board and management that might otherwise have been overlooked if only the views of board members were sought. These insights can often make a big difference in enhancing overall board performance. Moreover, management often notes that the board added value for them in a way that board members thought was "no big deal." This type of information enables the board to understand more fully where they are having positive impact, and how that impact can be maximized.

The board of directors of the New York Times Company was one of the first boards in the Fortune 500 to incorporate a management component into its annual assessment process. "In 2001, our nominating and governance committee requested that our annual board assessment include the views of those senior managers who regularly attend board meetings," said Chairman Arthur Sulzberger Jr. "We feel this has strengthened our process by serving as an important reality check on our board's assessment of its strengths, as well as indicating areas where there could be improvement."

Indeed, understanding how management perceives the board's effectiveness can be extremely helpful. We're not saying that management's view should dictate changes in how the board functions. However, it can be useful for boards to know where management thinks the board adds value or where they fall down on the job. Among other things, examining board performance through the lens of management prevents the board from forming an insular view of itself.

Any of the three methodologies previously discussed can be used to gather feedback from management on the board's effectiveness. One caveat: pick the same methodology that is being used for the board assessment so that management's views can be readily integrated with the other feedback. Only executives who regularly interact with the board should participate; usually four or five senior managers, including the CEO, are in such a position. If there are fewer, it can be difficult to incorporate management's views without making it obvious who the feedback is coming from.

SUMMARY

Board assessment is too often viewed as a necessary evil—a mechanical process of checking off items on a list that ultimately has little real value for the board apart from meeting compliance requirements. However, as the examples in this chapter illustrate, an effective board assessment process has the potential to be transformational.

The ideal starting place in effective board-building is to get an accurate picture of where your board stands today. Taking this snapshot—with a comprehensive, diagnostic assessment of the board—allows you to see clearly both your strengths and opportunities for change. It also helps you build a solid platform, one that can elevate your board from good to great.

PART THREE

Emerging Issues Outside the United States

CHAPTER TWELVE

Special Issues in Corporate Governance in Canada

Beverly A. Behan
Jason Ducharme
Richard D. Hossack

R egulatory reform of corporate governance evolved
nearly a decade earlier in Canada than in the United States, and in
some ways the countries have followed different paths. Nevertheless,
our work on both sides of the border clearly suggests that boards in
the two countries are grappling with many of the same issues as they
seek to improve the quality of governance.

Canada's governance reforms grew out of the Dey Report, the recommendations of a commission assembled by the Toronto Stock
Exchange (TSX). Since 1995, all TSX-listed companies have been
required to disclose in their annual proxy circulars whether or not they
complied with these governance guidelines. The substance of the
reforms closely resembles the listing requirements adopted in 2002 by
the U.S. stock exchanges, but there's a notable difference in how the
guidelines are used. In the United States, compliance is mandatory,
and noncompliance can lead to delisting. Canada, however, like Great
Britain, has adopted a "comply or explain" approach, and noncompliance carries no penalties. The Canadian view is that once investors

have been fully informed about the extent of a company's compliance, it's up to them whether or not they want to invest in it.

Many large Canadian companies began experimenting with changes in their board practices years before their U.S. counterparts, establishing governance committees, undertaking board assessments, and holding regular executive sessions. There has also been a cross-fertilization of ideas, since many Canadians sit on U.S. boards and vice versa. Despite the differences between the boards in each country, they face a common challenge: increasing their overall effectiveness and leveraging the talent at their board tables in an era of increased governance scrutiny and heightened board engagement.

In this chapter, we will focus on three issues that, although not unique to Canada, are notable within the corporate governance landscape there:

- The first is the widespread use of the role of nonexecutive chairman—one of the major differences that sets Canadian boards apart from their neighbors to the south. According to a Mercer Human Resources global disclosure database, 70 percent of Canadian companies separate the roles of chairman and CEO and choose an independent, outside director to serve as nonexecutive chairman.

- The second issue is the prevalence of crown corporations and other quasi-public company boards. Although these types of stakeholder boards also exist in the United States, Canadian governments (both federal and provincial) have historically been active in the country's economy and consequently figure prominently in Canadian governance.

- The third issue focuses on special circumstances surrounding boards of family-controlled companies, particularly those with dual-class share structures such as Molson's and Bombardier. Nearly 25 percent of large Canadian companies have dual or multiple voting rights, many of which involve family interests.

To supplement our own experience working with numerous Canadian boards, we conducted a series of confidential interviews with Canadian directors who serve on public company, crown corporation, and family-controlled boards. This material is referenced throughout the chapter.

CANADIAN NONEXECUTIVE CHAIRS

Unlike the majority of their U.S. counterparts, Canadian directors are strong advocates of separating the chairman and CEO roles. Moreover, they favor teaming the CEO with a nonexecutive chairman, a structure they prefer over the lead director model now gaining acceptance in the United States. In their view, nonexecutive chairs provide greater benefits in terms of sharing the workload with the CEO and providing two perspectives in board discussions; lead directors, they believe, are simply not as engaged or accountable as nonexecutive chairs.

The Canadian experience in effectively using the nonexecutive chairman role provides insights for U.S. boards that are considering a variety of leadership structures. For this reason, we asked Canadian directors to discuss the role in practical terms—exactly what it should be, what makes it effective, how the chair should be selected, and how to shape constructive relationships between the chair, the CEO, and other directors. In addition, we asked them to describe any problems they've encountered with the nonexecutive chair model.

Role of the Nonexecutive Chair

Several Canadian directors described the key roles played by their nonexecutive chairs: providing wise and thoughtful counsel to the CEO, setting the tone for governance and bringing clarity to the board's culture of integrity and ethics, engaging the board by running great meetings that cover the right topics, encouraging broad participation. Effective nonexecutive chairs create a healthy tension that leads to the development of the board as a team. This also means taking aside board members who are out of line to raise performance issues.

Most of the directors we spoke with thought the nonexecutive chair should avoid any public role in speaking for the company—apart from chairing the annual meeting—unless it was necessary during a crisis. Others, however, felt that it could be helpful to companies with a well-regarded nonexecutive chair to have that person comment publicly on various matters, so long as he or she was totally in sync with the CEO.

Qualifications of a Good Nonexecutive Chair

The fundamental requirements for a good nonexecutive chair start with personality and character—and the ability to create the right personal chemistry with the CEO and other directors. Many directors believe that former CEOs are particularly well-suited for the role because they understand the important distinction between governance and management. The job also requires someone who's not trying to act like a CEO or assume an authoritative role. As one director explained, "This means learning to disagree without being disagreeable, guide without leading, and taking pride in supporting others to succeed rather than being caught up in your own success."

Relationship Between the Nonexecutive Chair and the CEO

The nonexecutive chair has to manage two key dynamics: a relationship with the CEO and a relationship with the rest of the board. The goal is to maintain equilibrium in the relationship between the chair and the CEO. As one director said, you don't want to couple a deferential CEO with a nonexecutive chair who can't resist getting involved in management, nor do you want to pair a dominant CEO with a passive chairman.

Effective nonexecutive chairs give CEOs both space and support; they offer advice and counsel without abdicating their critical oversight role as a representative of the shareholders. Openness, trust, transparency, and mutual respect characterize excellent working relationships between CEOs and nonexecutive chairs, and the best of them develop these aspects of their relationship in conscious and thoughtful ways.

Finally, the CEO and the chair should share some deeply held values that set the tone for the board and flow through the organization. This goes beyond good chemistry and requires open communication and the ability to give each other candid feedback. As one nonexecutive chair observed, "This is a process of osmosis; it takes time to build the relationship, and to do that you need lots of contact." For the chair, in particular, this means taking both ego and personal prejudices and "checking them at the door," noted another director.

The presence of a nonexecutive chair has significant implications for CEO succession. For one thing, the model used by some U.S. companies in which the retiring chief executive gives up his CEO title but retains his role as chairman of the board simply doesn't work in Canada because the role of chairman of the board is already occupied by a nonexecutive chair in most cases. Indeed, the view in Canada is that when the CEO retires, he should not stay on the board. The nonexecutive chair often plays an important role in Canadian succession planning and provides coaching and mentoring to the new CEO. These relationships result in a win-win situation: the nonexecutive chair supports both the professional and personal journey of the out-going CEO, while ensuring a strong CEO succession process for the board and the shareholders.

Relationship Between the Nonexecutive Chair and Other Directors

Not surprisingly, many of the attributes that enable a good relationship with the CEO also apply to the nonexecutive chair's relationship with other directors. The chair must be adept at engaging all of them to maximize their contribution, and holding directors and committee chairs accountable. One director noted that a good nonexecutive chair communicates effectively, making sure the other directors "never find something out in the newspapers that hasn't already been communicated to them." Another emphasized that setting a tone of accountability and dealing with performance issues is an integral part of the role: "The nonexecutive chair must make it clear that a board is no place for people who just want to show up and collect their checks, but who don't carry their weight."

Notably, most Canadian directors felt strongly that the nonexecutive chair should not chair any of the board committees. This helps balance the workload, allows other directors to play a significant role in the board's work, and helps avoid confusion and undue influence when committees report to the full board. As one director noted, "The beauty of not having the nonexecutive chair serve as chair of any of the board committees is that it provides a check and balance." It can be helpful, however, to allow the nonexecutive chair to attend committee meetings and participate actively in such issues as CEO evaluation and succession planning in which one or more board committees may be taking the lead.

Selection of the Nonexecutive Chair

In most cases, the nonexecutive chair is selected by the governance committee or by a special ad hoc committee formed specifically for that purpose. Most directors support term limits for the role and believe that when the term expires, the nonexecutive chair should leave the board unless there are exceptional circumstances.

Drawbacks of the Model

Despite their unanimous support for the nonexecutive chair model, directors we interviewed acknowledged that it is not without problems. Many cited instances of meddling and micromanaging chairs. Frequently, these problems involved chairs who used the perks of office and secretary at the company site to become visibly engaged in company affairs, often establishing independent and unhelpful relationships with executive team members that left the CEO feeling undermined. Other problematic chairs engaged in public disputes with the CEO over fundamental policy matters.

In both Canada and the United States, it is not uncommon for a founder and majority shareholder to take a company public, and then wind up as chairman while another person is brought in as CEO. In such a situation, the chair can lose sight of the fact that he no longer owns or runs the company, resulting in conflict with the CEO and the board. Similarly, a nonexecutive chair who joins a board to represent the interests of a hedge fund or a venture capitalist who holds a significant stake in the company must also guard against the inherent conflict of interest between fiduciary duty to the company and the interests of the fund.

Because performance issues involving a nonexecutive chairman can be particularly challenging, many Canadian boards bar the chair from membership on the governance committee. This gives the committee's chair the responsibility to address such problems with the nonexecutive chairman.

CROWN CORPORATION BOARDS

Corporate-specific enabling legislation, rules, and regulations typically define the governance structure of crown corporations. Moreover, these boards are usually composed of a blend of operational and stakeholder representation, and in some cases, have directors who are political appointees.

This sector is large and very diverse in Canada, which makes it somewhat difficult to define and draw generalized conclusions. However, these organizations generally have three common traits:

• They are created by and subject to government legislation that defines their mandate, and to a greater or lesser extent, their governance structure and processes.

• There is an operational accountability relationship with government, especially in cases where taxpayer funds are provided to the corporation to help pay for operations.

• A board/CEO governance structure is used, with the government usually overseeing and sometimes directly controlling appointments to the board.

In this section, we'll use the term *crown corporation* to refer to a wide range of corporations, agencies, boards, commissions, and other operating enterprises that share the preceding characteristics.

Crown Corporations in the Canadian Economy

In the Canadian economy, a large number of crown corporations are found in virtually every sector. They are a diverse lot, including:

• Large operating enterprises (postal services, transit/rail, Canada Mortgage and Housing Corporation, liquor control boards)

• Utilities (hydroelectric, gas, water, and telecommunications)

• Hospitals and other public sector health care organizations

• Education (universities, colleges, nonprofits, and school boards)

• Special purpose corporations and agencies (airport authorities, tourism facility operators, waterfront redevelopment, economic development, police services)

• Subsidized housing (both nonprofit and public housing corporations)

• Regulatory/adjudicative agencies that make decisions or regulate economic activities

• Foundations and trusts that oversee assets or raise funds

The diversity and extent of public-sector corporations within the Canadian economy is significant. In the province of Ontario alone, there are more than 630 crown corporations directly controlled by the province, in addition to numerous municipal and federal agencies. Despite this diversity, most of these crown corporations use a board governance structure. As a result, they must deal with board-related issues of effectiveness, engagement, strategy, and succession planning.

The Relationship Between Government and Governance

Crown corporations are usually created through legislation and regulations that define mandates, authority, roles, and the board appointment processes. In addition, a variety of rules, protocols, and practice guidelines are issued (or imposed) to help manage the affairs of crown corporations, holding them accountable to the public benefit for which they were created. To the extent that crown corporations receive operating subsidies from the government, these "belts and braces" can become quite onerous in terms of audits, operational reviews, and approval requirements.

This underscores the view that, although arms-length crown corporations can help deliver a particular service, the government is ultimately accountable for both the performance of the corporation and its use of funds. Numerous federal and provincial governments impose some form of results-based management and accountability requirements, including risk-based audit and evaluations to set the objectives, business model, and expected outcomes for the crown corporation. More often than not, some form of operating agreement or memorandum of understanding is used as a structural tool to hold the corporation accountable for results.

Board Mandates Vary Widely

Our interviews revealed a broad range of board roles in crown corporations. In most cases, boards oversee the effective management of the enterprise, and in some cases they can become directly involved in management decisions. In other cases, board members are recruited to act as adjudicative decision makers, or even as fundraisers. These diverse roles clearly relate to the range of crown corporation mandates—for example, effective service delivery, fundraising, interest group advocacy, adjudication, regulation, consumer protection, and financial stewardship. The profound diversity of these mandates makes it difficult to generalize about the role of their boards.

Nevertheless, one theme that emerged from our interviews is the challenge of balancing the board's operational versus "public interest" roles. The legislation or regulation that creates a crown corporation spells out the board's role, but these rules can be unclear or ill-conceived. That lack of clarity can create significant concerns if it enables directors to become either overly involved in operations or excessively "hands-off," leaving the CEO relatively unchallenged in decision making.

Confusion and dysfunction can also arise when board roles include both public interest and operational oversight. Board members often have strategic roles that are intended to support the overall mandate of the corporation (for example, adjudicative decision making, fundraising, or stakeholder representation). These strategic roles may or may not be stacked on top of more typical director responsibilities for overseeing the enterprise's effective operations (such as strategy articulation, CEO succession, performance measurement, audit, and operational policy). This makes the issue of board role definition and level of engagement extremely complex, but of utmost importance to board effectiveness in crown corporations.

A more disturbing issue sometimes arises when board members who are recruited as stakeholder representatives face a potential conflict of interest when it comes to overseeing operational decisions. Some governments preclude these situations by limiting the number of stakeholder representatives to a minority and requiring board members to abstain from voting when there's a potential conflict of interest. But in other circumstances, it's up to individual board members to figure out how to manage their dual roles.

Evidence of Flawed Practices

Despite the precautions taken by governments to ensure the effectiveness of crown corporations, there is recent evidence of weak governance and flawed board practices. For example, a report in Ontario focusing specifically on board governance in hospitals found significant flaws in the boards' level of engagement and overall effectiveness. Frequently cited flaws included lack of clarity with respect to the board's accountability to government, lack of a clear board role, inappropriate skill sets on the board, lack of term limits for directors, inadequate and inappropriate information supporting board decision making, and lack of clear differentiation between governance activities and management responsibilities in the organization.[1]

Those same concerns have been echoed in the findings of the auditor general of Canada, whose report in 2005 focused considerable scrutiny on the potential for crown corporations to use taxpayer funds without adequate accountability or in ways inconsistent with their strategies.[2]

Crown corporation boards also find it difficult to decide what criteria to use in evaluating their effectiveness. In many cases, the desired results and outcomes are public benefits rather than purely financial results. Consequently, most crown corporations spend a significant amount of time articulating board performance dashboards to help them assess their effectiveness, not only in terms of operational efficiency but also in the achievement of the societal goals they were created to fulfill.

Dynamics of Board Chair, Director, and CEO Relationships

The enabling legislation that creates crown corporations is usually flexible, providing the corporation with some discretion to custom-tailor its governance and operations. But grey areas can lead to confusion, power struggles, and ultimately, ineffective boards. Crown corporations are no different than private companies when it comes to the potential for conflict and turf wars between the CEO and the board chair. The difference is that the dynamic can be further complicated by the relationship between the crown corporation's board and the government. This happens in a variety of ways:

- A CEO typically reports into a government ministry or department that has overall accountability for the crown corporation. This creates a dual reporting structure for the CEO, who is both a senior manager accountable to the board and a senior executive accountable to a government agency.

- Another potential problem arises when directors are strongly affiliated with the political party that was responsible for their appointment. They may see their duty as pursuing the government's agenda and directing the organization's operations in ways that will achieve politically desirable results. Such a near-term political agenda might conflict with the CEO's pursuit of long-term operational results. (There was no consensus on this issue among the directors we interviewed, and many respondents believe the appointment process for crown corporation boards has improved to the point where instances of "political meddling" have become rare.)

- In some cases, serious director performance issues are overlooked for fear of offending those in power who made the appointment.

Furthermore, because the director's term of appointment is fixed by legislation, there is often a feeling of inability to act on this issue by the chair/CEO.

A related issue concerns whether elected officials should serve on the boards of crown corporations. One view is that there is a potential conflict of interest when a director is accountable both to the electorate and to the corporation. In other jurisdictions (particularly at the municipal level), the appointment of elected officials is viewed positively as a way to align the corporation's priorities with the current public agenda. Because of these differing views, multiple appointment practices are in place at the federal, provincial, and municipal levels.

EFFECTIVE GOVERNANCE IN FAMILY-CONTROLLED COMPANIES

Another notable feature of the Canadian corporate governance landscape is the prevalence of family-controlled companies, often with a dual-class share structure. Under this structure, one class of shares is controlled by a family and held privately while another class of shares trades on a public stock exchange. Generally, the boards of these companies comprise both family members and outside directors. In many, family members also play key roles in corporate management, frequently serving as CEO or executive chairman. Some of the best-known Canadian companies—Molson's, Bombardier, and Rogers—have been governed this way. In fact, almost a quarter of Canada's largest companies have dual-class or other multiple voting share structures, many of these with one class of shares being family-controlled.[3]

The Canadian press has been filled with commentary on dual-class share structure companies. Critics of Hollinger, for example, have volubly decried them and urged regulators to all but dismantle them.[4] But proponents of family businesses, such as Paul Desmarais Jr., chairman and co-CEO of Power Corp., have passionately defended them, warning regulators not to get caught up in "governance hysteria."[5] The purpose of this section is not to add fuel to this fiery debate; our point of view throughout this book is that although the regulatory environment affects the way in which boards operate, regulations alone do not create either effective or ineffective boards.

Instead, we'll discuss some of the special issues faced by the boards of family-controlled companies and focus on how these boards can be most effective in a unique environment. The interviews to supplement our research and experience in this area were conducted with directors who serve on the boards of family-controlled companies in both Canada and the United States and were balanced between outside and family directors in order to understand both perspectives on this topic.

Outside and Family Directors

Boards of family-controlled, dual-class share structure companies are generally made up of both family members and outside directors. One of the first governance issues these companies grapple with is balancing the board with the appropriate proportion of family directors and those elected by public shareholders. Ronald C. Anderson, a finance professor at American University, was quoted in a recent article, noting that families who have a large economic stake in the company and don't want to see it destroyed can be useful, although, he warned, "if there are too many, you lose the oversight provided by independent professionals."[6] Several boards we researched had allocated roughly one-third of their board seats to family members, with the balance filled by outside directors. Boards of family-controlled companies are often slightly larger than public company boards to both accommodate family representation and provide the business skills and experience required from outside directors.

A constructive working relationship between family and outside directors is vital to the overall effectiveness of these boards. This requires mutual respect rooted in an understanding by family and outside directors of the unique capabilities and value they each bring to the board table.

If family directors view outsiders as a mere regulatory nuisance that must be tolerated to gain access to capital markets, it's unlikely they will maximize these directors' contributions. Even worse, there is great potential for conflict. If, however, family directors view their outsider counterparts as a valuable asset and source of sound advice and broad perspectives, there is tremendous potential.

Outside directors need to understand and respect the family's goals for the business. Moreover, they need to acknowledge the unique contributions that family members can provide through their sense of history, continuity, and commitment to the business.

As one director pointed out, family members "have a unique understanding of the business through their years of being part of the family that no outside director has." Even more valuable is the sense of legacy inherent in having a family's name and history closely associated with a business. "When your name's on something there's a personal attachment, which is quite different than anything a professional manager can ever have," the director said. "If you're running Molson's and your name is Molson, it's unquestionably more personal. The business is more important to someone like that both emotionally and reputationally." If outside directors fail to appreciate the unique value family members can bring to the boardroom, their unique contributions will likely be underleveraged, diminishing the board's performance overall.

Maximizing the Effectiveness of Family Directors

High-performing boards of family companies capitalize on the presence of family directors by designing processes to integrate them into the board in ways that facilitate effective contributions. This begins when the family selects members to serve as their representatives on the board. More sophisticated boards—and those where directorships have been passed to the third generation and beyond—have clear rules and guidelines to steer this process.

For example, one family now into its fifth generation of corporate ownership created a family trust structure where eight family members were elected to interface with the corporate board. They adopted a rule that the four family members who served on the corporate board must first have served on the board of the trust. As the chairman of this board explained, "There are two advantages to this. First, it would be a huge leap for someone who hadn't served on the trust to try to come onto the corporate board. Trustees get the board books and are involved in presentations and discussions about what's going on with the company and what happened in the board meetings. So right away, by having served on the trust, you have a much better idea about the business, its issues, and its players, which makes for a much easier transition onto the corporate board. The other advantage is that the trustees—who vote on who goes onto the corporate board—get to evaluate the suitability of their fellow trustees as corporate board members from serving with them on the trust."

Another family requires members who have an interest in serving on the corporate board to first build a track record of service on not-for-profit or other boards. Still others use well-established and explicit criteria that make it readily apparent why one family member's credentials are superior to another's when a board selection is made.

Some family-controlled company boards impose one more condition: every new family director must meet with the chair of the nominating/governance committee before his or her appointment is finalized. As the chairman of a board that has adopted this practice explains, "This is not a veto; selection of family directors remains within the purview of the family. But if the chair of the nominating and governance committee met with the proposed family director and told me that he had some real concerns about this person's ability to serve as a director, we'd take that very seriously. It would be raised openly with the individual and also with the family, and we might well change our minds about bringing that person onto the board."

Integration and education of family directors is critically important. Tossing a family member into the deep end of the pool to sink or swim does a disservice both to her and to the board.

"I've seen a situation where a family member named to the board was not integrated properly and therefore wasn't accepted by any of the other directors," one director explained. "He was ignored by both the family's side and by the outside directors. He didn't know much about the business, and no one had oriented him properly, so he asked a lot of dumb questions and never had anything worthwhile to add. It was clear that all the other board members treated him as persona non grata and that really must have been a terrible experience for him."

Orientation processes vary widely. Some boards require incoming family directors to attend their meetings as an observer for six months, or even a year, before they formally join the board. Others send the new family members to training programs either before or shortly after their appointment. "We have a practice of always sending a family board member to an outside director training course along with one of the people from top management," said one director. "This allows them to develop rapport, share their different perspectives when they're at the course, and learn from each other."

Some boards ask an outside director to serve as an informal mentor to the new family director. "A good lead director should serve as a go-between for the new family director and the board, helping to integrate them, answering questions they may have, being their sounding board," one outside director explained. "When a lead director takes a new family director under her wing, that validates the new person as a board member to the other outside directors."

The real value of integrating a family director onto the board was summed up by one outside director: "You want any new family director to be seen by the other outside directors as a 'real director,' not just someone filling a board seat. You want them to really contribute something as a board member, recognizing that their contribution will be different than what an outside director will make. It's when you maximize the contribution of both that these boards can work really well."

Unique Issues for Outside Directors of Family-Controlled Companies

"One of the big differences in a family-controlled company is that you have to look the major shareholder in the eye across the board table," one outside director explained. "That personalizes the situation a lot more than in a public company. It can make it more challenging in terms of dealing with sensitive issues. But it also makes it particularly rewarding in terms of really feeling the impact you're having in the boardroom."

Outside directors tend to do more due diligence before accepting board invitations to family-controlled companies than they would for other directorships. They want to avoid feeling compromised by having to "go along with whatever the controlling shareholder wants to do," an outside director said. One chairman noted that the greatest challenge in recruiting outsiders to these types of boards was "convincing them that this board runs just like any other public company board."

Many articles about family-controlled companies note the potential tension between the interests of public shareholders and the family. In reality, most of the directors we spoke to indicated that such conflicts are rare. When there is a significant disagreement with a controlling shareholder, however, the outside director's most powerful weapon is the threat of a noisy public resignation. This can have devastating consequences for the company, particularly if a small group of outside directors resigns en masse in protest. Outside directors who regularly play this type of brinksmanship can be a real menace. "Public resignation is the ultimate trigger and the family knows it," one outside director pointed out. "Obviously, you should only threaten to do something like that in really extreme circumstances." Privatization or sale of the business can be the family's ultimate resolution if conflicts prove impossible to solve.

Needless to say, it is generally best for all shareholders if major differences can be resolved without resorting to extreme measures. This typically requires a relationship between the family and outside directors that is grounded in an understanding of each other's goals and perspectives. If this foundation is not built into the board's everyday working relationship, it will not be there as support when major disputes arise.

Succession Planning at Family-Controlled Companies

CEO succession planning is a challenging issue for many boards, but at family-controlled companies where the family wants to continue to be involved in top management the task can be even more daunting. The talent pool is small by its very nature, and infighting over succession by family members can be intense and disruptive. There is always the potential for the conversation that every outside director dreads: telling the CEO that his son or daughter just doesn't have what it takes. The difficulties are reflected in the numbers: a survey released by consulting firm Grant Thornton in 2004 showed that in Canada, about 70 percent of family-owned businesses fail to transfer their operations to the second generation and 90 percent do not reach the third.[7]

Fortunately, the situation doesn't have to be so dire. Our research and experience suggest there are several key factors that can increase the chances of success:

START EARLY. This includes setting the right tone in the family. As one nonexecutive chairman explained, "It works best where you have a family who understands that the business is much more than their personal asset. The senior family members need to set the tone at the top on this, explaining to their kids when they're very young that if they want to contend for this job, it's not a hereditary right. There's a meritocracy aspect to it, and they're going to have to prove themselves and be willing to step up to that challenge."

ESTABLISH GROUND RULES AND STRUCTURES. This step is critical to the process. One company that has moved well past the third generation of family leadership developed a clear set of rules, such as requiring family members who have an interest in working at the company to spend a certain number of years working outside the company before they are eligible to apply. They also created a committee consisting of the chairman and vice chairman (both family members in this instance) and the CEO and vice president of human resources (both nonfamily members) to oversee the progress and development of family members in the company.

This structure eases the chairman's burden of being the sole decision maker about another family member's progress. More importantly, it helps ensure that family members get the honest feedback they need for their professional development, something that is inherently difficult when a midlevel manager is asked for a performance evaluation on the son or daughter of the chairman or CEO.

DEVELOP CANDIDATES' POTENTIAL AND BUILD THE ORGANIZATION'S COMFORT WITH THEM. Building a methodical approach to accomplish this is perhaps the most important step. It means "giving the board exposure to that person fairly early on and regularly, and giving that person jobs that present significant challenges," said an outside director. This allows a candidate to "show that he or she can deal with things— so that they earn their stripes both with the board and with other people in senior management."

One lead director recounted the story of how his current CEO (a third-generation family member) created his own extensive development plan to prove himself to the board, including allowing board members to regularly interview his executive coach without him being present: "That took a lot of confidence and determination and we respected that," the director said. "What I also have really respected about him is that six years later, he's still committed to his own professional development as a leader. If anything, he's done more than most public company CEOs to grow into this job and to grow within the job because he knows how much scrutiny he's under. He's genuinely keen to become a better executive, and he didn't just let that fall by the wayside when he was made CEO."

Of all the anecdotes we heard about how the CEO's baton has passed from one generation to the next, one company had a particularly comprehensive process. Members of the board's human resources committee conducted more than thirty interviews—with the candidate's former bosses and direct reports, key customers, and journalists and analysts who covered his industry. In addition, three prominent outside candidates were also interviewed for the job. This board's due diligence went well beyond the norm at widely held public companies to ensure they were completely satisfied before agreeing to choose another family member as CEO.

Exposure to the executive bench and talent pool can be even more important in succession planning for family-controlled companies because other members of the executive team are often used to "fill in" skills where a family candidate is weak. As one outside director explained, "Let's say I feel that the son has really proven himself, but he's weak on the numbers. If he's going to have an outstanding CFO to back him up, I can see my way to letting him be CEO. But I couldn't do that if I wasn't comfortable with the CFO's abilities." Several outside directors noted that self-awareness on the part of candidates and an openness to compensate for their weaknesses by working with others is vital. "In one case I know of, we could shore this guy up with a strong executive team, but he's not very open to that," said one director. "He has an overinflated view of his abilities and doesn't listen. In the end, the board just will not endorse him to become CEO."

Once a company gets into the third generation and beyond, hybrid corporate leadership structures often emerge. One of the most common is a family member serving as executive chairman while a nonfamily member serves as CEO. Another is to have the family member retain the title of CEO but bring in a strong and experienced manager as COO, who takes on certain aspects of the CEO role. Sometimes this is used as an interim step while the family member taking on the top job "grows" into the position; at other times it is a permanent structure.

Hybrid leadership structures can be very effective in maintaining the family's integral involvement in the company while supplementing the family leader's managerial expertise, easing the pressure on the leader to be all things to all people. In such scenarios, the family member frequently plays an enhanced public role, capitalizing on what one director described as "the magic of having Bill Ford talk to you about Ford." It's important to create and maintain an extremely candid and constructive working relationship between the individuals playing these two roles.

Although succession planning in family-controlled companies can be particularly challenging, it can also yield significant benefits. As one outside director noted: "Family members who are involved directly in the business, such as serving as CEO, really have a unique perspective, because in one person you have both the shareholder's perspective and the inside management perspective. There's a big, big difference between a family member who is involved as an active operator, such as a CEO, and a next-generation cousin who just sits on the board and has no involvement in day-to-day management." The chairman of a company with an enviable track record of passing the baton through numerous generations explained, "Having family members involved in management creates alignment between management and the family and builds cohesion within the family."

Family Governance Structures

Family cohesion, which plays an important part in the governance of family-controlled companies, becomes more difficult to maintain as time goes by and ownership spreads across the family. "Expansion is the enemy of cohesion," observed one outside director. "You aren't solving problems around the dining room table anymore. So you need to put structures in place to manage these issues effectively."

A separate governance structure for the family, independent of the business governance structure, provides a systematic way to deal with family issues outside of the boardroom. Without it, the business can become the only forum where these matters can be addressed. A lead director of a family-controlled company noted, "If you are going to deal with a significant issue, the family needs to hash out its position on the issue among itself before their directors come into the boardroom."

The most sophisticated companies with numerous generations of family shareholders actively involve family members in learning about the business outside of the boardroom and in working together better as a family. One chairman described what his family does: "We have two weekend meetings a year where our entire family gets together. One of these is purely social, a family reunion. The second is more structured. At this meeting, we spend time as a family on the business—for example, on the first day the CEO will make a presentation about the company. After that, we'll have breakout groups on topics of special interest, and participants can choose which of these they want to attend. After this full day, the family goes away on an offsite and spends two more days together talking about what they learned from the session and then delving into matters relative to the family and to elections."

When infighting develops between family members, it can create significant governance problems; in the most extreme cases, it can result in the company being sold. Short of that, however, family disputes can disrupt the boardroom, often creating polarized factions that can be difficult to unite. As one family director explained, "Making a family-controlled company work well requires honesty and cohesion among the family rather than a culture of individualism and people getting into entrenched positions. The cornerstone of this is an understanding of your family's goals. Is it growing your business, or maximizing your wealth? If you have a lot of infighting among family members, what you really need to do is try to get very clear about your goal as a family for this business."

Board leaders in family-controlled companies need to fully understand the family's goals and serve as a linkage point between the family and the company. Whether the board's leadership structure involves a family member as executive chair or an outsider as nonexecutive chair, that person needs to understand the family's goals and values as well as the board's perspective on key issues. "If the family wants to do something and the board disagrees, the family needs to understand why the board won't do it," explained one nonexecutive chairman. "Often you play an important role in helping them to understand the rationale behind the board's position and vice versa from the family to the board where the family doesn't support something that the board wants to do."

SUMMARY

We believe that Canadian and U.S. boards are grappling with many of the same issues as they seek to be most effective—and that topics covered throughout this book apply equally to boards on both sides of the border. In this chapter, we focused on three prominent, although by no means unique, aspects of the Canadian corporate governance landscape: the widespread use of nonexecutive chairs, the prevalence of crown corporation boards, and boards of family-controlled companies structured with dual- or multiple-voting rights.

Canadian experience with nonexecutive chairs has largely been very positive. Taking time to define the respective roles of nonexecutive chair and CEO, and creating a constructive working relationship between the nonexecutive chair, the CEO, and other directors are some of the keys to success with this structure.

Crown corporations bring with them myriad complex relationships, including those relating to board composition, roles, and the management of potential conflicts of interest. Often it is difficult for these boards to even define what "effectiveness" entails, given that their mandates are much broader than purely financial results. Some factors that both facilitate and impede effective boards operating in this arena have been addressed.

Finally, we discussed some of the ways to maximize the effectiveness of boards of family-controlled companies. This begins with an understanding of the respective contributions of both family and outside directors in the boardroom and a commitment to effective integration of family members onto the board. We also discussed the challenges of succession planning where family members continue to take leadership roles in the company, and the use of family governance structures apart from the corporate board itself.

CHAPTER THIRTEEN

U.K. Corporate Governance

Margaret Exley
Belinda Hudson

—∿∿— F or over a decade the United Kingdom has enjoyed a
well-developed corporate governance framework based on the principles of transparency and accountability. Indeed, for many years it
has been regarded by some as the most well-regulated and share-
holder-friendly market. This was most recently confirmed in a country ranking undertaken by Governance Metrics International, where
the United Kingdom scored highest among twenty-three nations in a
survey that included the United States, Canada, and Australia.[1]

The key features of the U.K. corporate governance regime are as
follows:

- The unitary board model
- Separation of the roles of chairman and chief executive
- No employee right to representation on the board
- A principle-based, rather than rule-based, approach with com-
  panies required to "comply or explain"
- A history of significant shareholder activism by institutional
  investors, particularly with regard to directors' remuneration

Over the past five years, in the aftermath of a series of high-profile cases of inadequate board performance, there has been a tightening and strengthening of the operation of U.K. boards. In this chapter, we examine these changes and how they affect the way corporate governance works in the United Kingdom. An increase in regulation, combined with sharper definition of roles, the addition of some new roles, clearer committee structures, and sharpened board processes have led to significant changes.

Although these changes have been evolutionary rather than revolutionary, and have built on the platform of reform that was kicked off in the early 1990s, some have been controversial—for example, the need to appoint a senior independent director and the recommendation that a chief executive not go on to be appointed as chairman of the same company. Yet these somewhat controversial changes are becoming the norm. There is more emphasis on induction of new board members, independence in their appointment, and evaluation of their performance and decision-making processes. More change is to come, and meanwhile, the risk-reward ratio for nonexecutive directors is shifting.

THE REGULATORY FRAMEWORK

The current governance framework was introduced following the Cadbury Report in 1992. The catalyst for that report was a spate of high-profile corporate scandals in the late 1980s and early 1990s, including Coloroll, Polly Peck, Bank of Credit & Commerce International, and the Maxwell empire. The framework was subsequently developed by the Greenbury (1995) and Hampel (1998) reports, followed by a single— or combined—code in 1998 and the Turnbull Report in 1999.

In 2002, the government appointed Sir Derek Higgs to undertake a review of the role and effectiveness of nonexecutive directors and Sir Robert Smith to review the role and responsibilities of audit committees.[2] This was in response to a number of high-profile cases in the United Kingdom, particularly Marconi and Equitable Life, where there was a dramatic loss of shareholder value. In the United States, many major corporate collapses were a result of alleged corporate malpractice and fraud. However, in the United Kingdom, the main factor was underperformance, which undermined investor confidence and raised questions about the role and performance of the board and nonexecutive directors in particular.

As the Higgs Review put it: "Against a background of corporate turbulence, it is very much the purpose of this review to let in some daylight on the role of the nonexecutive director in the boardroom and to make recommendations to enhance their effectiveness."

Most of Higgs's and Smith's recommendations were incorporated into the revised Combined Code on Corporate Governance, annexed to the Listing Rules by the Financial Services Authority. The recommendations were either incorporated in the "comply or explain" regime or appended to the code as best practice suggestions. The code contains main and supporting principles and provisions that apply for accounting periods beginning on or after November 1, 2003.

The code is supplemented by both the Directors' Remuneration Report Regulations, introduced by the government in 2002 to promote greater transparency in relation to directors' remuneration, and a host of guidelines from many different institutional investors and representative bodies, such as the Association of British Insurers and the National Association of Pension Funds.

The Directors' Remuneration Report Regulations made disclosure rules for quoted companies more stringent and required the directors of a company to produce a remuneration report for approval by shareholders in general meetings.

The array of guidelines from institutional investors has attracted much criticism from companies over the past few years on the basis that they cause added complexity for companies seeking to keep all investors happy. Sir Bryan Nicholson, the chairman of the Financial Reporting Council, recently called on investors to adopt a single code. Hermes Investment Management responded by sending a letter to all FTSE All-Share Index companies saying that the fund manager was replacing its corporate governance guidelines with the Combined Code in an attempt to lessen the confusion over conflicting guidelines. Morley Fund Management has taken similar steps, and many chairmen and companies are hoping that others will follow their example.

The Financial Reporting Council, which is responsible for monitoring the operation of the Combined Code and its implementation by listed companies and shareholders, has already carried out an informal assessment of its impact.[3] (It also proposed to carry out a formal assessment late in 2005.) Although many of the Higgs recommendations represented a major challenge for companies, the informal assessment concluded that encouraging progress has been made since the code took effect. Both investors and companies believed that the corporate governance climate had improved over the first twelve months of its operation and that many boards had raised their game and become more professional. The expectation is that as the provisions are put into use, the performance and effectiveness of boards will further increase.

In addition to the regulatory burden imposed by the U.K. government, U.K. companies that are also listed in the United States must comply with U.S. regulation provisions, and in particular, the far more onerous requirements of Sarbanes-Oxley. There is widespread concern that some boards are devoting too much time to compliance and regulatory matters and less time than they should to strategic direction and wider risk management, a concern mirrored in our firm's surveys of U.S. board members.

IMPACT OF THE HIGGS REVIEW

Higgs concluded in his 2002 study that the fundamentals of corporate governance in the United Kingdom were sound. He believed that the "comply or explain" approach offers flexibility and intelligent discretion and allows for the valid exception to the sound rule. He also noted that this approach was being increasingly emulated outside of the United Kingdom, in Canada, for example, and in the Tabaksblat Code in the Netherlands.

According to Higgs, "The brittleness and rigidity of legislation cannot dictate the behaviour, or foster the trust, I believe is fundamental to the effective unitary board and to superior corporate performance."

He recognized that the focus of governance had often been too narrowly directed at executive remuneration with insufficient attention to the real drivers of corporate success. He sought to "shift the focus to board performance and effectiveness and minimize the boardroom sins of commission or omission—whether strategy, performance, or oversight."

His underlying premise is that effective and robust boards are an essential feature of successful companies and that their absence in some instances contributed to underperformance and corporate failures in the United Kingdom. He set out to raise the professionalism and effectiveness of directors based on the premise that effective boards depend as much on behaviors and relationships as on procedures and structures.

The key areas examined in the Higgs Review were as follows:

- Board composition and role
- Roles and responsibilities of board members

- Committees
- Size and balance of the board

The recommendations and their impact on companies' behavior since the Combined Code was published follow.

Board Composition and Role

Under the United Kingdom's unitary model, the board usually includes a chairman and a number of executive and nonexecutive (outside) directors who are deployed on a number of committees. The board is supported by a company secretary.

Higgs recognized the need for much greater clarity on the roles and responsibilities of the board members, and he proposed definitions for the role of the board, its committees, the chairman, the nonexecutive directors, the senior independent director, and the chief executive.

The board's key roles were identified as follows:

- Provide entrepreneurial leadership of the company within a framework of prudent and effective controls that enable risk to be assessed and managed.
- Set the company's strategic aims.
- Ensure that the necessary financial and human resources are in place for the company to meet its objectives.
- Review management performance.
- Present a balanced and understandable assessment of the company's position and prospects.
- Maintain a sound system of internal control to safeguard shareholders' investment and the company assets.
- Set the company's values and standards and ensure that there is a satisfactory dialogue with shareholders.
- Ensure that obligations to shareholders and others are understood.
- Satisfy itself that plans are in place for orderly succession for appointments to the board and to senior management.

Director Roles and Responsibilities

The duties of the directors will also increase as a result of the new requirement on companies to produce an annual operating and financial review statement. In an attempt to shed more light on what goes on in the boardroom, Higgs also recommended that the annual report and accounts should include a statement describing how the board operates.

THE CHAIRMAN. Higgs recognized that the most critical element of board effectiveness is the chairman's leadership, and he stated that the chairman needs to ensure the following:

- The board is effective on all aspects of its role and setting the agenda.
- The directors receive accurate, timely, and clear information.
- There is effective communication with shareholders.
- There is effective contribution by nonexecutive directors in particular and there are constructive relations between executive and nonexecutive directors.

In addition, the chairman is required to meet the independence criteria on appointments. The code provides a definition of independence, but Higgs emphasizes that independence in both character and judgement is important, as well as an absence of relationships or circumstances that could affect a director's judgement.

SEPARATION OF CHAIRMAN AND CHIEF EXECUTIVE ROLES. Higgs emphasized that it is the chairman's role to run the board effectively and the chief executive's role to run the company's business. He strongly endorsed the prevailing view and practice that the roles of the chairman and chief executive should not be exercised by the same individual. The rationale for this is that "it avoids concentration of authority and power in one individual and differentiates the leadership of the board from the running of the business."

Specifically, he introduced the requirement that the division of responsibilities between the chairman and the chief executive should be clearly established, set out in writing, and agreed upon by the board.

At the time of his review, Higgs reported that around 90 percent of listed U.K. companies had split the roles, acknowledging the benefits envisaged by Cadbury. The number of FTSE 100 companies where the roles are combined has fallen further—with Unilever, British Land, and Amvescap falling into line with best practice—leaving only a handful that do not comply with this aspect of the Combined Code.

CHIEF EXECUTIVE SUCCEEDING AS CHAIRMAN. A more controversial recommendation from Higgs was that a chief executive should not go on to become chairman of the same company. The main concerns relating to such a promotion are these:

- The chairman may find it difficult to make room for the incoming CEO and may undermine him.
- The chairman may inhibit an objective assessment of the executive management and the strategy.
- The chairman may not appreciate fully the information requirements of the nonexecutive directors, taking for granted his inside knowledge.

The code went on to say that if a board decides that a chief executive should become chairman, the board should consult major shareholders in advance and set out its reasons to shareholders at the time of the appointment and in the next annual report.

Inchcape plc is an example in which the chief executive is moving into the chairman's role against Higgs's recommendations. However, the company consulted with about 35 percent of its shareholders and secured their support for the move. The rationale was that Peter Johnson, its chief executive, will be in a position to help maintain its relationship with its major Japanese customers, which account for more that 50 percent of sales. Johnson explained, "Our customers prefer relationships that are long-term. They don't like change, and if it does happen, they like it to be handled seamlessly."[4]

NONEXECUTIVE DIRECTORS. As for the nonexecutive directors—"the custodians of the governance process"—whose role had been "largely invisible and poorly understood," a clear definition was drawn up that set out their responsibilities:

- Provide oversight of executive management.
- Provide constructive challenge and contribute to the development of strategy.
- Satisfy themselves on the integrity of financial information and the robustness of financial controls and systems.
- Determine appropriate levels of remuneration of executive directors.

• Play a prime role in appointing, and where necessary, removing executive directors, and in succession planning.

Some of the problems in recent years have been the result of nonexecutive directors getting incomplete or poor-quality information. A recent high-profile example is Shell, where nonexecutive directors responsible for management oversight reportedly were not getting the information they needed to make good decisions on the issue of reserves. Consequently, they had insufficient knowledge for dealing with the reserves revaluation, which badly damaged the company's value and reputation.

Higgs also recommended that the nonexecutive directors meet without the executives present, and at least once a year, without the executive directors and the chairman present. The discussions would be informal and provide an opportunity to raise concerns on such matters as the provision of information and succession planning.

There will be even greater clarity on the duties of directors when the government produces its intended legislative statement of directors' duties expected in the forthcoming Companies Law Bill.

SENIOR INDEPENDENT DIRECTOR. Another controversial recommendation from Higgs was that the board should appoint a senior independent director who would be available to shareholders if their concerns aren't satisfied, or when it is inappropriate for them to communicate with the chairman, chief executive, or finance director. Higgs specifically recommended that the senior independent director should attend sufficient meetings with major shareholders. Much concern was expressed that the role would prove divisive and was unnecessary. However, experience to date shows that although the majority of FTSE 100 companies have now appointed senior independent directors to comply with this provision, shareholders have not requested access to them.

The only other specific responsibility of the senior independent director is to lead the nonexecutive directors in a meeting at least annually to appraise the chairman's performance.

Committees

Higgs recommended that every listed company should have the following committees: audit (at least three members—all independent nonexecutive directors), remuneration (at least three members—all independent nonexecutive directors), and nomination (made up of a majority of independent nonexecutive directors).

His research showed that in most companies, the nomination committee was generally the least well-developed, usually meeting irregularly and often without a clear understanding of its role and the appointment process. The number of companies that have established nomination committees has clearly increased over the past year or so.

The code introduced the specific recommendation that the audit committee should have at least one member who has recent and relevant financial experience. This requirement has increased considerably the employment prospects of retiring finance directors and partners in the major accounting firms. However, with the implementation of the new international financial reporting standards, knowledge and expertise in this area are in short supply. Over the past year, many boards have been changing the composition of the audit committee so that it is made up entirely of independent nonexecutive directors.

Higgs set out the key aspects of committee rules and recommended that all committees make available a written description of their roles and responsibilities. A significant number of companies have now posted these descriptions on their Web sites.

Size and Balance of the Board

Higgs reviewed the size of boards but decided against setting any detailed requirements other than two: the board should not be so large as to be unwieldy, and it should be of sufficient size so that the balance of skill and experience is appropriate to the business and that changes to the board's composition can be managed without undue disruption.

Recent research from Pensions Investment Research Consultants shows that in the FTSE 100 the average number of board members is eleven, although some companies have many more.[5] HSBC, in early 2005, remains one of the largest boards, with twenty members.

Higgs also recommended that there be a strong presence of both nonexecutive and executive directors on the board to ensure that power and information are not concentrated in one or two individuals and that no individual or small group of individuals can dominate the board's decision making.

He was concerned that there is a greater risk of distortion, withholding of information, or lack of balance in the management contribution to the boardroom debate when there are only a few executive directors on the board. His research showed that only twelve FTSE 100 companies had fewer than three executive directors.

Under the new regime, there is a provision that at least half the board, excluding the chairman, should be composed of nonexecutive directors who are determined by the board to be independent. Previously, the requirement was that one-third of the board should be nonexecutive. This new rule can be relaxed for smaller companies; for example, those below the FTSE 350 for the year immediately preceding the reporting year are only required to have at least two nonexecutives.

Companies have been busy over the past year or so reviewing and changing the composition of their boards in light of these rules, but it is an ongoing process and full compliance is still some way off.

APPOINTMENTS. Perhaps one of the areas where the Higgs recommendations have had the greatest impact is the appointment process. Companies are now required to have a formal, rigorous, and transparent procedure for appointing new directors to the board.

Higgs recognized that the nomination and appointment process is crucial to strong performance and effective accountability. In particular, it is essential to ensure that the board as a whole has an appropriate mix of skills and experience if it is to be a cohesive, high-performing, and effective decision-making body.

He found that a high level of informality surrounds the process of appointing nonexecutive directors and that a significant proportion of nonexecutive directors were appointed through personal contacts and friendships—and the "old boys' network."

Nomination committees are now required to prepare a description of the role and capabilities necessary for a particular appointment once they have evaluated the board's existing balance of skills, knowledge, and experience. They must ensure that appointments are made on merit and against objective criteria and that appointees have enough time available to devote to the job. They are also required to give an explanation in the annual report and accounts if neither an external search consultancy nor open advertising was used in the appointment.

DIVERSITY. Higgs's research found that the typical FTSE 100 board is composed of nonexecutive directors who were white males nearing retirement age with previous plc experience. These boards had very few nonexecutives who were under the age of forty-five, female, or not British. He found a number of factors that militate against wider representation in the boardroom:

- The "old boys' network," by which personal contacts as a main source of candidates tend to favor those with similar backgrounds to incumbent directors
- The attitude of boards when considering appointments, and in particular, a self-perpetuating process
- The tendency of search consultants to identify candidates from a narrow pool of "usual suspects"

He encouraged boards and nomination committees in particular to broaden the pool and increase the breadth and diversity of experience. Following on Higgs's research, a study was undertaken by a task force led by Dean Laura Tyson of London Business School with a view toward highlighting how a range of backgrounds and experiences among board members can enhance board effectiveness and exploring how a broader range of nonexecutive directors can be identified and recruited.[6]

Her report identified possible sources of talented candidates that traditional, largely informal search processes had tended to ignore, including:

- More executive directors or talented individuals from the so-called marzipan layer of corporate management—just below board level
- More individuals with international experience
- Executive directors or senior managers from unlisted companies and private equity firms
- Lawyers, accountants, and consultants who are used to working in an advisory capacity to businesses
- Individuals from charitable or public sector organizations who have developed strong commercial and market understanding

Evidence suggests that some progress has been made in introducing greater diversity into boardrooms. There has been a steady increase in the number of women and ethnic minority directors. Recent research from Cranfield University School of Management reported that women now occupy 17 percent of new FTSE 100 boardroom appointments.[7]

BOARD PERFORMANCE

Higgs realized that clarity of roles was not enough and focused on enhancing the competence, performance, and effectiveness of boards and increasing their accountability. He made recommendations designed to raise the quality of appointees and to ensure that nonexecutive directors are properly equipped for their role by specifying that they:

- Have sufficient time to devote to their role.
- Receive a full, formal, and tailored induction on joining the board.
- Continually update their skills, knowledge, and familiarity with the company required to fulfill their role.
- Have access to independent professional advice as well as the advice and services of the company secretary.
- Be subject to a formal and rigorous annual performance evaluation.
- Be submitted for reelection at regular intervals subject to continued satisfactory performance.

Higgs wanted to ensure that nonexecutive directors are in a position to devote sufficient time to the affairs of the companies on whose boards they sit. There was concern that some individuals spread themselves too thin by taking on too many appointments.

He imposed a requirement on nomination committees to ensure that new appointees have sufficient time for their duties. For the appointment of a chairman, the committee is required to assess the expected time commitment, taking into account potential crises. To encourage regular attendance at board and committee meetings as appropriate, the code requires disclosure of individual attendance at those meetings in the annual report and accounts.

Only two specific limits are imposed: no individual should be appointed to a second chairmanship of a FTSE 100 company, and a full-time executive director should not take on more than one nonexecutive directorship nor the chairmanship of a FTSE 100 company.

The outcome of the Higgs Review was a shift in focus away from compliance issues of corporate governance to the performance aspects, and in particular, the effectiveness of boards. Boards are increasingly in the spotlight, and their work now carries an unprecedented degree of visibility and accountability.

BOARD EVALUATION

The Higgs Review found that over a third of boards never evaluate their own performance and that fewer than a quarter of nonexecutive directors and fewer than half of chairmen ever undergo a personal evaluation.

It introduced "three-tier" performance evaluation, going one step further than the two-tier evaluation required in the United States. It stipulates: "The board should undertake a formal evaluation of its own performance and that of its committees and individual directors." In addition, the nonexecutives led by the senior independent director are responsible for appraising the chairman's performance at least annually. The reelection of directors should be subject to evaluation, showing that the individual exhibits commitment and that his or her performance continues to be effective. Any term beyond six years for a nonexecutive director should be subject to particularly rigorous review.

The Combined Code does not give any guidance on how evaluations should be conducted, although Higgs did state that "conduct of the evaluation by an external third party can bring objectivity to the process and its value should be recognised by chairmen."

Although a significant proportion of FTSE 100 companies have conducted or are planning to conduct a board evaluation, most chairman are adopting a "softly softly" approach and conducting such evaluations internally; this is, of course, also the less expensive option. A recent survey by Independent Audit found that only 18 percent of the 85 FTSE 100 companies that reported between January and August 2004 used external advisers.[8] Chairmen need to exercise caution in their choice of external advisers to ensure that there is no conflict or perceived conflict of interest. This is most likely where search or accountancy firms are appointed to offer the company advice on other matters.

Evaluations usually consist of informal discussions between the chairman and directors, and questionnaires, or a combination of the two. Many chairmen have indicated that they intend to use external consultants once the nonexecutives have grown accustomed to the concept and process.

The process also involves seeking the views of the company secretary, who typically attends all board and committee meetings. However, some chairmen are extending the scope of the evaluation to seek the views of other senior executives, advisers to the remuneration committee, and the auditors to give an external and objective perspective. Perhaps, in the future, the views of key investors may also be sought. The process is likely to evolve and become more rigorous, particularly as institutional investors take a keener interest in this aspect of governance.

RELATIONS WITH SHAREHOLDERS

As already mentioned, over the years institutional investors have played a significant and often high-profile and controversial role in the context of the U.K. corporate landscape. The main focus was often directors' remuneration, and in particular, those cases where there was perceived excess or rewards for failure. A high-profile example was when GlaxoSmithKline's remuneration report was voted against.

According to Michelle Edkins of Hermes Investment Management, "The changes in the relationship between shareholders and boards on corporate governance questions are reflected in a recent statement by Hermes. The focus of the corporate governance debate is moving away from the structural towards the behavioural aspect of running a successful company. Meaningful, periodic assessment of the effectiveness of the board is an essential part of ensuring our companies are run by the best people to the best effect."[9]

Already Pensions Investment Research Consultants has announced that, in 2005, it will switch its focus from director pay and auditor independence to issues such as boardroom appraisal and succession planning. Morley Fund Management also advised that succession planning is one of the key issues it will be focusing on.

The most recent high-profile cases include Sainsbury and Shell Transport and Trading. In 2004, Sir Ian Prosser was forced to withdraw as chairman designate of Sainsbury because of investor opposition, and there was great controversy over the termination payment to Sir Peter Davis. In the face of investor anger, the remuneration committee withdrew its support for the vesting of a share award after the incoming CEO analyzed the company's performance. However, the committee was then advised by its lawyers that it had a weak case, and Davis received his payment.

At Shell, the restatements of the value of proven reserves caused a huge slump in investor confidence. The group audit committee appointed a law firm to conduct a review, but Sir Philip Watts, chairman of the committee of managing directors, and Walter van de Vijver, CEO of exploration and production, resigned before the report was made public. The suggestion was that reserves booking had been aggressive and premature.

The relationship between investors and companies had become strained before the Higgs Review in a number of high-profile cases, and Higgs took steps to ensure that they were improved. He recognized that both boards and institutional investors have key roles to play in ensuring that they maintain a satisfactory dialogue and he imposed corresponding requirements on both groups.

He endorsed the requirement that institutional investors comply with the Institutional Shareholders' Committee's principles. In addition to imposing responsibility on the board as a whole, he recommended that the chairman, the senior independent director, and other nonexecutive directors maintain sufficient contact with major shareholders to understand their issues and concerns. He believed that nonexecutive directors often had virtually no direct contact with major shareholders and were unaware of their concerns.

The result has been a significant increase in the level of communication between companies and key shareholders on corporate governance issues over the past year or so.

Chairmen and senior independent directors have been taking an increasingly proactive approach to consulting with key shareholders and issuing invitations to shareholders to attend meetings with them. Indeed, some institutional investors are complaining that the pendulum has swung too far the other way, and they are inundated with such invitations. There is a creeping sense of "consultation fatigue" among some key shareholders who would prefer to engage in dialogue only when there is a significant issue relating to governance, such as strategy, succession planning, executive remuneration, or the need for a company to explain an issue of noncompliance.

Higgs also spelled out the role of institutional investors in making the "comply or explain" regime effective. Many companies had expressed concern that shareholders often adopt a mechanistic approach or "checklist" mentality, treating every departure from the Combined Code as a breach, resulting in a "comply or else" regime.

Although the onus is on the company to give a considered explanation where it does not comply with the provisions of the code, shareholders must evaluate and consider carefully explanations given for any departure and make reasoned judgements in each case. Further, they should put their views to the company and be prepared to begin a dialogue if they do not accept the company's position. Higgs emphasized that although shareholders have every right to challenge companies' explanations if they are unconvincing, they should not be evaluated in a mechanistic way, and departures from the code should not automatically be treated as breaches.

LIABILITY

In the United Kingdom under the unitary board model, executive directors and nonexecutive directors have the same legal duties and objectives.

Following the high-profile Equitable Life case, in which the nonexecutive directors are being sued for failing to fulfill their duties, nonexecutive directors should not be under any illusion as to the extent of their duties and liability.

The risks associated with being a nonexecutive director have increased significantly with a corresponding increase in the cost of directors' and officers' liability insurance.

Although the code states that the company should arrange appropriate insurance coverage with respect to legal action against its directors, which reduces directors' personal exposure, it does nothing to remove the reputational risk.

The Risk-Reward Ratio for Nonexecutive Directors

The burden on nonexecutive directors has increased significantly over the past few years. A survey undertaken by Independent Remuneration Solutions showed that nonexecutive directors of companies whose turnover exceeds £1 billion now spend up to thirty-eight days a year at each company, up from just twenty-one days five years ago.[10]

There has been a significant increase in the level of fees for nonexecutive directors over the past few years, reflecting this increase in commitment and risk. A report by Watson Wyatt in 2004 found that nonexecutive director fees had risen by 38 percent in 2004 among FTSE 100 companies that had reviewed their fees. The average fee at the time was £36,500 based on an average commitment of eighteen days a year. But among those who had reviewed board pay, the average was £40,000.[11]

Despite these increases in pay, the rewards for nonexecutive directors are relatively low compared to those of executive directors, but the risks are great because both carry the same legal responsibility. There is concern that the risk-reward ratio is now out of balance and that potential candidates may be deterred from seeking nonexecutive positions. Evidence suggests that this may be particularly true in general for the position of audit committee chairman, and even more specifically, in the cases of ailing companies or ones with potential governance issues.

Nonexecutive fees in the United Kingdom are typically paid in cash or shares. The code specifically provides that remuneration for nonexecutive directors should not include share options because they are likely to jeopardize their independence.

Over the past year or so, there has also been a significant increase in the number of companies paying an additional fee to those individuals who chair either the audit or remuneration committee, as recommended by Higgs. A PricewaterhouseCoopers survey showed that where companies have recently reviewed chairmanship fees, audit committee chairmanship fees tend to have been realigned 30 percent above those for the remuneration committee chairmanship. The survey also showed that relatively few companies pay an additional fee for the chairmanship of the nomination committee.[12]

THE FUTURE

Despite its favorable reputation, corporate governance in the United Kingdom remains under constant review and continues to evolve.

Significant changes are likely in the area of audit, financial reporting, and internal controls. In 2004 the Financial Reporting Council appointed a group led by Douglas Flint to consult and issue revised guidance, which is expected to come into force in January 2006. A recent Korn/Ferry survey showed that the cost to a U.K. company of complying with Higgs was an average of £820,000; in the United States, the average was $5.1 million to comply with Sarbanes-Oxley.[13] In reality, of course, many U.K. companies, which are listed on the New York Stock Exchange, must comply with both.

As the government seeks to raise auditor accountability to shareholders and as U.K. auditors seek to bolster trust in company accounts and win favor with the government—particularly in an attempt to secure approval for proportionate liability—there is likely to be some tightening of regulation and changes in best practice. The Audit Quality Forum, an influential group of accountants, shareholders, and executives, is recommending that the law be changed to allow investors to put written questions to auditors before annual general meetings and ask follow-up questions the day of meetings. They are also recommending that when an auditor resigns, a statement should be made outlining the circumstances of the resignation.

A recent suggestion is that taxes, and concerns from the general public that some companies avoid paying an appropriate amount, should become more central to corporate governance. The U.K. Inland Revenue has said that it will work with the accounting profession to place tax and the issue of tax avoidance more at the heart of the governance.

The general view among institutional investors is that the benefits of the compliance regime outweigh the associated costs. Not surprisingly, many companies are not nearly so convinced and worry that it distracts from the board's focus on key issues such as strategy and corporate performance. Although there is no conclusive evidence that good corporate governance raises performance, the general consensus is that it reduces the risk of major scandals and loss of shareholder value.

SUMMARY

In our experience working with chairmen and boards, we have found that the main challenges for chairmen are as follows:

- Ensure the board's composition meets the requirements of the Combined Code.
- Build a board that not only has the appropriate mix of skills but also is a cohesive and effective team that enjoys constructive debate and makes effective decisions.
- Undertake meaningful and effective performance evaluations.
- Ensure that the nonexecutive directors get accurate, relevant, and timely information and are appropriately well-informed and engaged.
- Ensure that sufficient time is devoted to the issues that are identified as critical, particularly the formulation of strategy.

The significance and importance of the chairman's role should not be underestimated. It is both time-consuming and demanding, and the demands will only increase. For example, boards are taking risk management much more seriously. They realize that it requires not only sufficient and timely information but also a social climate that encourages diverse perspectives regarding potential risks and enables directors to raise unpopular or uncomfortable issues. The best boards in the United Kingdom carve out time to pick up "weak signals" by standing back from the day-to-day questions and examining larger social, competitive, and economic trends.

The most advanced boards in the United Kingdom are prepared to question themselves and their companies, and to allow themselves to think about risk in a systematic and open-minded way. This is a long way from the "checklist" approach to corporate governance that has held back so many others.

Conclusion

Recommendations for Building Better Boards

David A. Nadler
Beverly A. Behan
Mark B. Nadler

T here's not much doubt that most boards and CEOs have heard the message loud and clear: times have changed, and so too must their roles as leaders and overseers of major enterprises.

Their motives are varied. Some are responding primarily to statutory changes and stock exchange listing requirements. Some are feeling intense pressure from major investors, activist shareholders, or government regulators. Some are driven by the looming threat of personal liability for negligent governance. And some genuinely understand that we are on the threshold of a new era in corporate governance that provides a historic opportunity for boards and CEOs to redefine their working relationship, with significant benefits for both their companies and shareholders.

Whatever the impetus, many CEOs and directors are seeing the need for change and asking, "Now what?" So far, there's been a visible gap between talk and action. To be sure, recent developments in the United States have cleaned up some of the most egregious shortcomings—obvious conflicts of interest, board audit committees with members who couldn't decipher a balance sheet, financial reporting that sometimes strayed from fact to fiction.

Yet, by and large, the recent structural changes in corporate governance have had more to do with preventing negligence than with achieving excellence. We're all in favor of the former, but also deeply committed to the latter—and constantly encouraged by the serious intentions of directors we've worked with who have set for themselves a more ambitious goal than simply filling out the required paperwork and staying out of jail.

Throughout this book, we've attempted to unfold a blueprint for excellence in governance that combines our best ideas on both theory and practice, drawing upon our firm's work with dozens of boards along with a wealth of research. The theory is fairly simple: boards that learn to function as high-performance teams, using the right processes to do the right work with the right leadership and in the context of the right culture, can create substantial value by striking the appropriate balance between overseeing and collaborating with senior management.

The practice is more complicated. It has a broader behavioral basis than mere compliance with technical requirements, and a more structured and deliberate approach than a hazy quest for "the right chemistry" in the boardroom. The creation of an exceptional board requires time, discipline, dedication, and a profound appreciation of the inherently unique social dynamics that mold working relationships at the pinnacle of the organization.

Our blueprint for building better boards has touched upon a wide range of topics, covering both how the board works and what work it should do. At each stage and in various ways, we've tempered our suggestions regarding specific practices with a consistent caveat: each board is different, and every process should be tailored to accommodate each organization's unique history, business context, and culture. And yet, although practices should vary, principles should not. So we'd like to conclude by summarizing and strongly recommending these seven core principles for building better boards.

1. *From time to time, every board should step back and take stock of its performance.* The technical requirements for board self-assessment can easily be met with a perfunctory paper-and-pencil survey, but those mechanical exercises are hardly worth the effort. Every few years—and certainly when there's a new CEO or board

chairman—we recommend that each board undertake a major effort, using a variety of information-gathering techniques, to assess how well it is functioning as a team, how effectively it is collaborating with senior management, and how conducive its leadership, work processes, and culture are to performing value-added work. The real benefit comes from designing and implementing an assessment process that not only raises the right issues but also engages the entire board in a healthy, candid dialogue that lays the groundwork for better performance.

2. *Every board and CEO should clearly specify their respective roles, shared responsibilities, and opportunities for collaboration.* There's no substitute for explicitly identifying every area of work related to governance and reaching a clear understanding about which work is primarily the board's, which is management's, and where collaboration between the two offers the greatest potential for creating added value for the organization. The real benefit lies in the combination of collaboration and constructive contention that results in top managers making better decisions than they would have made on their own.

3. *Every board should understand the difference between its current makeup and its ideal composition—and use every appointment to close the gap.* The selection of new board members, once the tightly held prerogative of the CEO, is rapidly becoming an area where the board exerts significant influence. Our sincere hope is that boards will use this power more wisely than the CEOs who regularly populated their boards with personal cronies, ineffectual celebrities, and deferential acquaintances. Today, the best boards are using each appointment to round out the collective profile of technical skills, professional experience, and personal attributes essential to doing real work in an atmosphere that balances collaboration with independence.

4. *Every board should step up to the issue of performance standards for individual directors.* No board can do the right work with the wrong people around the table. And yet, despite all the progress they've made, boards today are still more likely to remove a marginally effective CEO than a poorly performing director. The reluctance to deal forthrightly with directors' performance issues is the most glaring remnant of the "old boys' club" boardroom culture. Only a quarter of U.S. and U.K. boards have a formal

peer review process to generate performance ratings that are factored into decisions about renominating or removing directors.
That's just not good enough; every board should have one.

5. *Every board should formally designate a leader of the independent
   directors.* Although the issue has long since been settled in Great
   Britain and Canada, the debate rages on in the United States
   over whether the roles of CEO and chairman of the board
   should be separated. We take no side in that debate; there are
   good arguments for both positions, and we have seen situations
   where each model has been successful and where each has been
   inadequate. What's more important—and of more immediate
   concern—is that the independent directors, who now make up
   the overwhelming majority of each U.S. board, have a clearly
   designated leader to act as a counterbalance to the CEO. If the
   top roles are bifurcated, then clearly the nonexecutive chairman
   is the leader of the independent directors. If the CEO is also
   the chairman, then one of the outside directors should be designated as lead director or presiding director to play an ongoing
   leadership role.

6. *Every board should design work processes that enhance its ability to
   raise important concerns, explore important issues, and make fully
   informed decisions.* Boards find themselves at a distinct disadvantage when it comes to reviewing management's performance
   and proposals. Compared with full-time executives, the board's
   time for company-related work is relatively brief, and its access
   to complete, timely, and unbiased information is exceptionally
   limited. As a consequence, it is incumbent on board leaders to
   design agendas that allow the board to make the most productive use of its limited time together, and to manage the flow of
   information to ensure that directors are equipped to ask the
   right questions and fulfill their responsibility for informed
   business judgments. In addition, leaders should make the fullest
   possible use of executive sessions of the independent directors—
   in our view, perhaps the most significant of all the structural
   changes in governance processes.

7. *On every board, the most important responsibility of leaders
   is to foster and maintain a culture of openness, independence,
   broad participation, and constructive dissent.* Perhaps the
   greatest obstacle to sound governance has been the traditional

boardroom culture, characterized by passivity, deference to top management, and a propensity for ritual rather than real work. The crushing weight of the social system invariably silenced the scattered voices of dissent. It's essential for a board to have the right composition, to identify the right work, and to employ the right work processes, but at the end of the day, none of that matters if directors aren't encouraged to speak their minds, ask the tough questions, and espouse unpopular positions. It's up to the board's leaders—through their decisions, their actions, and most importantly, through their own behavior—to dismantle and replace the "gentlemen's club" culture that rendered so many boards so ineffective for so long.

In our blueprint for effective governance, these seven principles constitute the foundation upon which each board can build. All seven are not only important but universal; despite the vast differences in boards from one company and country to the next, it's difficult to think of a single case in which all seven won't apply. Once they're in place, the work of enhancing governance has only just begun. Nevertheless, they represent the essential starting point for building better boards.

~~~ Appendix: 2004 NACD Blue Ribbon Commission on Board Leadership

Shown here are the commission members and their affiliations at the time they served on the commission.

Co-chairs

Jay W. Lorsch, Louis E. Kirstein Professor of Human Relations, Harvard Business School, Boston

David A. Nadler, chair and CEO, Mercer Delta Consulting, LLC, New York

Commissioners

Edward C. Archer, managing director, Pearl Meyer and Partners, New York

Norman R. Augustine, retired chair and CEO, Lockheed Martin Corporation, Bethesda, Maryland

Patricia C. Barron, director, ARAMARK, New York

J. T. Battenberg III, chair, president, and CEO, Delphi Automotive Corporation, Troy, Michigan

Warren L. Batts, retired chair and CEO, Premark International, Chicago

Betsy Bernard, former president, AT&T, Morristown, New Jersey

Dennis Blair, president, Institute for Defense Analyses, Alexandria, Virginia

Frank J. Borelli, presiding director, Interpublic Group, New City, New York

Kenneth D. Brody, principal, Winslow Partners, Washington, D.C.

M. Anthony Burns, chair emeritus, Ryder System, Inc., Miami

Peter C. Clapman, senior VP and chief counsel for corporate governance, TIAA-CREF, New York

Jack Creighton, vice chair, Unocal Corporation, Seattle

B. Garland Cupp, chair, BMC Software, Inc., Edmond, Oklahoma

Gerald Czarnecki, chair and CEO, Deltennium Group, Inc., Boca Raton, Florida

Declan Denehan, principal, Mellon Financial Corporation, New York

Charles M. Elson, chair in corporate governance, University of Delaware, Newark

Barbara Hackman Franklin, former U.S. secretary of commerce, Barbara Franklin Enterprises, Washington, D.C.

Kenneth W. Freeman, chair, Quest Diagnostics, Inc., Lyndhurst, New Jersey

Wilbur H. Gantz, chair and CEO, Ovation Pharmaceuticals, Inc., Deerfield, Illinois

William W. George, former chair and CEO, Medtronic, Inc., Minneapolis

John J. Gorman, partner, Luse Gorman Pomerenk and Schick, Washington, D.C.

John R. Hall, former chair and CEO, Ashland Inc., Lexington, Kentucky

Robert E. Hallagan, vice chair, Heidrick and Struggles International, Inc., Boston

Alan G. Hassenfeld, chair, Hasbro, Inc., Pawtucket, Rhode Island

James E. Heard, vice chair, Institutional Shareholder Services, Rockville, Maryland

Thomas E. Holloran, professor emeritus, University of St. Thomas School of Law, Minneapolis

Michele Hooper, managing partner, Directors' Council, Chicago

Constance Horner, guest scholar, the Brookings Institution, Washington, D.C.

Allen Karp, chair emeritus, Cineplex Odeon Corporation, Toronto

William Earl Kennard, managing director, Carlyle Group, Washington, D.C.

Richard L. Keyser, chair and CEO, W.W. Grainger, Lake Forest, Illinois

Gwendolyn S. King, president, Podium Prose, LLC, Washington, D.C.

Reatha Clark King, former president and board chair, General Mills Foundation, Minneapolis

Kay Koplovitz, founding partner, Directors' Council, New York

Edward Ludwig, chair, president, and CEO, Becton, Dickinson and Company, Franklin Lakes, New Jersey

David C. Malmberg, chair, Kontron Mobile Computing, Inc., Eden Prairie, Minnesota

Henry A. McKinnell, chair and CEO, Pfizer Inc., New York

Nell Minow, founder and editor, Corporate Library, McLean, Virginia

Larry Mosner, chair and CEO, Deluxe Corporation, Shoreview, Minnesota

John F. Olson, senior partner, Gibson, Dunn and Crutcher, LLP, Washington, D.C.

Lawrence Perlman, chair, Arbitron, Inc., Minneapolis

James E. Rogers, chair, president, and CEO, Cinergy Corporation, Cincinnati

Hal Shear, president, Board Assets, Inc., Annapolis, Maryland

Robert B. Stobaugh, professor emeritus, Harvard Business School, Belmont, Massachusetts

John H. Stout, chair, Corporate Governance Group, Fredrikson & Byron, P.A., Minneapolis

Arthur O. Sulzberger Jr., chair, New York Times Company, New York

Mark C. Terrell, executive director, KPMG's Audit Committee Institute, Montvale, New Jersey

B. Kenneth West, senior consultant, Corporate Governance, TIAA-CREF, New York

William J. White, professor, Northwestern University, Evanston, Illinois

Ex-Officio

Roger W. Raber, president and CEO, National Association of Corporate Directors, Washington, D.C.

Peter R. Gleason, COO and director of research, National Association of Corporate Directors, Washington, D.C.

Expert Advisers

David W. Anderson, HRI Corporation, Toronto

Beverly A. Behan, partner, Mercer Delta Consulting, LLC, New York

John L. Howard, senior vice president, W.W. Grainger, Lake Forest, Illinois

Alexandra R. Lajoux, National Association of Corporate Directors, chief knowledge officer, Washington, D.C.

~~~ Notes

Chapter One

1. H. Kaback, "Felix Rohatyn: Taking the Measure of Today's Boards," *Directors & Boards,* Spring 2003, p. 20.
2. F. Kocourek, C. Burger, and B. Richard, "Corporate Governance: Hard Facts About Soft Behavior," *Strategy and Business,* 2003, *30,* 60. *Strategy and Business* is a publication of Booz Allen Hamilton.
3. A. J. Hill and T. Dalziel, "Boards of Directors and Firm Performance," *Academy of Management Review,* July 2003, p. 385.
4. C. Lucier, R. Schuyt, and J. Handa, "The Perils of Good Governance," *Strategy and Business,* 2004, *35,* 3.
5. 2003 and 2004 USC/Mercer Delta Corporate Board Surveys (New York: Mercer Delta Consulting, 2004, 2005).
6. J. W. Lorsch and D. Nadler, *Report of the NACD Blue Ribbon Commission on Board Leadership* (Washington, D.C.: National Association of Corporate Directors, 2004).
7. D. A. Nadler, "From Ritual to Real Work: The Board as a Team," *Directors & Boards,* Summer 1998, pp. 28–31.
8. J. A. Sonnenfeld, "What Makes Great Boards Great," *Harvard Business Review,* Sept. 2002, p. 106.
9. D. A. Bailey and W. E. Knepper, *Liability of Corporate Officers and Directors* (Dayton, Ohio: Matthew Bender & Co., 2002).

Chapter Two

1. *Spencer Stuart Board Index: Board Trends and Practices at Major American Corporations* (Chicago: Spencer Stuart, 2004), p. 7.
2. A. Raghavan, "More CEOs Say 'No Thanks' to Board Seats," *Wall Street Journal,* Jan. 28, 2005, p. B1.

3. M. Schroeder, "Corporate Reform: The First Year: Cleaner Living, No Easy Riches—Critics Say Sarbanes-Oxley Law Hobbles Stocks, Chills Risk Taking, But Upshot Is Far Less Dramatic," *Wall Street Journal,* July 22, 2003, p. C1.

4. E. Dash, "For Directors, Great Expectations (and More Pay)," *New York Times,* Apr. 4, 2004, p. C10.

5. *Spencer Stuart Board Index,* 2004, p. 7.

Chapter Three

1. *Spencer Stuart Board Index: Board Trends and Practices at Major American Corporations* (Chicago: Spencer Stuart, 2000), p. 14.

2. J. R. Engen, "Boom Times for the Director Emeritus," *Corporate Board Member,* Jan.-Feb. 2005, *8*(1), 30–32.

3. *The Conference Board Commission on Public Trust and Private Enterprise* (New York: The Conference Board, 2003), p. 21.

Chapter Four

1. *Split of CEO/Chairman Roles* (Portland, Me.: Corporate Library, Mar. 2004). http://www.thecorporatelibrary.com/Governance-Research/ spotlight-topics/spotlight/boardsanddirectors/SplitChairs2004.html. Accessed Mar. 2005.

2. C. Lucier, R. Schuyt, and J. Handa, "The Perils of Good Governance," *Strategy and Business,* 2004, *35,* 3. *Strategy and Business* is a publication of Booz Allen Hamilton.

Chapter Five

1. I. M. Millstein, "A Self-Correcting Course for Governance," *Directors & Boards,* Spring 2003, pp. 26–31.

2. *Spencer Stuart Board Index: Board Trends and Practices at Major American Corporations* (Chicago: Spencer Stuart, 2004), p. 30.

Chapter Six

1. D. A. Nadler, "From Ritual to Real Work: The Board as a Team," *Directors & Boards,* Summer 1998, pp. 28–31.

2. D. A. Nadler, "Building Better Boards," *Harvard Business Review,* May 2004, pp. 102–111.

3. J. A. Sonnenfeld, "What Makes Great Boards Great," *Harvard Business Review,* Sept. 2002, p. 106.

4. M. Langley, "After a 37-Year Reign at AIG, Chief's Last Tumultuous Days," *Wall Street Journal,* Apr. 1, 2005, p. 1.

5. K. M. Eisenhardt, "Strategy as Strategic Decision Making," *Sloan Management Review,* Spring 1999, pp. 65–72.

Chapter Seven

1. A. J. Slywotzky and D. J. Morrison, *Profit Patterns* (New York: Times Business, 1999).

2. *The Conference Board Commission on Public Trust and Private Enterprise* (New York: The Conference Board, 2003), p. 9.

3. D. A. Nadler, *Champions of Change* (San Francisco: Jossey-Bass, 1998).

4. P. Plitch, "Ready and Able?" *Wall Street Journal,* Feb. 24, 2003, p. R3; J. S. Lublin, "More Work, More Pay," *Wall Street Journal,* Feb. 24, 2003, p. R4.

Chapter Eight

1. S. Craig and K. Brown, "Schwab Ousts Pottruck as CEO," *Wall Street Journal,* July 21, 2004, p. A1.

2. J. A. Conger, E. E. Lawler III, and D. L. Finegold, "Holding Leadership Accountable," *Organizational Dynamics,* Summer 1998, pp. 7–20.

3. R. E. Berenbeim, *Corporate Boards: CEO Selection, Evaluation, and Succession* (Report No. 1103–95-RR) (New York: The Conference Board, 1995), p. 36.

4. C. K. Brancato and D. Hervig, *The Compensation Committee of the Board: Best Practices for Establishing Executive Compensation* (Report No. R-1306–01-RR) (New York: The Conference Board, 2001), p. 33.

5. Berenbeim, *Corporate Boards,* p. 28.

6. *Evaluating the Chief Officer* (Los Angeles: Korn/Ferry International/ University of Southern California Marshall School of Business), 1998, pp. 10–11.

7. J. A. Conger, E. E. Lawler III, and D. L. Finegold, *Corporate Boards: New Strategies for Adding Value at the Top* (San Francisco: Jossey-Bass, 2001).

Chapter Nine

1. W. A. Pasmore and R. Torres, "Choosing the Best Next CEO: Succession Should Be a Process, Not a Horse Race," *Mercer Management Journal,* 2003, *16,* 67–75.

2. 2004 USC/Mercer Delta Corporate Board Survey (New York: Mercer Delta Consulting, 2005).

3. "The First 100 Days: The New CEO's Challenge," *Mercer Delta Insight,* 2001.

4. R. Charan, S. Drotter, and J. Noel, *The Leadership Pipeline: How to Build the Leadership-Powered Company* (San Francisco: Jossey-Bass, 2001).

Chapter Ten

1. M. Langley and I. McDonald, "Marsh Averts Criminal Case with New CEO," *Wall Street Journal,* Oct. 26, 2002, p. A1.

2. C. Roux-Dufort, "Why Organizations Don't Learn from Crises," *St. John's University, College of Business Administration, Review of Business,* 2000, *21*(3), 25–30.

Chapter Eleven

1. B. Behan and J. Brant, "Building a Better Board Assessment," *NACD Directors Monthly,* June 2004, pp. 9–11. *Directors Monthly* is a publication of the National Association of Corporate Directors, Washington, D.C.; see http://www.nacdonline.org.

Chapter Twelve

1. M. Quigley and G. Scott, *Hospital Governance and Accountability in Ontario* (Ontario, Canada: Ontario Hospital Association, Apr. 2004), p. 5.

2. *A Status Report of the Office of the Auditor General to the House of Commons* (Canada: Minister of Public Works and Government Services, Feb. 2005), ch. 7.

3. G. Bragues, "Dual Shares Do Work: Shareholder Democracy Has No Place in Equity Markets: Investors Can Vote with Their Pocketbooks When They Have a Choice," *National Post,* May 19, 2004, p. FP19.

4. J. Kay, "School for No Scandal: In the Post-Enron-Worldcom-Hollinger World, Pressure Is on Boards and Directors to Reform Themselves," *National Post,* Apr. 1, 2004, p. FP11.

5. P. Desmarais, "Control Means Control: Applying Independent-Director Proposals to Existing Closely Held Public Companies Would Constitute an Expropriation, an Attack on Property Rights," *National Post,* Jan. 31, 2004, p. FP11.

6. G. Fabrikant, "Do Families and Big Business Mix?" *New York Times,* Apr. 24, 2005, p. C1.

7. S. Prashad, "Family Business No Guarantee of Success: Research Shows Firms Often Fail in Second or Third Generations," *Toronto Star,* Sept. 2, 2004, p. ONT D22.

Chapter Thirteen

1. *2004 Global Governance Ratings* (New York: Governance Metrics International, Mar. 2005). http://www.gmiratings.com. Accessed Mar. 2005.

2. D. Higgs, *Review of the Role and Effectiveness of Non-Executive Directors* (Higgs Review) (London: The Stationery Office, June 2002), pp. 3–23.

3. Financial Reporting Council, "The Combined Code—One Year On," Jan. 13, 2005. http://www.frc.org.uk/press/pub0738.html. Accessed Mar. 2005.

4. L. Urquhart, "Inchcape Appoints Chief Against Higgs' Recommendations," *Financial Times* (London), Mar. 1, 2005, p. 25.

5. *Corporate Governance Annual Review 2004* (London: Pensions Investment Research Consultants, 2004).

6. L. Tyson, *Report on the Recruitment and Development of Non-Executive Directors* (London: London Business School, June 2003).

7. *Female FTSE Report 2004* (Cranfield, Bedford, United Kingdom: Cranfield University School of Management, 2004).

8. *Reporting Board Effectiveness: A Survey of FTSE 100 Annual Reports, 2004* (London: Independent Audit Limited, 2004).

9. B. Hudson, "Evaluating the Board: The Chairman's Role," *Mercer Delta Board Development Series,* 2004, p. 3.

10. *The Independent Chairman and Non-Executive Director Survey* (London: Independent Remuneration Solutions, Jan. 2005).

11. *Executive Reward Survey* (London: Watson Wyatt, Oct. 2004).

12. *Non-Executive Directors' Fees Post Higgs* (London: PricewaterhouseCoopers, 2004), p. 3. http://www.pricewaterhousecoopers.co.uk. Accessed Mar. 2005.

13. *Annual Board of Directors Study 2004* (Los Angeles: Korn/Ferry International, 2004).

—ᴠᴠ— References

Chapter Two

Behan, B. A. "Research to Do Before Joining a Board." *Directors & Boards,*
First Quarter 2005, pp. 49–51.

Lorsch, J. W., and Nadler, D. A. *Report of the NACD Blue Ribbon Commission
on Board Leadership.* Washington, D.C.: National Association of
Corporate Directors, 2004.

USC/Mercer Delta Corporate Board Surveys, 2003 and 2004. New York:
Mercer Delta Consulting, 2004, 2005.

Chapter Three

Lorsch, J. W., and Nadler, D. A. *Report of the NACD Blue Ribbon Commission
on Board Leadership.* Washington, D.C.: National Association of
Corporate Directors, 2004.

USC/Mercer Delta Corporate Board Surveys, 2003 and 2004. New York:
Mercer Delta Consulting, 2004, 2005.

Chapter Four

Andrews, P. "Bill Gates Hopes Career Future Will Bring Return to Software
Focus." *Knight Ridder Tribune Business News,* Jan. 16, 2000. Accessed
July 2004.

Hopkins, N. "Founder Logs Off as Dell's Chief." *The Times,* Mar. 5, 2004,
p. 29.

Lorsch, J. W., and Nadler, D. A. *Report of the NACD Blue Ribbon Commission
on Board Leadership.* Washington, D.C.: National Association of
Corporate Directors, 2004.

Reidy, C. "Staples CEO Makes Way for Successor." *Boston Globe,* Sept. 6,
2001, p. C1.

USC/Mercer Delta Corporate Board Surveys, 2003 and 2004. New York:
Mercer Delta Consulting, 2004, 2005.

Chapter Five

Lorsch, J. W., and Nadler, D. A. *Report of the NACD Blue Ribbon Commission on Board Leadership.* Washington, D.C.: National Association of Corporate Directors, 2004.

USC/Mercer Delta Corporate Board Surveys, 2003 and 2004. New York: Mercer Delta Consulting, 2004, 2005.

Chapter Six

Hackman, J. R. *Leading Teams: Setting the Stage for Great Performances.* Boston: Harvard Business School Publishing, 2002.

Lorsch, J. W., and Nadler, D. A. *Report of the NACD Blue Ribbon Commission on Board Leadership.* Washington, D.C.: National Association of Corporate Directors, 2004.

Nadler, D. A., and Spencer, J. L. *Executive Teams.* San Francisco: Jossey-Bass, 1998.

Schein, E. R. *Organization Culture and Leadership* (3rd ed.). San Francisco: Jossey-Bass, 2004.

USC/Mercer Delta Corporate Board Surveys, 2003 and 2004. New York: Mercer Delta Consulting, 2004, 2005.

Chapter Seven

Lorsch, J. W., and Nadler, D. A. *Report of the NACD Blue Ribbon Commission on Board Leadership.* Washington, D.C.: National Association of Corporate Directors, 2004.

USC/Mercer Delta Corporate Board Surveys, 2003 and 2004. New York: Mercer Delta Consulting, 2004, 2005.

Chapter Eight

Bailey, D., and Knepper, W. *Liability of Corporate Officers and Directors.* Dayton, Ohio: Matthew Bender & Co., 2002.

Bonsignore, F. N. "Constructive Thinking on CEO Evaluation." *Directors & Boards,* Summer 1997, pp. 35–39.

Carver, J. *Board Assessment of the CEO.* San Francisco: Jossey-Bass, 1997.

Charan, R. *Boards at Work.* San Francisco: Jossey-Bass, 1998.

Cornwall, D. J. "Succession: The Need for Detailed Insight: Evaluating a Company's Chief Executive Officer." *Directors & Boards,* June 22, 2001, p. 28.

Corporate Governance Core Principles & Guidelines. Sacramento: California Public Employees' Retirement System (CalPERS), 1998.

Current Board Practices, 2001. New York: Society of Corporate Secretaries, 2002.

Goldstein, M. L. "Grading the CEO." *Industry Week,* Jan. 21, 1985, pp. 48–49.

Hann, D. P. "Emerging Issues in U.S. Corporate Governance: Are the Recent Reforms Working?" *Defense Counsel Journal,* Apr. 2001, p. 191.

Lawler, E. E., III. "Appraising Boardroom Performance." *Harvard Business Review,* Jan. 1998, p. 136.

Lear, R. W., and Yavitz, B. "Boards on Trial." *Chief Executive,* Oct. 2000, p. 40.

Lipton, M., and Lorsch, J. W. "A Modest Proposal for Improved Corporate Governance." *Business Lawyer,* Nov. 1992, p. 59.

Lorchner, P. R., Jr. "Lessons in Evaluating CEO Performance: Tell It Like It Is." *Directorship,* Oct. 2000, p. 1.

Lorsch, J. W., and Nadler, D. A. *Report of the NACD Blue Ribbon Commission on Board Leadership.* Washington, D.C.: National Association of Corporate Directors, 2004.

Muschewske, R. C. "CEO Evaluation: A Process That Works." *Directors & Boards,* June 22, 1995, pp. 26–29.

Orlikoff, J. E., and Totten, M. K. "CEO Evaluation and Compensation." *Trustee,* 1996, pp. SS1–SS4.

Performance Evaluation of Chief Executive Officers, Boards, and Directors. Washington, D.C.: National Association of Corporate Directors, 2000.

Statement on Corporate Governance. Washington, D.C.: Business Roundtable, Sept. 1997.

TIAA-CREF Policy Statement on Corporate Governance. Charlotte, N.C.: Teachers Insurance and Annuity Association–College Retirement Equities Fund, 1997.

Twenty-Eighth Annual Board of Directors Study 2001. Los Angeles: Korn/Ferry International, 2001.

Tyler, J. L. "Practical Governance: CEO Performance Appraisal." *Trustee,* 2001, p. 14.

USC/Mercer Delta Corporate Board Surveys, 2003 and 2004. New York: Mercer Delta Consulting, 2004, 2005.

Ward, R. D. *Improving Corporate Boards.* New York: Wiley, 2000.

Chapter Nine

Cheloha, R. "Diamonds in the Rough: Developing Leaders Through the Group Evaluation Method." *Mercer Management Journal,* 2004, *28,* 60–66.

Khurana, R. *Searching for a Corporate Savior: The Irrational Quest for Charismatic CEOs.* Princeton, N.J.: Princeton University Press, 2002.

Lorsch, J. W., and Nadler, D. A. *Report of the NACD Blue Ribbon Commission on Board Leadership.* Washington, D.C.: National Association of Corporate Directors, 2004.

Chapter Eleven

Hallagan, R. E., and West, B. K. *Report of the NACD Blue Ribbon Commission on Board Evaluation: Improving Director Effectiveness.* Washington, D.C.: National Association of Corporate Directors, 2001.

Lorsch, J. W., and Nadler, D. A. *Report of the NACD Blue Ribbon Commission on Board Leadership.* Washington, D.C.: National Association of Corporate Directors, 2004.

Nowlan, S. E., and Carlucci, A. "Self-Help: Board Evaluations Become de Rigueur." *Chief Legal Executive,* Fall 2003, pp. 73–75.

USC/Mercer Delta Corporate Board Survey, 2003. New York: Mercer Delta Consulting, 2004.

Chapter Thirteen

Audit Committees Combined Code Guidance (Smith Report). London, United Kingdom: Financial Reporting Council, Jan. 2003.

The Combined Code: Principles of Good Governance and Code of Best Practice. Toronto, Canada: Committee on Corporate Governance, May 2000.

The Combined Code on Corporate Governance. London, United Kingdom: Financial Reporting Council, July 2003.

Directors' Remuneration: Report of a Study Group Chaired by Sir Richard Greenbury (Greenbury Report). London, United Kingdom, CBI, July 17, 1995.

The Dutch Corporate Governance Code. Toronto, Canada: Committee on Corporate Governance, Dec. 9, 2003.

Final Report: Committee on Corporate Governance (Hampel Report). Toronto, Canada: Committee on Corporate Governance, Jan. 1998.

Financial Aspects of Corporate Governance (Cadbury Report). London, United Kingdom: Burgess Science Press/Professional Publishing Press, Dec. 1992.

Internal Control: Guidance for Director on the Combined Code (Turnbull Report). London, United Kingdom: Institute of Chartered Accountants in England and Wales, Sept. 1999.

The Responsibilities of Institutional Shareholders and Agents—Statement of Principles. London, United Kingdom: Institutional Shareholders' Committee, Oct. 21, 2002.

U.K. Parliament. *The Directors' Remuneration Report Regulations 2002.* Whitehall, London, United Kingdom: Queen's Printer of Acts of Parliament, July 2002.

USC/Mercer Delta Corporate Board Surveys, 2003 and 2004. New York: Mercer Delta Consulting, 2004, 2005.

⟨⟨⟨ Acknowledgments

Any undertaking as comprehensive as the one reflected in this book involves the contributions of a great many people, whose efforts we want to acknowledge.

Clearly, this book is the direct result of the hard work of our chapter authors—our colleagues at Mercer Delta Consulting. But their work also reflects the experience and insights of our many colleagues at Mercer Delta who, at one time or another, have contributed to our work with boards. In particular, we'd like to acknowledge the contributions of those directly involved in our corporate governance consulting: David Nygren, Elise Walton, Rick Hardin, Chuck Raben, Peter Cairo, Michel Daniel, Richard Hossack, Rick Ketterer, Roselinde Torres, Bill Pasmore, Lela Tepavac, and JoAnn McNutt.

The National Association of Corporate Directors (NACD) project was a collaborative effort with Harvard Business School. Professor Jay Lorsch was a true partner in this effort, and his staff, including Ashley Robertson and Katharina Pick, were great collaborators. The Mercer Delta staff on the project, including George Manderlink, Judy Roland, and Lynn Roberts, were also major contributors. Roger Raber, the president and CEO of the NACD, and Peter Gleason, the director of research for the NACD, were our primary sponsors and sources of guidance at the NACD.

The USC/Mercer surveys and reports have also involved many different contributors. Edward Lawler, our longtime friend and colleague who heads up the Center for Effective Organizations, was an active member of the research team. David Finegold, who was at USC and now is at the Keck Graduate Institute of Applied Life Science, was the principal investigator. Again, our colleagues at Mercer Delta, including Fusako Matsui, Lela Tepavac, and Carlos Rivero, were major contributors.

Finally, a special word of thanks to our Mercer Delta colleagues without whose tireless work and endless patience this book would have been impossible: to Lynn Roberts, our editorial director, both for her outstanding editing and for her assistance in putting all the pieces together; to Agnes Schlenke for her work on the graphics; to Jon Howley and Veronika Cveckova for their research support; and to Tina Wong for her assistance in editing, proofing, and production.

D.A.N.
B.A.B.
M.B.N.

—ᴡᴡ— **The Authors**

Dᴀᴠɪᴅ A. Nᴀᴅʟᴇʀ is chairman of Mercer Delta Consulting, where he was CEO, 1980–2005. He consults at the CEO level, specializing in large-scale organization change, executive leadership, organization design, senior team development, and board effectiveness. He is well-known for his research and writing on organizational change, feedback, group performance, management, corporate governance, quality improvement, and organization design. He has written or edited fourteen books, including *Organizational Architecture, Prophets in the Dark: How Xerox Reinvented Itself and Drove Back the Japanese; Competing by Design: The Power of Organizational Architecture; Executive Teams;* and *Champions of Change: How CEOs and Their Companies Are Mastering the Skills of Radical Change.* His numerous published articles include "Building Better Boards," which appeared in the *Harvard Business Review* in 2004. He has served on the faculty at the Graduate School of Business at Columbia University. He holds a B.A. in international affairs from The George Washington University, an M.B.A. from the Harvard Business School, and an M.A. and Ph.D. in psychology from the University of Michigan. He is a member of the Academy of Management, was elected a Fellow of the American Psychological Association, and is a member of the board of Mercer Inc.

Bᴇᴠᴇʀʟʏ A. Bᴇʜᴀɴ, a partner in the corporate governance practice of Mercer Delta Consulting, has worked with more than fifty boards in the United States and Canada over the past ten years. She primarily works with board chairs, governance committee chairs, and CEOs of publicly traded companies to enhance the effectiveness of their boards. She also has worked with boards in other sectors, such as hospitals, crown corporations, pension funds, and not-for-profit organizations. She has spoken on corporate governance for the National Association of Corporate Directors, the Toronto Stock Exchange, the American Management Association, and the Caribbean Corporate Governance

Forum, and was a founding faculty member of the Conference Board of Canada's director education program. Before joining Mercer Delta in New York, she worked with Mercer Human Resources in Canada, specializing in executive compensation and corporate governance. She holds a law degree from the University of Western Ontario and two business degrees, including an M.B.A.

MARK B. NADLER is a partner and the executive editor of Mercer Delta Consulting, overseeing the firm's publications and editorial operations. He led the firm's strategic communication practice from 2000 through 2004, and continues to consult with CEOs and senior executives on communication strategies, processes, and functions in the context of organizational change. Before joining Mercer Delta in 1995, he worked for twenty-two years in the newspaper business as a reporter, editor, and senior newsroom executive at papers including the *Wall Street Journal* and the *Chicago Sun-Times,* where he was vice president and executive editor. He has coauthored and assisted in the writing of numerous publications concerning the management of organizational change, including two books—*Competing by Design: The Power of Organizational Architecture,* by David Nadler and Michael Tushman, and *Champions of Change: How CEOs and Their Companies Are Mastering the Skills of Radical Change,* by David Nadler. He holds a B.A. in English from The George Washington University.

JASON DUCHARME is a partner at Mercer Delta Consulting. He has an extensive background in business planning, organizational architecture, and public sector transformation, and has twenty years of consulting experience, specializing in public sector governance, performance measurement, privatization, strategic planning, and agency effectiveness. He has been retained by the public sector to assess financial and policy issues and recommend innovative transformation strategies. He has undergraduate degrees in economics and geography, and a master's degree in urban planning, all from the University of Toronto, where he is a guest lecturer.

MARGARET EXLEY is the nonexecutive chairman of Mercer Delta in the United Kingdom. She is well-known for her work in the United Kingdom and Europe, and has spoken and written widely on change management and leadership, including writing a regular column in *Management Today.* Before joining Mercer Delta, she cofounded

Kinsley Lord, a change management consultancy, and led Towers Perrin's European management consultancy practice. Her consulting has included work with global companies on organizational change, leadership development, mergers and acquisitions, and turnarounds. She has a first degree in economics and a master's degree from Warwick Business School, followed by a research fellowship at the Manchester Business School. In 2001, she was publicly honored with the award of a CBE.

RICHARD HARDIN is a partner with Mercer Delta Consulting and a member of the firm's corporate governance practice. He has consulted at the CEO and board level with numerous corporations and institutions on organization design, executive leadership, board effectiveness, mergers and acquisitions, strategy, and other areas of large-scale change. Before joining Mercer Delta, he was a consultant with the IBM Consulting Group's worldwide business transformation practice. He was a managing principal for Nolan, Norton & Co. in that firm's New York office, was cofounder of its Utrecht, Netherlands, office, and directed its European Research Institute from Brussels. He was on the faculty of Boston University Medical Center. He received a B.S. in education from the University of California, Santa Cruz, and holds an M.S. and Ph.D. in organizational behavior from Cornell University.

RICHARD D. HOSSACK is the president of Mercer Delta Consulting Canada. He works with boards, CEOs, and top management teams, dealing with both personal and enterprisewide transformations. He specializes in board effectiveness, strategic planning, mergers and acquisitions, transformation leadership, leadership development and executive coaching, restructuring, and organization design, development, and renewal. Before joining Mercer Delta, he led practices for IBM Business Consulting Services and was a senior partner in the PricewaterhouseCoopers Consulting Group. He has worked in the private sector and with a range of public sector organizations. He holds a Ph.D. in organizational development from the Fielding Graduate Institute, an M.B.A. in finance from the University of Toronto, a bachelor of commerce in economics and marketing, and a bachelor of science in math and physics, both from the University of Manitoba.

BELINDA HUDSON was a principal with Mercer Delta in London and a European partner for Mercer Human Resources. She has broad-based experience with a range of FTSE 100 and global private companies on aspects of leadership, corporate strategy, and people programs in support of organizational change. She also has extensive experience in dealing with institutional investors. She is qualified as a chartered accountant and has an honors law degree from Bristol University.

WILLIAM A. PASMORE's consulting work has focused on advising CEOs and senior executives in executing strategies to improve organizational performance and shareholder returns. His work has spanned strategy formulation, organization design, change management, succession planning, executive development, and senior team effectiveness. Before joining Mercer Delta in 1997, he was a professor in the Weatherhead School of Management at Case Western Reserve University, where he taught courses in the school's M.B.A., executive M.B.A., Ph.D., and executive Ph.D. programs for over twenty years. He was a visiting professor at Stanford and a faculty member in the executive education programs there. During the time that he was teaching, he also headed his own consulting firm, Pasmore & Associates, which offered public workshops and supported efforts in organizations to bring about large-scale change. As a thought leader in the field of organization development, he has published nineteen books and numerous articles, including *Designing Effective Organizations, Strategic Change,* and *Relationships That Enable Enterprise Change.* He holds a B.S. in aeronautical engineering–industrial management and a Ph.D. in administrative sciences, both from Purdue University.

J. CARLOS RIVERO is president of U.S. operations for Mercer Delta Consulting, and previously led the firm's global practice in organization research. He works in the areas of organization diagnosis and change, collaborative strategy development, corporate governance, organization culture, and action research with emphasis on measurement and feedback. Before joining Mercer Delta, he was on the faculty of The George Washington University with a joint appointment in industrial-organizational psychology and applied social psychology. Other teaching appointments include Columbia University and New York University. He has also worked at Goldman Sachs and AT&T, specializing in management development. He has published several articles and book chapters in the areas of CEO evaluation, executive team effectiveness, strategic human resources, management development, and e-business. He holds a B.A. from Columbia University and an M.A. and Ph.D. from New York University in industrial-organizational psychology. He is a member of the Academy of Management and the American Psychological Association.

JUDITH A. ROLAND was a principal at Mercer Delta Consulting, where she was a member of the firm's strategic communication practice, helping clients articulate their need for change, develop a change communication strategy, and implement communication processes and programs. Before joining Mercer Delta, she headed her own public relations firm for ten years. She worked principally on top-level intellectual capital projects for clients, including two books she wrote for the chairman and vice chairman of executive search firm Spencer Stuart, *CEO Succession* and *The Human Side of M&A*, both published by Oxford University Press. Previously, she was communications director for executive search firm Egon Zehnder International and an account executive with a research-based public relations firm. She holds a B.A. in behavioral sciences from Drew University and an M.A. in urban studies from the University of Chicago.

ROSELINDE TORRES is group executive for Mercer Delta Consulting, where she oversees the firm's five worldwide practices and global marketing. Prior to this role, she was president of U.S. operations. She consults to CEOs, board directors, and senior executives on leading change to achieve business results. She has been a longtime adviser to some of the most prominent chief executives in business on issues of CEO succession and evaluation, mergers and acquisitions, reorganizations, culture change, new strategies, enhanced executive leadership, and executive team development. Before joining Mercer Delta, she was a member of the senior leadership team at the Ethicon Endo-Surgery division of Johnson & Johnson. She also worked at Connecticut Mutual Life Insurance Company, where she held positions as a training officer and an underwriter. She speaks frequently at national business forums on organizational transformation and leadership and has been featured in the major business press, including the *New York Times*, the *Economist*, the *Corporate Board*, and *Chief Executive*. She has an A.B. double major degree, with honors, in English and Spanish from Middlebury College and an M.S. degree in human resource development from American University and the NTL Institute for Applied Behavioral Science.

—~~— Index